The Last Flight of the Daisy Mae

A Story of Heroism and Hope at 17,000 Feet

Wayne F Perkins

ISBN-13: 978-1519558336
ISBN-10: 1519558333

http://www.thelastflightofthedaisymae.com

Dedication

To All the Men and Women who sacrificed and fought
to end World War II.

From the People of a Grateful Nation...

Table of Contents

Chapter 1

Heroism and Hope

The story begins far away from the battle site. On a warm, dark July day not far from a quiet ocean, the Marine Color Guard is escorting an airman to his final resting place.

Looking into the eyes of a lanky, young marine in the burial detail, there is the focused stare of a man doing his job for his country. There is no room for emotion. His eyes are dry. After all, the marine has seen many of his friends killed doing their jobs, working and dying for their friends, their families and their country during a time of great stress and peril. For this lanky marine, it is the time and the place to complete his job of folding the flag and presenting it with spent M1 carbine shell casings from the twenty-one-gun salute for the resting airman. He gently tucks the shell casings inside the folded US flag neatly and efficiently. His eyes stare straight ahead as he hands off the flag.

The bugler sounds taps and there is a familiar rumbling in the far off clouds. The marines from the burial detail stand at attention. As the chaplain recites, "On behalf of the President of the United States and the People of a grateful nation," I wonder what happened on the airman's last mission…the last flight of the **Daisy Mae**.

The Perkins Clan

The airman's name is Francis J. Perkins Jr. He goes by Fran. He is a senior at Calumet High School in Chicago, Illinois. He lives with his father, mother and four brothers in the area called Washington Heights next to Evergreen Park. The Brainerd Park District keeps the boys busy in the summer months with sports. It is early afternoon when Jim and Bob, his two older brothers, are talking about taking a bus to downtown Chicago to begin some Christmas shopping.

"Do you want to come along, Fran?" asks Bob.

"No, I am having dinner with Elaine and I don't want to be stuck downtown and not make it to dinner on time."

"It sounds like Fran's getting married soon," the oldest brother, Jim says sarcastically. "Remember what Dad always says, you have to graduate from high school in June. Then we'll all be working for the City of Chicago together. They don't want a dummy you know. Even if you are a dummy in love."

"You are nuts, Jim, nuts," Fran retorts.

Dad comes into the living room and turns on the radio. "We'll listen to some music while we figure out where everyone's going today. I'm staying home to help your mother. We're going to bake a cake together."

"That sounds like real fun, Dad. You can get little Fran to help. That'll help him keep from thinking about his new girlfriend, Elaine, all day," Bob jests.

"Don't listen to your brothers, Fran. They're just trying to get you rattled," says Dad.

Dad, who goes by Frank, turns on the monstrous radio that looks a fine piece of furniture. The walnut cabinet stands about five feet high and is three feet wide. Television was nonexistent in homes back then.

As radio tubes heat up the sound begins; however, no music plays.

"That's the voice of the President," says Bob excitedly. "What's going on?"
The three boys and their dad huddle in front of the radio and listen.

A reporter's voice interrupts the President's voice. "Today, December 7, 1941, the Islands of Hawaii, Wake Island and Midway, as well as the

Philippines have been attacked by the Empire of Japan. American naval ships anchored at Pearl Harbor are sinking, as well as ships between Hawaii and San Francisco, California are sinking. Hickam Air Field and other airfields in the Hawaiian Islands have hundreds of burning airplanes on the ground. This cowardly attack by Japan is on the same day we are receiving a Japanese Ambassador in Washington DC. Tomorrow, on Monday, December 8, 1941, an emergency session in Congress will take place to vote on an official Declaration of War on the Empire of Japan."

After listening to the emergency bulletin that goes on for hours, Frank Perkins turns off the radio. He looks at his sons. He cannot smile.

Francis J. Perkins remembers World War I. He fought the Germans, over there. Over there are the battlefields of France and Germany in 1919. Frank Perkins fought bravely to end war forever. World War I was the War to End All Wars. He fought that war over there. "Over There," the famous George M. Cohan song, was playing while a younger Frank boarded the troop ship leaving for the European battlefields in 1917. Many of his friends never made it back.

Looking at his young boys today, Frank knows they will learn war from firsthand experience rather than from books. He is too dumbfounded to speak, the memories vivid in his consciousness even after over twenty years.

The oldest brother, Jim, in his early twenties takes over the conversation. "Dad, it's our time to be adults and take care of you. You did a great job raising us. You did it with one hand tied behind your back because of Mom's stroke after giving birth to Ray. Now we must fight for our country and our family. I appreciate everything you have done for us, Dad. Tomorrow, I am joining the Army. Bob, are you coming with me?"

"Yes, I want to join the Army Air Corps and bomb those bastards straight to hell."

"What about me?" young Fran asks. "I'm going too."

"You are still in high school. I want you to finish in June before going anywhere," Frank demands. "You won't be able to get a good job at the city anymore without a high school diploma."

"Not to worry, Dad," Bob pipes up, "By the time Fran enters basic training, Jim and I will finish the war. They'll send Fran right back home so he can marry Elaine."

Fran defends, "There'll be plenty of War left by the time I get in. The Germans are next, after you take care of the Japanese. I'll be in one of those fast little fighter planes knocking down everything in the sky."

What Fran does not realize is that in four days on December 11, 1941, Germany declares War on the United States, mostly because they want Japan to help them defeat the Russians. Hitler feels Japan is not strong enough to take on the United States, but they will definitely be able to take the pressure off the European Front with Japanese invading Russia from the West. The only question is how strong is the United States of America?

Fran asks, "What's war like, Dad?"

Dad says nothing but quickly and quietly walks out of the room.

Jim explains, "Dad never talks about the war, Fran. World War I veterans never talk about the war."

"That is right," Bob adds. It was like living through a horrible nightmare every single day. Dad never complains but I know he has nightmares still over twenty years after the war."

Jim clarifies, "Now that nightmare is ours to share. All three of us need to enlist first thing tomorrow morning. We need to show those Japanese that the Perkins boys stick together. Blood is thicker than water like Dad always says."

The Birmingham Family

Later on Sunday, Fran leaves the house in the Brainerd District of Chicago and heads over to Elaine's house at 9336 S. Clifton Park Ave in Evergreen Park.

1-1 Birmingham Home in 1941

He politely knocks on the door and Clarence Birmingham, Elaine's father, turns off the large console radio looking much like the one in the living room of the Perkins home. The radio was airing his favorite show, The Jell-O Program Starring Jack Benny, his favorite comedian.

"Welcome, Fran," Clarence smiles as he opens the door. "Mae and Elaine are in the dining room setting the table. I hope you enjoy yourself this evening."

Clarence Birmingham is a kind man who works for the transportation system in Chicago. He was born in 1888 in Silver Spring, Maryland, not far from Washington D.C. Clarence dropped out of school in the fourth grade to assist his brothers working in the family bakery business. As a young boy, Clarence drove a horse drawn wagon delivering bread, pies, cakes and other baked goods in Washington D.C. He delivered bread to the White House and occasionally handed the fresh bread directly to President William McKinley. McKinley was a war hero in the American Civil War and won the Spanish-American War while President. As a young boy Clarence was easy going and not awestruck by the Presidents and Congressmen he served.

Clarence Birmingham, like Frank Perkins, served in World War I. He had a strong, steady focus that made him invaluable in the trenches of war.

He does not talk about it.

Mae greets Fran as he walks through the enclosed porch to the dining room. She smiles, takes Fran by the hand and sits him at the head of the table.

Mae grew up on a large dairy farm in Wisconsin. Her father makes the best-churned butter in all of Wisconsin. In fact, he won a Blue Ribbon at the Columbian World Exposition, also known as the Chicago World's Fair in 1893.

Mae is very sociable. She loves to have visitors. She has a way of making a dear friend of every stranger. Today her natural talent of helping strangers feel comfortable affects young Fran Perkins.

"Fran, I know you're upset by the radio broadcast. How do you feel right now?"

"I don't know what to think. Tomorrow I'm skipping school and joining the Army with my brothers Bob and Jim. Bob and I are enlisting in the Army Air Corps and Jim in the Army. We want to fight this war so my little brothers Eddie and Ray won't have to fight."

Elaine enters the room, looking radiant in a suitable Sunday dress. She is finally in a public high school, Calumet High School, after spending grade school in a Catholic grade school called Longwood Academy in nearby Washington Heights. Elaine carries a notebook. She writes for the school newspaper and the school yearbook called Temulac, which is Calumet, spelled backwards.

Conversation leads to Fran asking questions about the home, the Christmas tree and decorations, while Elaine is taking notes.

"Hey, Elaine, what're you writing?" Fran queries.

"I know this is an important day in history. A World War starts this day for America. I want to record everything now so I can write articles for the school paper or even write a book someday about World War II. Fifty years from now, no one will remember how people felt on Sunday, December 7, 1941. I want to help them remember today and all the events of this day."

Fran looks around the room as it is growing darker outside and now the dining room is taking on a different tone. Fran relaxes and feels safe and warm in the Birmingham household. Fran silently hopes he will marry Elaine someday and he can spend more evenings in the candlelit dining room belonging to Clarence and Mae Birmingham.

Mae and Clarence are in a mixed marriage. Mae is a devout Catholic and Clarence never attends church of any kind. Mae is a poster child for the way a true Catholic should live her life. Faith, hope and charity are inborn behaviors. Mae never has a bad word to say about anyone. She respects people of all faiths, colors and creeds.

Clarence, on the other hand, never talks about religion nor goes to church, however, he lives his life the same way Mae does. Even though he has no one or no religion to account to, he lives a life of charity and goodwill toward others. He and Mae go through life seeing the best in everyone they meet. Silently he gives to the poor without allowing the beneficiary the opportunity to lose any dignity. There were no income tax breaks for charity back in those days. He gives from his heart and soul, not because of any fundraiser or outside request. Clarence is a deeply spiritual man yet never talks about what he believes, even to Mae. Clarence quietly and privately helps others.

"Clarence and I are going down to the Ford Plant this week to see if we can help out. Ford is manufacturing engines for bombers for the Allied countries, England, Canada Australia and India. The Ford Plant in Chicago makes the engines and the new Willow Run factory in Detroit is making the largest bombers in the World. I imagine some of those bombers will bomb Japan as well as Germany to win the War."

Fran is impressed. He makes a mistake, though, when he turns to Clarence and asks, "Sir, what was it like to be in battle?"

Clarence says nothing. His eyes look downward as he quickly and quietly leaves the room.

Fran is stunned. He said the wrong thing again. By the time, Fran speaks, he stutters from the embarrassment.

"Mae, I am sorry. I must have said the wrong thing to Clarence."

"Fran, Clarence understands your interest in finding out about his war experience, but he never talks about World War I. Many of his friends died over there. Many of his friends died over here on training exercises. He said that war is just about bullets, bombs and poison gas. He feels fortunate that he came back. He lives his life because of how he survived World War I and then the Great Depression. He always worries about supporting Elaine and me. He's a very responsible person. Fran, can you please excuse me a moment while I check up on Clarence?"

Fran feels he messed up their relationship and looks at Elaine who says. "Fran, everything'll be okay. When you're in the Air Corps, I'll write to you every day just as Mom & Dad did. Mom wrote letters to Dad that were so inspiring that Dad shared her loving letters with the other soldiers. My mom loves everyone and within a few sentences of her uplifting words, each man wanted to hang on to the letter as his very own. I hope I can write like that someday."

Clarence and Mae emerge from the hallway leading from their bedroom. Clarence acts as if nothing happened when he abandoned his young guest. He has something in his hand.

"Fran, when I was a little boy, my father took me to Buffalo Bill's Wild West Show. Buffalo Bill came to Washington D.C. for a huge outdoor performance. There were real Indians like Crazy Horse and Geronimo acting out Custer's Last Stand. My brothers and I had a wonderful time. My father gave each one of us a wooden nickel from that event."

Clarence hands young Fran his wooden nickel and with a gleam in his eye says, "Never take any wooden nickels." Clarence laughed long and hard at his own joke. Understanding this, Fran laughed along with his new friend and possible future father-in-law.

1-2 Fran's new lucky charm

Clarence solemnly asks Fran, "Will you take this wooden nickel as a token of our friendship tonight? Keep it with you as a good luck charm. I kept this with me overseas during the War and it got me home safe. I want you to be safe."

"Thank you very much, sir. I'll keep it in my pocket for good luck," Fran says as he pictures a younger Clarence with his brothers enjoying a Wild West Show. Clarence has many brothers just like Fran.

After dinner Mae, Clarence, Elaine and Fran walk to the door. Mae tells some motivational stories for him to remember on his long, dark walk home in the wintry Chicago weather. She then asks Fran a question.

"Fran, Americans in battle have two weapons that defeat the enemy. Do you know what the two weapons are?"

Without thought Fran replies, "Guns and ammo."

"No, the weapons I am talking about are the greatest weapons in the world. The weapons are heroism and hope. With hope in your mind and in your heart, heroism will spring forth at the very moment you need it. You and your fighters will see how easy it is to trade your lives for each other. This will come to you without any forethought on your part. With acts of heroism by you and your soldiers, hope springs forward. We will win this war. All of us, working together behind the scenes, will win this war. Nothing will ever defeat us. We are Americans. We will win because we have heroism and hope."

When Fran reaches home, he finds his brothers in the same place he left them. They never left on the bus to go Christmas shopping. Today it is more important to stay home. Fran learns that on this same day, December 7, 1941 the Japanese also invaded Midway, Wake Island, Hong Kong, the Philippines, Malaya, and Thailand, called Siam at the time.

It seems as if the Japanese Armies and Navies are everywhere at once. At the same time, the Russians and Germans stall in heavy winter fighting on the Eastern Front and the British Army is engaged in heavy desert fighting in North Africa.

December 7, 1941 is called the Day of Infamy as expressed by President Franklin D. Roosevelt the next day as he addresses a joint session of Congress. The purpose of the joint session is to declare War on Japan.

As Fran reunites with his brothers on this dark, cold Chicago night, he visualizes the entire world at war. Fran looks at his older brothers and sees grown men. Their lives will never be the same after today. Soon they find themselves training for battle. Tomorrow Fran joins Jim and Bob at the enlistment center in Chicago. Fran will stay in school until this coming July at the request of his father. In July, he goes to the Induction Center by himself to swear into the Armed Forces of the United States. His brothers will be through with most of their training by then. Fran Perkins will meet his personal Day of Infamy in the not too distant future. He arms himself with his new lucky wooden nickel and a smidgen of hope. He will always remember Mae's uplifting words about heroism and hope.

"I know my brothers are ready. I'm ready, too. I hope."

Chapter 2

Molly and Her Lib

They called her Molly. She was born in 1911 just prior to World War I. The other workers at the Consolidated Aircraft B-24 Plant in San Diego, California, called her Molly because none of them could pronounce her first name or last name, which were very long and chocked full of consonants. Therefore, Molly was good enough for now. Her boss called her Molly Alphabet to distinguish her from the other Mollies under his management.

The rumor was she came from Yugoslavia, Czechoslovakia, Bulgaria or Romania. She could have been from some other country most Americans did not learn about until World War II was well underway. Her husband may still be over there, although she never talked of having a husband. Molly was not born in America; she chose to live here. She was a naturalized citizen and was extremely proud to live and be free in America.

During her citizenship ceremony, Molly was moved to tears hearing the following words in the Naturalization Oath of Allegiance. She used the Oath as a blueprint for the career she chose at the Consolidated Aircraft B-24 Plant. She accepted each word of the oath into her heart and soul.

Those words are as follows:

"...that I will support and defend the Constitution and laws of the United States of America against all enemies, foreign and domestic; that I will bear true faith and allegiance to the same; that I will bear arms on behalf of the United States when required by the law; that I will perform noncombatant service in the Armed Forces of the United States when required by the law; that I will perform work of national importance under civilian direction when required by the law; and that I take this obligation freely, without any mental reservation or purpose of evasion; so help me God."

Molly knew the work that she needed to pursue. She would "perform work of national importance under civilian direction" and would take her "obligation freely, without any mental reservation or purpose of evasion."

War was breaking out in her country of birth and in countries all over the world. Molly decided that she could best serve her new home by finding work in the Defense Industry.

She wanted to repay Uncle Sam for the opportunity to work in this country and to raise her children in a free society. Having lived under a dictator's rule in the past, Molly was proud and grateful to be an American because America has so much more to offer her family. She vowed never to live anywhere where hopes and dreams did not have a chance to come true.

The project at the Consolidated Aircraft B-24 Plant was called Project 32, where men and women worked on a new bomber they nicknamed the "Lib." The B-24 Liberator was originally called the LB-30. LB stood for Land-Based Bomber. It was the heaviest land-based bomber in service at that time in the entire world.

Molly smiled and her eyes lit up whenever other employees called the B-24 by its full name. It was the Liberator. Liberator sounded much better to Molly than names like Flying Fortress or Super Fortress. In her mind, she saw the Liberator as an instrument to bring peace around the world. The Liberator would free people around the world from tyrannical governments bent on destroying the hopes and dreams of millions of good people. In Molly's eyes, the Liberator was a symbol of hope for oppressed people everywhere. Yes, the Liberator was the center of her life. The Liberator was the passion in her soul that kept her focused on her job and her family.

The American Declaration of Independence does not guarantee happiness. It guarantees the pursuit of happiness. In other words, America guarantees hope for all of its citizens.

Molly raises two small children while working at the defense plant, her son Dale who is eight years old and her daughter Linda who is six years old in 1942. Molly's mother cares for the children while Molly works. They all live in an apartment near downtown San Diego.

Molly is a very spiritual person. At lunch every day, she opens her lunch pail and closes her eyes for a few seconds in prayer. She does not belong to a church but chooses to honor her God in her own personal way. Molly is a very intelligent person. She speaks with a thick Slavic accent but she reads and understands English much better than she speaks it.

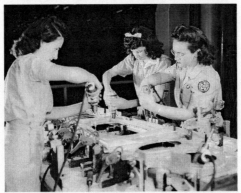

2-1 Heroes Helping the War Effort

Back in the 1940s, women didn't earn much money because they were usually housewives and were expected to take care of children while their husbands worked to pay the bills. In the fledgling Defense Industry of the late 1930s and 1940s, a woman could support herself quite well working at the defense plants. Women were paid the same wages as men in the Defense Industry, which was greatly appreciated by Molly who was the only financial support for her children and her mother. It was no wonder why women left their kitchens by the millions to work at these defense plants.

Molly and Her Lib

Molly works a nine-hour shift beginning at noon. She likes the hours because she has time to spend with her two children before going to work and is able to tuck them in before they go to sleep at night. Molly does not have any friends, as she is too busy working during the week and spending time with her mother and two children.

Molly works on a small team that assembles and welds the machine gun mounts that fit in the ball-turret of the new B-24D Liberator. Molly can read blueprints. This makes her invaluable to her team constructing the machine gun mounts and harnesses that fit inside the turrets. She knows exactly where everything is supposed to go and how everything is supposed to fit.

Molly has a quiet confidence the other women on her team respect. She does not speak much while working but when she does speak, the other women listen. They know that Molly knows her job well and the team works together to achieve all of the production and quality goals that Consolidated Aircraft Manufacturing demands.

There is not much time for idle chitchat and gossip while on the job. The women understand they need to work like men to keep enjoying the compensation that supports them. Therefore, they work like the men at that time in history. Workers didn't allow themselves the luxury of being burned out or stressed out. If the women did not feel well, they just sucked it up and kept working, as did the men of that era. The men and women who worked in Consolidated Aircraft Manufacturing and the entire Defense Industry around the country were the unsung heroes of World War II. Each and every worker in those plants should have been awarded medals for their almighty work.

Machine Guns and A Note

The ball-turret was a retractable housing that was located in the belly of the B-24. On bombing missions, a gunner climbed into the ball-turret, which was in the turret housing and then released a motor driven turret that spiraled down outside of the aircraft just beyond the bomb bay doors. The ball-turret or belly gunner climbed into the turret while still inside the bomber and then lowered himself and the Plexiglas turret down to the outside of the aircraft while the bomber was thousands of feet above the ground. The gunner must be small and thin to be able to move around in the retractable turret. He had to be mighty strong to handle the heavy, vibrating machine guns. A young man with the skills of a Kentucky Derby jockey would be the perfect fit for an assignment as a ball-turret gunner on a B-24 Liberator. The gunner must also withstand confinement in tight places. He could not be claustrophobic.

Twin fifty-caliber machine guns were placed on the machine gun mounts that Molly and her team built and were housed inside the retractable ball-turret located in the belly of the B-24. The Plexiglas and metal turret stayed inside the bomber until needed on a bombing mission or on a patrol to find lost seamen, downed aircrews and enemy submarines.

The "D" Model B-24 was different in many subtle ways from previous models, the most noticeable difference being the front turret mounted in the nose of the bomber just below the pilots. This area, known as the greenhouse because of the amount of glass used, also housed the bombardier and sometimes the navigator. The nose gunner, bombardier, and navigator were all located in the greenhouse. The navigator also had a table behind the pilot and co-pilot that made it easier for the pilots to get their bearings especially if their communications over the intercom system were interrupted or damaged.

Every workday, after finishing the machine gun mounts for the B-24 ball-turret, Molly tapes a printed set of installation instructions onto one of the mount subassemblies. Then she writes her own note on a heavier grade of paper measuring four inches by six inches in size, carefully folds and places it inside the middle of the instruction packet between two sets of instructions. She prints by hand, each note very carefully so that any crewmember can read and understand it fully. She prints rather than writes because she is left-handed.

Molly and Her Lib

When she was a child growing up in the 'old country', as she always referred it, she had been disciplined for using her left hand to print or write, scolded in public for using a knife, fork or spoon with her left hand. Her parents told her that using her left hand was demonic. This was a common belief at that time. Many Americans living in the early and middle part of the twentieth century also felt that way, that there was something bad about being left-handed. Molly did not want anyone reading the note to judge her negatively because of her penmanship skills. She was very careful at all times to make straight up and down characters instead of a noticeable left-handed slant.

After she finishes writing, she closes her eyes with the note pressed against her heart and says a few words to herself. The note is always the same for each gun mount subassembly.

The note reads, "Angels are flying with you now."

Molly knows the ball-turret gunner will eventually find her taped instructions when he inspects the equipment to make sure the guns are mounted properly before going into battle.

Molly's Work Day

The noon whistle blasts are heard for several miles triggering the salivary glands of thousands of workers who began work earlier at 8AM. For Molly the noon whistle triggers the beginning of her workday on the gun mount assembly line. Upon entering the building, workers stop at two security desks where armed security officers check any bags or lunch pails, then open the doors and escort the workers inside. As she ends her shift at 9:30PM, Molly takes a ten-minute free bus ride that takes her within just one block of her apartment.

She works in a pod with three other women, Betty, Sandra, and Marie. Because of her extensive knowledge of blueprints and her ability to read and understand instructions even though English is her second language, she became lead man on the job. Her team of four consistently exceeds production and quality goals and all four women take great pride in their work. The three co-workers are in their early twenties and all have husbands who joined the Navy the day after the Pearl Harbor attack on December 7, 1941. Betty, Sandra, and Marie's husbands are in the Silent Service of the United States Navy.

The Silent Service was submarine duty and because of the secret nature of the Silent Service, letters from their husbands did not come as frequently as other branches of the service. Rumors had it that all three men were stationed on the same submarine in the North Atlantic Ocean off the coast of either France or England. No one knew for sure. The women rarely talked at work even if they knew where their husbands were located because of the creed that they lived by. "Loose lips sink ships" was printed on posters everywhere. The phrase did not fall on deaf ears for the wives. They knew their husbands were working every day at sinking enemy ships and were very aware of the risks. They were working with a woman with a foreign accent. In fact, the accent was one that matched up closely with the Axis Forces of the Nazis fighting the Russians at Stalingrad this very minute. Even though these women liked Molly, they remained quiet around her. Their silence was America's best secret weapon in defeating their enemies and saving the lives of those they loved. The women also knew that in addition to the B-24 Liberators, they were also building the PB4Y bombers that were assigned to the US Navy. Skillful naval officers piloted the PB4Ys that patrolled the waters looking for downed ships, airmen and watching out for Nazi submarines. They knew the bombers they were building would be assisting their husbands on submarine patrols in the Atlantic Ocean. They considered themselves the protective eyes and ears for their husbands' submarines.

Late in 1942, the Consolidated Plant was turning out over 300 bombers a month. Considering there were over 1,250,000 parts in each airplane, turning out even one Liberator a day was an enormous task. The goal was to turn out a Liberator every hour of the day. Henry Ford's Willow Plant near Detroit, Michigan was turning out over 750 Liberators a month. American bomber plants throughout the country employed this new kind of hero. The hero could be male or female and could be of any race or creed.

2-2 The B-24 Liberator

Terror on Tuesday

Tuesday before Thanksgiving in 1942 was a terrible day for Molly at the plant. She had finished her last gun mount assembly and hurriedly put it on a pallet to be picked up and moved to the Welding Department at the far end of the plant. After the material handler picked up the pallet with his hand truck, Molly noticed that the last packet of instructions was laying on the floor where the pallet sat a few minutes earlier.

Molly was horrified! "How could I be so stupid?" she thought. "I didn't include the note! I have to write a note for that gunner. He needs to have my note."

She took off running, ignoring the strict factory rule forbidding workers to leave their assigned pod without strict permission. As she ran, she had horrible visions of a B-24 high in the sky ambushed by many fighter planes and the gunner helpless to fire back. Molly saw the Liberator spiraling and crashing into the sea. She had never run this far or this fast since she was a little girl back in the old country. Running as fast as she could, Molly caught up to and stopped the material handler before he reached the Welding Department. She examined the gun mount on the top of the pile and found that it was missing the instructions and her hand-printed note. She was panting heavily as she pulled out her pen and paper. Making things worse, in her panic, she forgot to print the note, but instead she wrote out the note using her left-handed slant to each character.

Molly was terrorized by the incident and as she walked back from the material handler and the gun mount pallet, tears rolled down her face. When she reached her team in their work pod, the women reached out to console her. This was the first time and the only time that they hugged at work. They had to act and work as men so hugging would not have been the first response; a masculine response would be sarcasm. These female co-workers did not exhibit any sarcasm that day. Betty reached out first and whispered in her ear, "I'll watch the mounts as you place them on the pallets to make sure the instructions are included. Together we'll make sure every ball-turret gunner in the Air Corps finds his instructions."

Betty never told her that she once opened a set of instructions while Molly was in the restroom and read Molly's note to Marie and Sandra just about a month earlier. Betty justified the invasion to her co-workers because of Molly's accent. The team had no idea what Molly might be telling those ball-turret gunners and they did not trust her. She could be a spy.

Thanksgiving Weekend

The family spent weekends at the library or in the small city parks located around the city. When World War II began the city's largest park, Balboa Park, was closed and turned into a military camp. Balboa

Park became Camp Kidd named after Admiral Kidd who was killed at Pearl Harbor during the attack on December 7, 1941.

Thousands of bunkers and gun emplacements were constructed along the beautiful beaches of Southern California. Some beach areas were restricted because the military was wary of a Japanese invasion of California, as some of the largest naval facilities and some of the world's largest bomber manufacturing plants were located there. Soldiers, artillery and tanks were everywhere. Every day there were rumors of attacks by the Japanese and enemy submarines that were sunk off the coast, but these were just rumors. The people of San Diego and other coastal cities tried to live their lives the best they could in spite of the rumors.

Molly and her family like to spend time at a variety of smaller parks throughout the city and found small areas of beach where bathers are allowed to swim.

After working on Friday after Thanksgiving, Molly came home a little after 10PM to both Dale and Linda. The children could stay up late since there was no school on Saturday when the family would be taking a trip to the San Diego Public Library.

Dale is very excited to go because he is interested in science. Linda is just beginning to read and does not know what books to look for, so Dale, the ever-protective big brother, suggests that she find books about George Washington, Abraham Lincoln, Benjamin Franklin and Dale's personal hero, Thomas Edison. Little Linda is reading the books and enjoying every moment. She is being a 'big girl' reading books about the same heroes that inspire her mother at work.

Dale asks his mother why she feels history books are so important. "My teacher told me that history is important to learn so we don't repeat the same history. He told us that the One Hundred Years' War over in Europe actually lasted over three hundred years."

Molly laughs saying, "Your history teacher is correct. War seems to never end over in the old country. That's one of the reasons I worked so hard to bring all of us over here to become American citizens.

"There is another reason you should learn history," Molly adds. "All of the characters, who won battles, became leaders or created new and exciting inventions had one thing in common. They all used the power of hope. Hope wakes us in the morning and puts us the sleep at night. Living in America just these few years taught me that hope is the most powerful force in America and should be the most powerful force on earth. Unfortunately, there are tyrannical leaders of countries that try to destroy that power of hope in the people they rule. The heroes of the world teach us that hope can change things for an oppressed people. As you learn more history, you learn more about the power of hope in your own lives."

On this Saturday in late November, although it is normally warm all winter in San Diego, a severe cold front hits Southern California and the family wears coats as they celebrate their day together in their adopted city.

After the library, Mother, Molly, Dale and Linda take a bus over to a restaurant to finish their Saturday adventure. The restaurant is large, resembling the cafeteria inside the Consolidated Aircraft Plant where Molly works. Normally it would be noisy inside the restaurant but today there are very few people, due to the cold weather to which most San Diegans are unaccustomed.

As they sit down, they hear a record playing that warms them. It is the song written by Irving Berlin while staying at the Biltmore Hotel in Phoenix, Arizona a short time earlier and made popular by the famous singer and actor, Bing Crosby. No one talks while the song plays because the words of the song exemplify the lessons learned today. The song is about a White Christmas, "just like the ones we used to know." The song is about hope.

22

Sunday flies by very quickly for the family and they stay warm in their apartment reading the books from the San Diego Public Library. Mother gladly washes and irons clothes for the family and cooks the meals, grateful be living with her daughter and grandchildren in relative harmony. Molly prepares for the workweek and gets the children ready for school the next day. Before tucking them into bed, she reads the *Biography of Davy Crockett King of the Wild Frontier* to the children. Just before closing the book, she reads one of Davy's well-known sayings, "Always be sure you are right and then go ahead."

As the family sleeps peacefully, around the world many disturbing events cause a sense of urgency in the American Defense Industry. However, during the weekends, life for the family seems to be almost normal in a land that is still free.

Over there, many large battles raged. The Battle of Stalingrad in Russia was taking place between the Russians and the Nazis along with their Hungarian and Slavic Allies. This one battle alone claimed more lives than were lost by the Americans during all of World War II on all fronts. A key battle in the Pacific raged on the Island of Guadalcanal. Naval ships, Army Air Corps Bombers and US Marines were fighting the first land battle against the Japanese. Some of the same B-24 bombers on which Molly worked were key weapons used in this bloody battle.

Molly, Mother, Dale and Linda did their best to live with the world events in 1942. They believed the War would end someday.

It just may not end today.

Nightmares Begin for Molly

Not all was perfect for Molly. Sometimes she felt lonely but most of the time she could deal with it. She never felt comfortable confiding in her co-workers. She sensed early on that her co-workers did not trust her. Molly's life in Europe had been much worse than any stress she faces here. However, ...

She began to have nightmares about a lonely ball-turret gunner aboard one of her bombers. It would come to her right after a day at work that went a little amiss. Fortunately, there were few days like that but when there was, she could count on the nightmare as she fell asleep at night. As a worker in the Defense Industry during World War II, Molly created a fearful vision about the ball-turret gunner in mortal combat and turned it into a recurring nightmare that would follow her for a long time. Without being in combat herself, she was experiencing some of the same "shell shock" combat veterans experience, today known as PTSD.

Molly remembered her father was wounded during World War I, the War to End All Wars. As a young girl, she could hear her father screaming out at night in his sleep. When Molly's brothers or sisters asked him what he did in World War I, he would talk for a while and then leave the room. Molly and her siblings understood and did not press for more information. They knew something horrible had happened and they prayed for his release from suffering.

Molly sometimes wondered if her efforts were truly making a contribution. She knew that her fellow workers were doing all they could to help the war effort. They seemed happy and positive but who knows how they felt when they went to bed at night after a long day working in the plant. She wondered if they felt the same stress. She wondered if her work would help her children live in a country where they worry of war no more. Molly struggled to release the worry and fill her soul with hope. Molly knew she was not alone and she held fast to the confidence that her intelligence and strength would triumph in the end. She never knew how she influenced lives of others around her. She just held on to the belief that all would end well and that world war would be over soon.

Chapter 3

The Farm Boy

At the end of rows and rows of one of the largest soybean fields ever seen in Illinois, Jacob Nelson sits cross-legged on the thick, black soil with his face buried in his hands. Out near the little town of DeKalb, Illinois, farmers were just beginning to enjoy the benefits of the end of the dust bowl. Illinois corn grew as tall as the famous Iowa corn and farmers reveled in its splendor. Jacob Nelson appreciated the abundance, but right now, he had an overwhelming problem: with current limited resources how to harvest soybeans before they spoil?

Jacob's job as a farmer is professional but also very personal. Sitting in the bean field in despair, he thinks about his older brother, John, who lost his life in battle over in the trenches of France during World War I. World War I was the War to End All Wars, but in the summer of 1942, an even larger war was consuming life in every corner of the planet.

3-1 Food for Freedom poster

Jacob's only help, along with his three daughters, was his brother John's son, John Jr., also known as Deuce. Deuce dropped out of grade school to work the farm with his Uncle Jacob. He was a good farmer and his greatest value came from being able to keep the rickety old tractor working. Some area farmers were still plowing their fields using horse-drawn plows, but Jacob's farm was mechanized, using a tractor for all of his acreage.

Jacob grew soybeans this year because he had heard that they are not only used for making margarine and other food products, but supply more nitrogen into the soil and when he plants corn in the field for the harvest next year, he should have a record crop. The blood, sweat and tears expended by the Nelson family today to produce abundant crops will feed the American Armed Forces in their many battles around the world, as well as the refugees and even the prisoners from the battle-weary countries. Jacob's job is to feed the world.

Over ten years earlier Japan invaded Manchuria and restricted export of all soybeans and now it was up to Jacob to help fill the void thus created. The benefits of harvesting a new crop of soybeans far outweighed the benefits of his corn. Rotating corn in the fields that soybeans grew the previous season insured a strong corn crop because of the nutrients left behind by the beans.

Jacob's memory of the dust bowl just a few years earlier reminds him that soil is his most precious asset and he is the caretaker of the soil.

Camp Grant near Rockford, Illinois

At the same time, at Camp Grant near Rockford, Illinois, Private Fran Perkins sits on his lower bunk bed of an Army barracks contemplating the forced field march scheduled for tomorrow, his first such forced field march.

The Farm Boy

On a forced field march, the men dress up in all of their US Army gear including a steel pot helmet, fatigue shirt and pants, a pair of heavy wool socks and Army boots. In addition, each soldier packs a small shovel, canteen kit, tent ropes and pegs, and one-half of a tent, called a shelter half, that attaches to another soldier's shelter half. Fran packed extra socks and his K-rations to eat during the day.

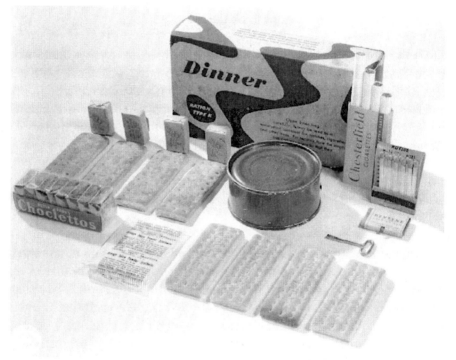

3-2 K-ration dinner 1942

Fran is excited but disturbed at the same time. It is summer time and lugging all of this gear will make the heat unbearable. He is in his 5th week of basic training and he wonders if he has the endurance to march for twelve miles with a thirty-pound pack on his back. Even though he is a young, healthy eighteen-year-old, doubt enters Fran's mind.

"What happens if I can't do it?" thinks Perkins. "My brothers Jim and Bob will be sick. My Dad will be disappointed and think I'm a failure. Jim's fighting with General Patton's army in North Africa and Robert's with the Eighth Army Air Corps stationed in England. They've both proven themselves in combat. How did these two city boys ever make it through basic training? We never hiked or lived in the woods growing up. We never exercised as we do now in basic training. I'm not familiar with this stuff and I don't want to be the one who fails."

Fran looks around his barracks, now empty. There are twelve bunk beds on the first floor of the barracks and eight upstairs. The Drill Sergeant Dale McDowell and his assistant Corporal Tom Hevey have a bedroom in part of the upstairs barracks. Outside groups of soldiers are talking and laughing but Fran is deep in thought about tomorrow's activities. "I just hope I can do this," Fran says in a whisper.

Just then, Fran hears a loud whistle from outside the Company B barracks, coming from the DI or drill instructor, Sergeant Dale McDowell.

The whistle is a signal commanding every soldier to line up at a marked location. The phrase "fall out on the company street" is one that every soldier understands and obeys immediately without question. They snap to in a formation of four squads consisting of ten men each that forms a unit called a platoon and four platoons that form a Company of one hundred sixty men. This Company is Bravo Company or just plain Company B. Every time Fran hears the term Company B, he thinks of the popular song by the Andrews Sisters, *the Boogie Woogie Bugle Boy of Company B*. Sometimes he daydreams about being the famous trumpet player, Harry James, and playing this very song.

As the whistle sounds several times, Fran hears Sergeant McDowell yelling, "Bravo Company fall out in formation. Company B fall out on the company street."

The Farm Boy

Where is Deuce?

Jacob gets up from his sitting position and scans the bean fields and the cornfields, calling for Deuce. His wife, Tina, responds to his calls bringing daughters Ailie, Bobbie, and Becky. The youngest daughter, three-year-old Bonnie, is napping back at the farmhouse.

"What's wrong?"

Jacob shakes his head from side to side, "Where is Deuce? He should be back from Rockford with those spare parts he thinks he needs. I told him this tractor will never run again and he is off on a wild goose chase getting some spare parts. We have enough spare parts now to turn one of the cornfields into a junk yard."

"Now don't get your bowels in kink, Jacob. Deuce is Brother Johnny's boy and we swore to love him and take care of him for the rest of his life. We both know your nephew Deuce is doing his best to help this farm," exclaims Tina.

"But..."

"I know we don't have enough help to harvest the entire bean field but we'll work as much and as hard as we can. We'll work all day and all night if we have to. The girls will help and we'll be fine. We'll turn this hard work into fun. You need to have hope, Jacob. Farming's a tough life and when you give in to fear and frustration, you lose yourself and you lose your farm. We've been through hard times before on the farm and so have our parents. Tomorrow will bring a new day. We need to fill that new day with hope. Deuce is not the problem, our fear and hopelessness is. When we plant the seeds of hope, we'll harvest a brighter future."

Jacob smiles at his wife saying, "Tina, this is why I married you. You sound like our Pastor but you're much prettier. Sunday morning when we're finished with the beans, we'll take a long look at our tall corn, our

29

farmhouse and our huge front yard. We'll hope for the best and be grateful for what is. We'll count our blessings."

Bravo Company Fall In

Fran races out to the company street just outside the barracks compound remembering to wear his fatigue pants and cap, knowing that he would receive a stern reprimand if he had not. The drill sergeant would command him to "drop and give me twenty," that is twenty good pushups before ordered back into formation. Fran would be humiliated in front of the other one hundred sixty troops, much to their personal amusement and delight. Sometimes Sergeant McDowell or Corporal Hevey will yell, "Drop and give me fifty, or drop and give me a hundred." Attention to detail in all drills and learning exercises was necessary to turn the young boys into a disciplined fighting unit. Fran is in "B" or Bravo Company. Alpha, Bravo, Charlie and Delta Companies form a Battalion and four Battalions form a Brigade.

Right now, only Company B's one hundred sixty men from the First Platoon, Second Platoon, Third Platoon and Fourth Platoon are standing in formation on the street.

The company commander, Captain Joseph B. Korn, steps up on a riser to address the troops. Drill Sergeant McDowell and Assistant Drill Instructor Corporal Tom Hevey face and salute Captain Korn. McDowell then completes an about face movement and salutes the troops of Bravo Company and shouts, "Ten hut!" The company stands at attention with arms pressing down with hands along the seams of their pants, thumbs curled at the forefinger.

Captain Korn then orders "At ease men!

"You are scheduled to go on a twelve-mile forced field march with full pack tomorrow at 0600 hours. In the Army and Army Air Corps, we sometimes get lucky and receive a target of opportunity, which takes

30

priority over the best-planned attack. I want a volunteer to go after a target of opportunity."

Fran Perkins feels an invisible force shoving him forward and instantly breaks rank from his squad and stands in front of the Third Platoon of Bravo Company. At the very same moment, the words of his father and his brothers are ringing in his ears, "Never volunteer for anything," Fran's overwhelming sense of duty overcomes the common sense that is his hallmark. How could he retract his forward movement and comply with the warning in front of officers and his entire company? "It is too late now," Fran, whispers to himself. "Everyone is looking."

Company Commander Korn smiles saying, "Thank you for volunteering. What is your name, Private?"

Perkins shouts as a basic trainee learns to shout back to a superior officer, "Private Francis J. Perkins Jr., Sir!"

"Are you a city boy or a farm boy?"

"I am a city boy from Chicago, Sir!"

"Private Perkins, the Army and Army Air Corps have a long tradition in history. We plan military campaigns and carry out our campaigns successfully and with military precision. When we have a target of opportunity that will bring us a greater victory, we immediately adjust to that target of opportunity. Do you understand what I am saying, Private Perkins?"

"Yes Sir!"

Fran may not understand anything, but he must yell out yes sir or Sergeant McDowell will order Fran to drop and give him fifty pushups.

The Farm Boy

"I need a volunteer who is a farm boy to fall out next to Private Perkins." Immediately a tall, handsome well-built young man falls out next to Perkins.

"What is your name, son," bellows Captain Korn.
"My name is Private John Paul Olsen, Sir!"

"Tomorrow you will face the enemy," says Captain Korn gravely.

"Your enemies are not the Germans, Italians, or Japanese. Your enemy is time. There is a large farm needing to get their soybeans picked within twenty-four hours or they may lose the crop. Jacob Nelson is the farmer's name. I know that we can pick the field in 12 hours because of my background in agriculture. We need 12 hours for our forced field march as well. This is not easy work, men. You have a decision to make. If I can get every man here to stand beside Private Perkins, a city boy, and Private Olsen, a farm boy, we can achieve our mission and Sunday morning we will leave the farm and you will have your Sunday off. After picking all of these soybeans, you might feel the same kind of pain as if you were on a forced field march, however, you will have the satisfaction of knowing your new enemy has been defeated and you are helping to feed your fellow soldiers and airmen in combat around the world. It is the job of every American farmer to feed the entire world at war.

"Everyone who is going to volunteer step forward in line with Private Perkins and Private Olsen," commands Captain Korn. Quickly and quietly, every soldier advances.

"It is settled then. Company B will fall out on the company street at 0700 hours tomorrow morning and you will mount up in several busses. We will all advance about forty miles from here to DeKalb, Illinois. We will break down in four platoons when we get there and each platoon will be led by one of the farm boys. Fall out of formation now and go back to your barracks for more instructions from your drill sergeant and platoon leaders. Do your job and defeat the enemy tomorrow. Good luck men. That is all."

Amber Waves of Grain

Saturday morning at 0600 hours, the drill sergeant is running into the barracks with a large empty garbage can, banging it loudly to wake up the young men inside. "Get up, get up, and get your buddy up!" the drill sergeant yells. "We have a battle to fight today."

All of the men get up and stand at attention by their bunks. The sergeant races upstairs to make sure the second floor of recruits have heard the message and soon comes back downstairs and orders everyone to the mess hall for breakfast. "Eat and move out," orders the drill sergeant. "We have work to do today."

The men dress and advance on the mess hall, a cafeteria large enough to hold several hundred men. The drill sergeants and officers have a special table on a raised platform about four feet above the rest of the cafeteria. They can view all of the troops eating below.

After eating, all of the troops of "B" Company load up on several troop busses and begin the forty-mile drive to Jacob Nelson's farm near DeKalb, Illinois.

Fran and John walk to the first bus. They will be riding with their drill sergeant who wants to learn as much as he can from Private John Paul Olsen about the harvesting of beans, so he can successfully lead his troops into this battle against time.

As the bus departs, Fran looks out the window and sees rural Illinois for the first time in his life. He arrived at Camp Grant a few weeks ago at night by train and could not see anything outside the dark windows. Blackout curtains covered most of the windows. Since we are at War, public and private transportation services use blackout curtains to prevent presenting an easy target should enemy bombers attack the

United States. Now he has a close-up and personal view of the enormous fields of tall corn and wheat. As large oceans of wheat fields pass by under the rising sun, the words from Kathy Lee Bates' song *America the Beautiful*, float through Fran's mind. "O beautiful for spacious skies, for amber waves of grain." Perkins views tall corn on stalks that seem to rise six to ten feet high. He gets up and looks out the window on the opposite side of the bus where again, he is overcome by the enormous, bountiful, beautiful cornfields.

As a city boy growing up in Chicago, Illinois, he never saw such grandeur. Perkins learned about agriculture from black and white photographs in schoolbooks. No photos in those books come close to the full color visual feast for Private Perkins. He imagines being outside the bus and walking through the cornfields. Looking at Private Olsen he says, "No wonder other countries want to take us over. We have so much for everyone. Do you want to go back to farming when the war is over?" asks Perkins.

Olsen stares out the window for a second, turns his head toward Perkins and says, "I enjoy farming. All of us Olsen kids grew up in these fields. My uncles all live in the farm country of Minnesota, Wisconsin, Illinois, and the Dakotas. However, I love history and if I can get into college after the War, I want to become a history teacher."

Sergeant McDowell, sitting directly behind Olsen, jumps in on the conversation and with a wily smile, sarcastically addresses Olsen, "What do you know about history, farm boy?"

Without hesitation, Olsen gives the drill sergeant and Perkins a quick and effective history lesson. "We will be arriving in DeKalb in a few minutes. It is exactly 42 miles from Camp Grant. The city was named to honor a Revolutionary War hero, Johann DeKalb, who was a German citizen and served under Lafayette. Johann DeKalb died in the Battle of Camden in South Carolina. He was shot off his horse. He died three days later. DeKalb wanted to die in a battle that would help win freedom for others. He wanted people to remember him as a Liberator."

The Farm Boy

Sgt. McDowell smiles, slaps Olsen on the back and proclaims loudly, "I like you, Olsen! You're smart and can think quickly. You should consider Officer Candidate School. The Army needs good officers to help us win the War and I can see those leadership qualities in you. Come to my office after breakfast on Monday and we will talk further. After you help us win the War, you'll become the best history teacher you can be."

Olsen looks startled and says, "Thank you, Sergeant."

McDowell taps Perkins on the shoulder and asks, "What do you want to do when you get out of the Army?"

"Honestly, I don't know, Sergeant," says Perkins. "I'm leaving for the Army Air Corps right after Basic Training. Hope to become a Pilot. I'd love to see a large body of water from high in the sky. I come from Chicago and my older brothers and I worked on a tugboat out on Lake Michigan. The water goes on for miles and miles. I want to pilot a plane over the Lake. I can't imagine how the lake would look from the air."

Sergeant McDowell slaps Fran heartily on that back and proclaims, "Someday you will get your chance, Perkins!"

Just then, the convoy of busses stops on the road in front of Jacob and Tina Nelson's sprawling farm.

Bean Company, Fall in!

Army busses circle the property. All of the doors open and young soldiers fall out on the road across from the farmhouse.

"What's going on!" shouts Jacob.

Deuce, having arrived a few minutes earlier, replies, "I got us some help for the soybean fields."

"Glory be!" says Jacob shaking his head from side to side. "You got the whole Army out here!"

"Company Beans, fall in!" roars Sergeant McDowell now with a rare yet noticeable grin on his face.

Four platoons of young fighting men snap to and fall in four separate lines on the dirt road. Deuce grabs Uncle Jake by the arm and both walk up to Captain Korn who leads them to a high point on the front yard, facing the troops. Deuce introduces Jacob Nelson to Company Commander Captain Korn, who is going to lead his troops into battle to save the beans. Surprisingly, Nelson remembers Korn as the man who sold him the now broken down tractor years earlier.

Four platoons of forty men each are standing in perfect lines on the dirt road facing the farmhouse. Captain Korn, Sergeant McDowell, Corporal Hevey, Jacob Nelson, Tina Nelson and Deuce Nelson are facing the troops.

Sergeant McDowell yells, "Company," and as he holds the "e" sound for several counts each platoon leader standing in front of each of the four platoons yells, "Platoon!" holding the long "oo" sound for several counts. Then Sergeant McDowell shouts "Ten hut!"

Snapping to attention, all one hundred sixty men stomp their boots creating a large cloud of dust that lingers for a few moments. An emotional wave engulfs the Nelson family watching the precision and commitment of these brave young men. Captain Korn addresses the men.

"Years ago as a civilian, I sold a tractor to Jacob Nelson to use on the farmland we are standing on. I promised him that he would always be able to bring his crops to harvest. Well, the tractor is broken and his nephew Deuce is trying to fix it. I have a promise to keep. Your job, men, is to help me and help Jacob Nelson harvest his crop.

The Farm Boy

"I understand you are ready to go into battle. You may not think that this battle is as important as taking a beachhead, taking prisoners, or bombing the hell out of a strategic target, but I assure you, it is. Farmers and ranchers from all over the United States of America are working with one hand tied behind their backs. They need to not only farm enough food for every man, woman and child in the United States, but also for all of the people on every continent that has experienced the destruction and devastation of their crops at the hands of our enemies Japan and Germany. I chose you today, men, for your first important battle in World War II. Volunteers Perkins and Olsen led you to these soybean fields. This is where we will make our stand. Do your best work and help this farmer save lives and feed the world. Right here and today we will win the Battle of the Beans. That is all."

From about 9AM until 8PM the "bean boys" labored to harvest the soybeans, each city boy soldier and farm boy soldier highly motivated. Even with hands sore, raw and bleeding and backs aching this was still a better substitute for the long field march that was originally promised. Twice during the day, squad leaders passed out K rations to the men and they took only a few minutes to choke them down.

This duty presents a nice break in all of the constant drilling, discipline and exercise. During basic training, there is little time for idle conversation. As these soldiers find success in harvesting the soybeans, they talk more and the country boys and city boys swap stories. This is the perfect time for them to relax while achieving a hard-earned goal. It is also a wonderful bonding exercise as these men will be in combat soon and it is nice to have these moments on which to reflect when they are in battle.

Perkins talks with Olsen and realizes he is just like his brothers Jim and Bob whom he misses deeply. Both are also keenly aware not to bond with any of these men too closely as the heartache of losing a friend in battle is too much to bear at this moment.

The Farm Boy

As night approaches women begin cooking sweet corn and put it out for all of the hungry young men. Along with the sweet corn, a woman from an adjoining farm brings freshly churned butter.

Faraway lights announce a convoy of cars, trucks and farm equipment peeling toward the farmhouse. Headlights are banned because of the wartime blackout. Gasoline rationing is enforced as well, but these farmers have enlisted in winning the Battle of the Beans.

The Battle of the Beans, taking place in DeKalb, Illinois is won by Jacob Nelson, his family, the soldiers of Bean Company, and local farmers ignoring their own duties to help a fellow farmer. The soldiers in the field shout out a hip, hip hooray, as the vehicles emerge on the new company street. Captain Korn, who is stripped down to his tee shirt and fatigue pants, smiles at the sight. He and Sergeant Dale McDowell shake their heads at each other, as each man knows that the tough training they give their men to survive in battle is already paying off with this battle raging in the quiet Illinois soybean fields.

Fran Perkins and John Paul Olsen sit on a couple of tree stumps at the edge of the largest bean field looking over all of the ground they covered today and are impressed. "The battle is over, Fran," says Olsen as he smiles with pride and satisfaction. "We win." Olsen then points to the sky and says, "Do you see that star formation in the sky that looks like a frying pan? That's the Big Dipper."

"My brother, Bob, in the Army Air Corps says that the pilots and navigators sometimes use the stars to navigate their planes at night."

The budding history teacher Olsen adds, "Yeah, people from around the planet have been navigating vast seas and oceans by the stars. You can always count on this navigating device. It's a navigating tool that gives you hope. It's like us seeing all of the farmer's friends showing up to help. Friendship is like navigating with the stars, you can always count on it."

The Farm Boy

"When I fly my first airplane," Fran says, "I hope to learn how to navigate by the stars. That'll be fun."

"You'll get your chance someday, Fran. You'll get your chance."
The rising morning sun brings relief for the soldiers and farmers. Sergeant McDowell orders everyone to fall out on the new company street, the dirt road in front of Jacob and Tina Nelson's farmhouse. As the four platoons line up to board the buses, Olsen hears a loud engine starting up. He sees Deuce, Jacob, and Tina standing by the tractor with Captain Korn in his tee shirt and fatigue pants sitting on the tractor's seat. A large puff of black smoke shoots out of the tractor exhaust and the hard work Deuce put in all night pays off. Deuce figured out what parts he needed and put the tractor back in service. An elated Captain Korn pounds the air with his fist and whoops, realizing that he kept his promise to Jacob. Jacob will never have to worry about harvesting his crops.

The sounds of the buses starting their engines and the men boarding, all happily looking forward to a day off, is balanced by the sound of a tractor purring loudly that it is alive and well. It is back in action for the Nelson family to help feed the world at war.

Jacob pulls Tina aside and they view the now empty bean field and the lush cornfields. This was a battle fought and won by farmers, friends and the US Army and Army Air Corps. As he scans his vast cornfields, with a smile Jacob says," I'm counting my blessings, Tina. I'm counting my blessings."

Monday Morning

After a quiet Sunday, going to the Chapel and returning to clean their gear and write letters to their families, the men from B Company turn in for a quiet, restful sleep.

Monday morning starts at 0500 hours and the troops pile out onto the company street at Camp Grant. After a few short announcements,

The Farm Boy

Sergeant McDowell has Olsen and Perkins fall out of formation and report to Captain Korn. The Company Clerk orders both men to sit while the captain prepares and then directs Olsen to Korn's office.

Olsen salutes the officer and Korn orders Olsen to sit. Captain Korn is short and direct with Olsen. "Private Olsen, Sergeant McDowell feels you will make a good officer. I watched you in action on Saturday and I agree. Here are your orders. You will get on the next train to Chicago and then you will take a train to Fort Sill, Oklahoma, to begin your officer training. The Army needs good officers."

Captain Korn comes to attention and both men salute each other. Olsen does an about face, heads out the door with official orders inside a brown envelope, and smiles at Perkins with two thumbs up. Fran knows it is great news for his friend.

Perkins enters Captain Korn's office and both men salute each other. "Perkins, you are to report to Sheppard Field in Wichita Falls, Texas, where you will be testing for your assignment in the Army Air Corps. You test for pilot, navigator, radioman and a host of gunner positions on heavy bombers. I am excited for you and I wish you well."

Fran leaves the office and runs back to the barracks where Olsen is packing for his next assignment. "I guess this is it, John! I'm being sent to Wichita Falls, Texas, to be tested for a bomber crew."

"And I'm being sent to Officer Candidate School at Fort Sill, Oklahoma. I never imagined being an officer. It's hard to believe. I hope I can cut it."

"Are you kidding? I have no doubt you'll make it. The next time I run into you, I'll make sure I address you as Sir and give you an official salute."

"The next time I see you, Fran, I had better get a plane ride, maybe over Lake Michigan. You can navigate by the stars! I hope there'll be a next time, but we really don't know what's ahead, do we? At least I know that I am one step closer to being a history teacher." Swinging his duffle bag over his shoulder, giving Fran a thumbs up, he gallantly adds, "Let's go make some history!"

Olsen leaves the barracks and Fran stands alone. "See ya, John." The rest of the third platoon is out in the field training. The two-floor barracks is silent. As his gaze circles the empty room, many disjointed thoughts flood his mind.

"Many men have slept in this building, who are now deployed in combat units all over the world.
Many young men have stood on this spot where I'm standing now.
Many are dead.
Many more men will be needed to fill their shoes.
Many men will be here someday to celebrate victory."

"I hope I make it," Fran whispers to himself. "My dad and my brothers are counting on me. When I become a pilot, Elaine will be happy for me. She'll brag to all of her girlfriends." With determination he vows, "I will make it!"

Fran removes his uniforms from his wall locker and picks up the remaining items from his footlocker. He stuffs his duffle bag to overflowing. To rectify that situation Fran pretends he is the heavyweight boxer Joe Lewis, the Brown Bomber. After reigning several punches on the defenseless duffle bag, the bag gives up and Perkins stuffs more items in the submissive bag. Fran raises both arms high in the air and declares, "I am the champion. Hear me roar!"

Perkins and Bean Company fought the Battle of the Beans on Saturday, two days ago. On another Saturday, less than a year from now Fran will find himself in a much deadlier battle than the Battle of the Beans. He will be fighting in his own Brown Bomber over the skies of the Pacific Ocean. He and his crew will be fighting for their lives.

41

The Farm Boy

The battle is the Alamo in the Sky, the last flight of the famous and beloved **Daisy Mae**.

Chapter 4

Advanced Airman Training

Fran flies to Texas the following day. He rides in an Army Air Corp jeep on a long trip from the airport to Camp Sheppard also known as Sheppard Air Field located on the Northern Texas border not far from Wichita Falls. Camp Sheppard will be home for several weeks.

An Army Air Corps poster circulates across the land. The poster shows a handsome young Army Air Corps Pilot standing in front of a scene showing large bombers flying across a blue sky and large white puffy clouds. It illustrates how glorious the service looks to young Fran Perkins who is only eighteen years old at the time. The clouds resemble angel wings. These young men are on a mission from God.

4-1 Army Air Force recruitment poster

Advanced Airman Training

The airbase is an exciting place. Fran will be training for all positions on the B-24 Bomber including gunner, radio communications and armorer.

Davy Crockett

The first training Perkins is excited about is Small Arms Fire Training starting with the M1 Garand Rifle and the smaller version, the M1 Carbine. The M1 Rifle is the bread and butter gun for the US Army fighting the Nazi's and the M1 Carbine is the bread and butter gun for fighting on the Pacific Islands and the jungles of the Asian Continent against the Japanese Empire.

Perkins is a raw recruit when it comes to firing a gun but is more than willing to learn.

Fran's company of one hundred sixty men, the same size as his basic training company at Camp Grant, marches down the road and reaches the rifle range.

The range is over three football fields long and about two football fields wide. The men wait their turn several yards behind a firing line marked with lime that marks where no one other than the men shooting can cross until a whistle signals.

Perkins is nervous, yet excited to get the chance to shoot a real weapon. Playing cops and robbers with sticks as a child during the Great Depression is not the same as smelling gun smoke and firing heavy metal.

One instructor is assigned to every four soldiers. Fran's instructor shows him how to point the rifle at the target, how to aim the weapon and how to squeeze the trigger. Fran lines up the rifle sight with the target and fires. The weapon practically rips out of his hand with the recoil received from a thirty-caliber bullet traveling at a thousand feet per second toward the target. He misses the target wide to the left. His second shot compensates for missing wide to the left and goes wide right of the silhouette target.

From the corner of his eye, another instructor, Sergeant Billy Lewis, spots Perkins having trouble and approaches to relax an agitated and frustrated private. "Ah see what yer problem is thar, Perkins, 'n' Ah kin fix it fer ya," Billy Lewis shouts to be heard over the gunfire.

Billy Lewis grew up in Cleveland, Tennessee. Cleveland was named for Benjamin Cleveland who was a Colonel during the Revolutionary War. Billy is proud of his hill country heritage and rarely wore shoes in the summer, even when it rained. He is uncomfortable wearing the required Army boots in August, and when he is off work, his boots remain by his footlocker. Billy has a big, strong Southern smile on his face as he speaks.

Lewis asks Perkins to hand over the weapon and then hits the target with four shots in a one-inch shot grouping. He hands the M1 over the Perkins and shows him how to place the rifle on his shoulder and lay his cheek on top of the stock.

"This'a way, Perkins, ya keep yer cheek on the weapon 'n' don't worry 'bout recoil. Yer body'll move wi' the gun. Think a the rifle connecting ta yer body. Have it connect ta yer arms, fingers, shoulder 'n' yer right cheek. Now, aim at the target, take a deep breath 'n' as ya exhale, squeeeeeze the trigger."

Perkins obeys and the bullet tears out of his gun hitting the target dead center. Perkins empties his clip and all bullets hit their mark.

"This is unbelievable. I like it," says Perkins. Billy Lewis grins with satisfaction.

Billy trains thousands of young men each month with similar results. He has shot all kinds of guns from the time he was five years old. He grew up in a small family that could not afford to purchase meat. Learning to shoot meant they were able to eat meat every day as deer and squirrels were plentiful in the hills of Tennessee.

Perkins thinks of Billy Lewis as his own personal Davy Crockett, the King of the Wild Frontier.

With the help of Lewis. Fran Perkins becomes an expert marksman. The introductory training gives him the confidence to move up to the bigger guns. Soon he will train on fifty-caliber machine guns, the same guns he will fire on the **Daisy Mae.**

Airman's Testing and Evaluation

These young men test to meet the current needs of the Army Air Corps. Many crews have been lost in combat already by the end of 1942. Thousands of young men have died. Every time a bomber is lost in combat, ten young men are gone forever both in the B-17 and the newer B-24 Bombers.

In class instructors explain, "The reason we have two eyes is to take two pictures simultaneously and then allow our brain to calculate the proper distances to understand the depth of the object. If you are flying in a plane, you can spot aircraft flying at you or away from you, but you need an internal compass to determine exactly where he exists in space. It is very easy to see length and width but you also need to see the depth if you are assigned a gunner position in a B-24 Bomber. Once you leave the ground, flying thousands of feet above the earth your vision is disoriented."

Fran tests in the physics of flight, mathematics, aeronautics, deflection shooting, and thinking in three dimensions. He tests off the charts in his three-dimensional viewing, as well as three-dimensional thinking. This makes him an ideal candidate for a gunner position on a B-24 Liberator Bomber. Next, he needs gunnery practice on the ground in the hot desert of Nevada before a future assignment to attend aerial gunnery school, shooting at targets while a plane is flying and executing maneuvers. This will be the real test of Fran's visual aptitude.

Major Perry 'Tosh' McIntosh

Major Perry McIntosh Jr. is in charge of turning raw recruits into much needed bomber crews for deployment to North Africa, England, the Pacific Front and the Middle East. He is responsible for all aspects of training the ten-man crews for the workhorse B-17 Flying Fortress and the newer, larger B-24 Liberator Bombers. Just coming home from a successful tour in the Pacific, he is new to the base.

Perry led a squadron of B-17 Bombers at the Battle of Midway, which precipitated an ambush against six of the Japanese aircraft carriers that launched the United States into war after their attack on Pearl Harbor. Major McIntosh with his B-17s, many other American fighter planes, and torpedo planes, found the enemy aircraft carriers at sea. They sank four of the six carriers and destroyed other ships in the fleet as well. Over three hundred eighty enemy planes fell from the sky. Many other enemy fighter planes broke up when they ditched into the ocean because their carriers sank and there was nowhere to land. This was at a cost of only one American carrier and one destroyer warship.

The Battle of Midway represented the worst naval loss for Japan in almost one hundred years and the momentum change in World War II. Japan was invincible in Asia, Southeast Asia and Indochina (Indonesia). With this turn of events, Japan understood they could not defeat the United States of America.

Major McIntosh is going to infuse the successful feeling of this enormous victory into every man training for battle. His enthusiasm during his one-on-one talks with each trainee is infectious. He is the right man for the right job. The entire training operation exudes excitement.

Morale is high.

Advanced Airman Training

A One-On-One Meeting

On a Monday morning after falling out in formation on the company street at Sheppard Field, Fran Perkins receives an order to fall out and report to the training officer in charge of all training, Major Perry McIntosh Jr. Perkins comes to attention and gives a crisp salute to the officer. He stands with both feet together with his right arm bent at the elbow. Fran's thumb is in perfect alignment with his forefinger and his fingers extended and joined. His forefinger aligns at a mark just above his right eyebrow. Heart pounding, Perkins extends a perfect salute as he expects to be informed that he is assigned to attend pilot flight school training.

Major McIntosh is a tall, handsome and extremely intelligent man. He has rows of medals streaming down his uniform. The son of a marine drill sergeant "Tosh," as he is hailed by his civilian friends, wanted more than ever to become a pilot and not a ground pounding marine. Now his father boasts to all of his ex-marine buddies how his son is winning the air battle around the world by training their crews. A proud father, Perry McIntosh Sr. is not exaggerating, but merely stating fact.

Returning Fran's salute McIntosh invites Fran to be seated. Rather than sit behind his desk, the Major takes another chair the same size as Fran's and places it directly across from him. They are sitting so close together that their knees almost touch. Major McIntosh wants to make sure Fran understands him and understands there is nothing to hide. This kind of treatment from an officer is unusual in the Armed Forces as officers follow strict military protocol with enlisted men.

The officer gets right to the point. "Private Perkins," the Major begins, "You are not going to be a pilot for now. We are sending you to gunnery school in Nevada." McIntosh pauses a few seconds as he watches Fran's reaction and then adds, "This is not because of your test scores. We made the decision because of your unique skill set."

"Is it because I am short?" asks Perkins

"It is because of three very important factors," says the Major.

"Number one, you are short and strong, and that gives you an advantage for the ball-turret or belly gunner position that rides beneath the bomber. Number two, you have exceptional three-dimensional vision and three-dimensional thinking aptitude. These skills are crucial in air-to-air battles with our enemies. Finally, you are a team player.

"When you arrived here at Sheppard Field, I received a letter from Captain Korn, your commander back at Camp Grant. Korn talked about how you and another private led a company out on a farm to save a crop. Korn explained how you and the other private worked all day and all night without any rest and you looked as fresh as when you started. You see a job through, Perkins. You are motivated to help and give 110% in order to achieve the goal for the greater good. That is something we cannot teach. Individuals never win battles. Many men working together win battles.

"After the Battle of Midway, the Army Air Corps gave me orders to report here and take over the training program. When I heard that, I felt as if Joe Lewis punched me in the stomach. I wanted to again, lead my men in the air as a bomber pilot. I wanted to see the job through to the very end."

"The Brown Bomber," Perkins whispers, eyes lowered.

"Yes, the Brown Bomber.

"I knew I must get over that feeling because the Army Air Corps discovered something about me that is going to serve the greater good of the Air Corps and my men. Someday, you will have your chance at flying, Private Perkins, but your value for the greater good is to become the best gunner you can possibly be.

"Do you feel any better now, Private Perkins?"

"No, not really, Sir. However, I will someday. As you said, I'll get my chance to fly someday and I believe you. I have four brothers and two of them are fighting right now. They wrote to me and told me not to get my hopes up because we don't always get what we want in life."

"That is good advice, but I want to add something, Private Perkins.

"Never give up on hope. Never, ever give up on hope. Hope is what keeps dreams alive. Hope is what will help you and your shipmates through the War.

"During the Battle of Midway our bomber was surrounded by several Japanese Zeros. Those fighter planes travel over three hundred miles per hour. However, our waist gunners, tail gunner, nose gunner and ball-turret gunner never gave up. They gave each other and me the power of hope to make it through the battle safely. They trusted me to fly them home safely. I felt like a bus driver. I felt so helpless because I had no weapons to fight back. My job was to keep flying no matter what was going on around me. I could not let death and destruction take me off course. I had to trust my men and my plane. I had to have hope. The truth is every job on the bomber is equally important. There is no one hero on board; there are ten heroes.

"When you get on your bomber, you make sure you remember that, okay?"

Fran nods in agreement.

"A single pilot, a bombardier, or a ball-turret gunner does not win a war. We win because of teamwork. The Battle of Midway, which in history someday will go down as America's greatest battle, is a lesson in teamwork."

Top Secret Trust

"Perkins, get up from your chair and follow me over to this chart by the front of my office."

Fran complies, wondering why this high-ranking officer is giving him so much of his time. Maybe this is why the Army Air Corps put him in charge of turning out bomber crews. McIntosh knows how to connect with enlisted men and raw recruits.

"Perkins, take a look at this B-24 Bomber in action.

4-2 B-24 dropping bombs

"Follow the trail of bombs up to the bottom of the aircraft," lectures McIntosh.

"The bomb bay doors represent a top military secret. I am going to tell you highly classified information well above your rank and military clearance. Can I get your promise you will never tell anyone about this, even after the war is over? We never know what new enemies await us as the dust settles down across the world after this war is over."

"Yes Sir!" Fran shouts enthusiastically as he did in basic training.

"Easy, Perkins, we are not in basic training anymore.

"The bomb bay doors, as well as some other critical parts of the B-24, are made of aluminum not steel."

"Why use aluminum instead of steel?" asks Perkins.

"Because the reduced weight will help the bomber fly faster. That is the official word from Air Command. However, the real reason and one you are ordered never to reveal, is because we can build the plane much faster than the B-17 or any other large aircraft. Henry Kaiser is an industrialist who consulted with the Defense Department and found he can build planes and naval ships quickly. Private Perkins, can you imagine if you lived in Tokyo and you saw hundreds or even thousands of B-24 Bombers flying overhead? You would want to give up immediately."

"Yes Sir," responds Perkins.

"Kaiser and Henry Ford got together and figured out a production system with the added aluminum bomb bay doors in the B-24 to turn out one B-24 every hour at the Willow Run Plant in Detroit, Michigan. We have other plants including the Consolidated Plant in San Diego. It is just unbelievable how fast they can build these planes. It takes twenty to twenty-four years to grow a pilot and only one hour to grow the fastest and largest bomber in the world. Do you have any doubts who will win this war?"

"No Sir!"

"There is one more advantage to the aluminum doors on a B-24 Liberator and this will be the most important advantage in the end. As the war is ending and we are liberating nations from tyranny, you and your B-24 Liberators will use those lightweight aluminum doors to airdrop tons of food to the millions of people around the world that will be starving to death because of all the agricultural destruction in their countries. All of Europe and Asia are in need of food now. Can you imagine now if you are a citizen of Tokyo and the war is finished? How would you feel looking up in the air to see a vast armada of Liberators flying at low levels dropping food from the sky to feed your family?"

"Wow, I think I would be overjoyed, Sir." Perkins responds.

"This is why the Liberator will be the largest family of planes ever built. We need these planes to carry all of the food that the farmers in DeKalb, Illinois can harvest, as well as all of the farmers in all regions of the United States. Now you may understand how your training here, including your temporary duty as a farm boy, is all part of a larger plan."

"Yes, Sir, I understand."

Why You Are Here, Private Perkins

"You must understand why you are here, Private Perkins. You must understand why you are so necessary to the larger plan.

"Since the bomb bay doors are lighter, Japanese Zero fighter planes are going to attack that area first, so recently we added a bottom ball-turret with twin fifty-caliber machine guns to protect the soft underbelly of the B-24. This model is the B-24D Liberator.

"The perfect profile of the man to work the ball-turret guns is one who not only possesses excellent marksman skills on the ground but expert skills in space. He needs an extraordinary talent to operate his guns in space. He must be able to instinctively calculate speed and direction of enemy fighters and be able to prioritize the moving targets. Do I shoot at the one on my right first or the one on my left? Do I attack the one coming up from below or do I shoot at the one coming straight at me that is directly in front of my guns? You make quick decisions based on gut feeling. This gut feeling comes from our training and more importantly, it comes from your unique God-given talents."

"Private Perkins, just as I was born to train young men to become effective bomber airmen, you were born to protect the B-24 at its most vulnerable point. Of course, you are also protecting the lives of nine young fighting men just like yourself. You are a man who was born of small size with a wiry frame. That is a great advantage in maneuvering in such a small defensible space. You were born with amazing three dimensional eyesight and multidimensional thinking ability. No matter what you accomplish in your life, after it is done and the world is gone, you know how you fit into the grand scheme of life.

"Have you ever watched a live thoroughbred horse race?"

"Yes, I saw Hardtack and later his little boy, Seabiscuit," answers Perkins.

"Did you notice how small the jockeys are riding those large animals? Some are smaller than you are. They are traveling over forty miles per hour and bouncing all over the place. I am six feet four and over two hundred pounds and I cannot control a running horse. Those jockeys do it with a superior sense of balance and body strength. They can see and maneuver in space. They live in three dimensions. You, Perkins, have those same unique qualities. When a horse is running fast, he can get all four feet off the ground at the same time. In other words, he can fly just a few inches off the ground for an instant. A jockey becomes a pilot, just like me. When you are flying and shooting, hanging below the airplane in your rotating Plexiglas turret, you are now the championship jockey and you are the pilot. You are riding Hardtack or Seabiscuit to the finish line."

"Yes Sir." Perkins agrees with McIntosh, even though he feels he is listening to a load of bull. Fran thinks to himself, "This is a large load of bull but this is my personal load of bull. This officer is a pilot and a hero from the Battle of Midway. If he has that kind of confidence in me, I cannot ask for a greater compliment from anyone. I can handle this. I will not let him down."

McIntosh ushers Fran back to his chair and displays a map of the Pacific Ocean stretching from Alaska, diagonally across huge areas of blue, down to Australia.

"This is your briar patch, Perkins. This is where the Seventh Army Air Corps protects our country. You are representing the last line of defense for America against the Empire of Japan. After taking Midway and Hawaii, the United State West Coast is the next to fall.

"Your job, Private Perkins, is to perform submarine watch, watching out for enemy fleets, and offensive bombing runs in support of the United States Marines pushing the enemy from those islands. You will also search for downed soldiers, sailors, airmen and marines. There are plenty of targets out there. Your bomber, Private Perkins, will be in the air flying over vast areas of open sea between twelve and eighteen hours a day. Most of the time you will not have the support of fighter planes because the distances are just too far for them to fly. The B-24 flies longer missions than any other airplane in the world. This is going to be the tactical advantage over our enemies in the Pacific as well as our enemies in the Atlantic and Mediterranean Sea. You can fly almost as fast as the Japanese Zero at 17,000 feet. Your speed and your guns are your only protection on these missions."

"Sir, what's it like to fly over a vast body of water?" Perkins inquiries.

"I remember my last takeoff from the Midway. First, you are watching the pavement on the ground and the horizon off in the distance. The engine starts and you move quickly down the runway and finally you feel the wheels leave the ground from beneath you. Then you feel a sense of freedom only felt by the birds that have been here long before man. You look down when you reach the water and see hundreds of fish near the shore in the shallow waters. You can see ten to twenty feet below the surface on a clear day. It is an incredible feeling.

"I am certain your travels will take you to Midway. It is our last line of defense before Hawaii, Hickam and Pearl Harbor. I hope you will enjoy the journey."

"Sir, do you think I will ever fly a plane?"

"Yes, of course, you will fly someday. However, until that day, your mission is to protect the Big Brown Bomber and every man in your crew."

"That is an order and that is all, Private."

Both men stand and salute. Major McIntosh escorts him from the office. It is almost 1700 hours by the time Perkins walks across the parade grounds, about a block from his barracks. Just then, he stops to watch a small military detail march by. They halt a few feet in front of Fran, by the flagpole.

At 1700 hours each day on Army and Army Air Corps bases around the world, a bugler sounds Retreat. Retreat is a short bugle call to mark the end of a workday.

Two soldiers are lowering the flag of the United States. Perkins' heart fills to overflowing as he snaps to attention and gives the flag the respect he received just a few minutes ago by a superior officer and a true hero in World War II. He hopes he will get his chance at flying a plane over Lake Michigan near his home in Chicago where he and his brothers worked on the tugboats. He hopes he will fly over Midway and see the fish ten to twenty feet below the surface in calm, clear waters.

Whatever happens now, Fran will complete his mission with the Air Corps and accept whatever they ask of him. His life and the lives of nine other men flying thousands of feet in the air are counting on him as much as they are counting on each other.

Fran will not let them down.

As the Colors return to an awaiting soldier at the base of the flagpole, Perkins holds his salute until the two soldiers are finished folding it neatly in accordance to official military regulations.

Proper respect for the flag and for other military customs are drilled into every airman, seaman, marine and soldier. Fran and his brother Robert serving in the Eighth Air Corps and his brother Jim serving in the Army, all concur on this subject. Their father, Francis Joseph Perkins Sr. instilled patriotism in all of his boys at a young age. Frank served with distinction in the Army in World War I and learned firsthand the high price paid for freedom.

After watching the ceremony and finishing his salute timed with the end of the bugle call, Fran pensively walks up the wooden steps to his barracks.

The barracks resembles the barracks Perkins left back at Camp Grant in Rockford. Until Fran deploys overseas, the Army barracks will look the same from duty station to duty station. A standardization in every duty station allows these young men to feel more at home. They do not have to ask for directions to find the mess hall, the chapel or the day room that are always located in the same relative positions.

Fran thinks about his mother, father, and his two younger brothers, Edward and Raymond who are back home in Chicago. His older brothers James and Robert are fighting overseas for their lives and the lives of their comrades at this very moment. Fran's girlfriend, Elaine, is at home in Evergreen Park, Illinois. When he addresses Elaine, he refers to her as "Lady Elaine." Fran is very protective of his Lady Elaine and is working so hard just for her, her family and his own family.

As he moves through the barracks and finds his Army cot, Fran decides to write a letter back home to Elaine. He wants to write about his amazing discussion and advice from Major Perry McIntosh. However, he stops right after "Dear Lady Elaine," because he remembers everything told to him by the Major is highly classified information and he made a promise never to discuss the conversation. He remembers that the aluminum doors on the B-24 Bomber make it faster, albeit vulnerable to the enemy firing from pursuing fighter planes. He also remembers how the Major told him in confidence that industrialists, Henry Ford and Henry Kaiser, insured our victory in World War II by building manufacturing plants that turn out the largest bombers in the world every hour of every day. We are also turning out ships faster and faster. With the Top Secret information Fran received from the Major, Fran is confident we will win the war regardless of how long it takes.

Perkins wants to write this down to assure Elaine everything will work out between them in their trying, long-distant relationship, but he cannot take the risk. In addition, Fran is very aware of military censors who read all of the mail going in and out of the base. In a moment of weakness or forgetfulness, Fran might say something in the letter that would bring dishonor on himself, his family and Major Perry McIntosh, who trusted Fran implicitly.

The Note

Fran puts down his stationary pad for a moment and notices a brown envelope sticking out from under his pillow with an official Army Air Corps seal on it. As he opens the envelope, he looks around to see who might have left it there or if anyone is watching. All of the other trainees are at the beer hall located about two city blocks from the barracks. After duty hours, the young men go down to the beer hall to listen to the latest music, have a beer and relax, taking an opportunity to forget training and the war for the rest of the evening.

Advanced Airman Training

From the brown envelope, he pulls out a small handwritten note that reads:

> Fran,
>
> When your plane lifts off the ground at Midway, picture me saluting you.
>
> Regards,
> Tosh

Fran holds the note in his left hand and studies it repeatedly. Being the consummate analytical thinker, Fran wonders how the sealed note arrived at his barracks before he got there. He left the Major's office and cut across the parade grounds. The encounter with the retreat detail took less than two minutes. Fran shakes his head from side to side in disbelief then he smiles as he imagines the six foot four-inch frame of Major McIntosh standing below, as his airplane is flying overhead. "At least I'll be able to pick him out in a crowd," Perkins chuckles to himself.

Lady Elaine

Since no one is around and the barracks is quiet, Perkins begins to write:

> Dear Lady Elaine,
>
> I received the news today that I cannot go to pilot school but in instead will have the best gunnery position on the bomber. I plan to do the very best job I can because when all of my missions are done, I will apply for pilot training and I know I will get it this time. I was disappointed at first but I understand that the position I am working is the most important assignment on the bomber.
>
> Tell Mae and Clarence that I love them and will learn as much as I can to insure the safety and freedom of my new family. Get good grades in school. Say hi to your friends Marge and Sophie.

Love,
Fran

He keeps his letter to Elaine short because he wants to make sure she receives a letter every day. He also wants to make sure he does not slip up and tell her of the exciting insights on how we are winning the war with our manufacturing techniques. Fran addresses the envelope and places it in a mail slot near the entrance to the barracks.

He is one-step closer to an assignment on a bomber crew. After training here at Camp Sheppard, he will receive orders for gunnery school. Fran knows he must excel in gunnery school in order to achieve his destiny as a ball-turret gunner.

In August of 1942, the United States gains control of territory occupied by Japan as the 19,000-man First Marine Division lands on Guadalcanal and Tulagi. The marines kick ass and take names. The Japanese command who doubted the bravery and resolve of the American fighting man are keenly aware that they woke the sleeping giant and the sleeping giant is ready to win.

In Europe, over 400,000 Jews die and the Russians are winning against the Germans in Stalingrad. More men die in the Battle of Stalingrad then the United States loses in all of World War II.

World War II is raging full force.

Soon Fran will be part of a silent but deadly history of World War II. First, he must complete gunnery school in the Nevada desert. Then he will fly with the crew that culminates in his personal day of infamy, the last flight of the **Daisy Mae**.

Chapter 5

Armorer School Training

Flying in a C-47 transport plane from Sheppard Field, Fran views the vast desert terrain around Las Vegas for the first time.

The C-47 Skytrain is a large two-engine transport plane that is cavernous inside with benches running along the length of the aircraft, hard benches that offer little comfort on a long trip. The Skytrain, a workhorse for the military that serves in all theatres around the world, can transport jeeps and all kinds of heavy equipment, in addition to transporting troops.

Getting off the transport plane, Perkins reports to the company clerk's office at the Flexible Aerial Gunnery School at McCarran Field near the current city of Las Vegas where an aide shows him to the barracks he will call home for several weeks. Fran locates his all familiar Army cot, wall locker, and footlocker and begins to unpack his large, fist-pummeled duffle bag wondering, "How many times will I pack and unpack this bag in my military career?"

The barracks is a bit different, narrower than his other barracks and the building feels more Spartan. This is an all-work-no-play environment, as the serious business of destroying enemy aircraft is the main objective around here.

Two other trainees unload their duffle bags on adjoining beds, Earl W. Conley and Larry A. Calhoun. Already Conley and Calhoun are sharing funny observations about the Spartan barracks, mentioning rats and cockroaches and soon Perkins is laughing more than he can ever remember in his civilian life. Calhoun approaches Perkins and takes two dead cockroaches out of his pocket. "We haven't eaten in a week,"

Calhoun says. "Conley and I caught ten cockroaches today, and I only have two left, but you're welcome to 'em."

Fran turns red, sneers and does an about face. Calhoun doesn't realize Fran Perkins is one of five boys. This kind of banter goes on every night back at the Perkins home on South May Street in Chicago. Fran thinks to himself, "I am no rookie."

First Sergeant Masters

First Sergeant Robert Masters, all spit and polish, greets the new trainees in Gunnery School. He passionately maintains strict discipline, speaking in short sentences, abrupt and always very loud. He meets any deviation from proper protocol by trainees with considerable wrath. Cleaning and repairing guns is Sergeant Masters' life and he is at it 24/7.

Perkins, Conley, and Calhoun sit down at their desks and Sergeant Masters calls roll. Then he begins the first of what will be many speeches during the training, all executed in loud, short sentences.

"You are going to be gunners!" Masters shouts. "You will need to learn in a very short time, everything necessary to defeat the Axis. You will take our bombers through to smash the Axis! You and you, and the guy sitting next to you," directing a strong palm at each trainee. "Every man in gunnery school must want to be a gunner. Otherwise, he will waste his time, and ours. Every man must want to get into the fight. He must want to win it and finish it! He must want the rank and pay of a Sergeant's pay in just five short, quick weeks! He must want his badge of courage and skill, the gunner's wings, which proves him a flying fighter!

"You will be wondering exactly what you will be doing in Gunnery School. You are in a small group of men called a Flight. Perkins, Conley and Calhoun make up one of those Flights of the ten Flights in this classroom. My job is not to pass or eliminate you from Gunnery School.

My job is to teach you. America needs your help to win the War against the Axis. The Axis Powers include Germany, Japan, and Italy.

"Hour by hour, your progress will be reported on a progress sheet. Everything you do and everything you say will be on record. You are required to understand everything about your guns and shooting in order to win this war.

"In the first class today, you will meet your two closest friends in the war, the thirty-caliber machine gun and the heavier, harder hitting, fifty-caliber machine gun. You will become intimate friends with these guns, on a first-name basis! The parts of the machine are bolt, barrel, cover plate, lever, slag, spring, pin, and stud.

"You will learn how to take the machine guns apart and put them together again. You will learn how each gun reacts in succession as the gun is fired. You will learn what to feed big guns and small guns and how to doctor them when their digestion goes bad."

"You will know your guns inside and out and what happens after the trigger is pulled. You will learn the path of a bullet's flight. A bullet flies a curved path. You will have to find out why, if you want to shoot straight and on target. The problem with hitting a target with a bullet that drops and drifts will bring you to the question of sights. You will make the acquaintance of ring and bead sights and reflective or optical sights. The introduction of sights will bring you to the problem of sighting a moving target. A gunner uses his sights to figure how much faster or slower than himself, an attacker is flying. The instructor will show you how to estimate the apparent speed of an enemy by how long at a given range it takes the enemy to fly across part of your sights. You will learn how to use your fighting platform, the power driven turret, which is the fighting fortress inside your bomber. You will learn how to use several different types of turrets mounted on test stands."

"You will move the guns as if you are tracking an enemy fighter. The feel and control will become easier for you. Later in the course, you will learn how these turrets are put together and how to install the guns. You will also learn how to disassemble, clean and repair the guns while flying thousands of feet off the ground. Turret manipulation gets you closer to fighting in the air. The bombers that carry these turrets fly at high altitudes where the air is cold and thin. Your medical officer will explain what equipment to use and what clothes to wear to make you fit to fight.

"You will be up in the air, fully alert as you patrol the skies looking through your turrets for enemy aircraft, ships, and submarines. You take out enemy submarines and enemy troops. You look out your turrets for missing or stranded soldiers, sailors, marines and airmen.

"Your first experience in shooting real machine guns is on the malfunction range where your first duty is to fire broken guns and figure out what is wrong with them. Then you will fix the gun and continue firing at a fixed target until you consistently hit the bull's eye located in the center of the fixed target.

"Fixing guns is hard to do. You will learn how to diagnose and treat your machine gun as a skilled doctor treats his patient during surgery. You will doctor your guns back to health!

"In the very first class after a ten-minute smoke break, you will learn how to disassemble machine guns, clean them, and reassemble them. By the end of the day, you will know the machine gun better than its mother does!

Take a ten-minute break. Then return to the first training room on the right to become an Air Corps gunner!

As Perkins, Conley and Calhoun leave the classroom, Conley asks, "What do you think?"

Calhoun speaks first, "Sounds like we'll have a good time once we get through with all of this training. I mean, how hard can it be to fly and shoot all day?"

"I hope I'm strong enough to take those guns apart," says Perkins. "I'm the smallest guy in class."

Conley laughs, "I am not that far behind you, Perkins."

Ten-minutes flies off the clock and the "Flight" consisting of Perkins, Conley and Calhoun go back into the first training room on the right. There are several long tables displaying machine gun parts. There is a thirty-caliber and a fifty-caliber machine gun mounted on stands by the end of the line of long tables. The tables look like they double as mess hall tables, about eight feet long and three feet deep. First Sergeant Masters is standing on the other side of the tables facing a long blackboard.

"Today we learn how to assemble and disassemble guns. Your guns are your best friends. Treat them well and they will treat you well!"

The instruction proceeds and everyone catches on and actually has fun with their guns. About two hours into class, First Sergeant Masters pulls out a dozen black hoods. Now that each student has disassembled and reassembled his gun with the loose parts on the tables, each man is directed to repeat the procedure blinded by the hoods!

The hoods create great difficulty. Private Larry Calhoun assembles and disassembles his guns perfectly and in record time. First Sergeant Masters is pleased.

Private Earl Conley has no trouble and comes in second place with his performance. Private Francis Perkins comes in dead last. He is devastated to be last out of his Flight and out of the entire Armorer School class of thirty.

"Why do we have to learn how to take our guns apart with hoods over our heads so we can't see? This is stupid," Fran remarks.

Hearing the comment, Sergeant Masters dismisses the class but signals for Perkins to remain. "You stay after class, Trainee. You and I are going to become best friends!"

Calhoun and Conley walk back to the barracks without Perkins. "I wonder what's going to happen to Perkins," says a concerned Conley.

"First Sergeant Bastard Masters is going to eat Perkins for breakfast," smiles Calhoun.

Back in the classroom, Masters shouts to Perkins even though they are the only two people in the classroom. "Trainee Perkins, tomorrow is Saturday. You, your two best friends and I are going to be here at 0700 hours. Do you read me, Trainee?"

"Yes, First Sergeant," Perkins says dejectedly.

"I can't hear you, Trainee!" shouts Masters.

"Yes, First Sergeant!" Perkins shouts as if he is in Basic Training.

Perkins meets up with Conley and Calhoun at the mess hall. "You look shorter, Perkins," laughs Calhoun. "Did Sergeant Bastard Masters chew you up and spit you out?"

Conley adds, "You definitely have to keep your opinions to yourself with that guy."

"Yeah, while you guys are off on Saturday, I have to go in for a personal class with Sergeant Bastard Masters."

Conley and Calhoun have an eight-hour pass to go off base so they plan to go into the little gambling town of Las Vegas, Nevada. It was also a large cattle town. Ranch boys and farm boys liked to visit and watch the large herds pass through.

Calhoun is from the city and has another idea how to spend the day with Conley. "Let's go by the wedding chapels and pretend we are in the wedding parties, free food and booze." Conley is not too keen on the idea, but knows that by hanging around Calhoun, something interesting and fun is probably going to happen. Fun seems to be Larry Calhoun's middle name.

Perkins awakens early Saturday morning and heads right over to the Armorer's classroom, arriving early to find First Sergeant Masters already there.

Masters is old school Army, hence the First Sergeant's rank. He is on loan to the Army Air Corps and despite some of his quirks; he is always able to train gunners to excel. He has many methods and is about to use a powerful one on young trainee, Private Perkins.

"Perkins, do you want to be a gunner?"

"Yes, First Sergeant, I do want to become a gunner."

"A gunner in the Air Corps must learn how to assemble and disassemble a machine gun!" shouts Masters. "You must learn the techniques I give you or you will not become a gunner!"

"Yes, First Sergeant," Perkins says with an agreeing nod of his head.

For four straight hours, First Sergeant Masters has Perkins assembling the fifty-caliber machine gun. Masters knows that turret gunners in the Air Corps use fifty-caliber machine guns and he does not want to miss a minute of training diverted to any other gun in the school's arsenal. Perkins understands this is his best chance of learning everything about the guns he will use in combat after he finishes his five-week course at Flexible Gunnery School.

Perkins finally gets it and after successfully assembling the fifty-caliber machine gun repeatedly with the parts on the table, he blocks out any unnecessary comments by Masters.

Masters brings out the black hood and this time Perkins accepts it graciously. The instructor orders Perkins to sit on the floor and position the hood over his head, then Masters dumps the parts randomly across the floor. He turns up the volume of a recording of actual combat sounds. Fran hears the sound of fifty-caliber rounds hitting against solid steel as if he is riding in a B-24 Bomber, the sound of four huge aircraft engines and the sound of anti-aircraft shells exploding around him. Masters ties the hood securely over Fran's face blocking out all light. Fran cannot peek out anywhere so he is essentially blind. Masters gives Fran a few minutes to get accustomed to the feeling of being blind and then instructs him to reach for the machine gun parts scattered on the floor and assemble the weapon.

At first, it takes Fran several minutes to assemble the weapon. The loud noise of explosions, engines, and gunfire distract the trainee, but he does not give up. He pictures Conley and Calhoun fighting from the tail and the nose of the bomber and imagines he has to fix his machine gun to help his shipmates. His sense of duty toward his shipmates will not allow him to give up. His mind relinquishes control allowing the muscle memory in his hands to complete the tasks.

After an hour of hooded training, Masters unties Fran's hood and instructs him to take a break. Sporting a large grin over his face he continues, "Congratulations Trainee, you did fine. You can leave now but if you want to stay and practice, you can."

Masters puts a hood over his own head, sits on the floor filled with broken machine gun parts and good machine gun parts, and works at the same exercise Fran just completed. Fran takes that as a challenge, grabs another hood, and goes over to another fifty-caliber machine gun station, scatters the assorted machine gun parts on the floor and starts the record player with the sound track of the bomber in battle, turning it to full volume. Masters and Perkins repeat the exercise for two more hours after Masters gave Fran permission to leave.

Training Day

On Monday, Perkins sprints to class early while Calhoun and Conley remain sleeping in their bunks. First Sergeant Masters is writing on the blackboard and Perkins requests a fifty-caliber machine gun and a hood to practice before class begins.

Masters nods at a fifty-caliber machine gun on a stand near the door. Perkins grabs a hood and ties it securely under his chin and around his neck, so tightly he coughs and gags for a few seconds. Masters is inwardly impressed with the private's enthusiasm.

The other classmates enter the classroom and stand quietly by their seats as they watch Fran attack the gun. Masters turns on the soundtrack and cranks up the volume. Fran is sitting cross-legged on the floor and Masters pours out machine gun parts and spreads them all over the floor so Perkins needs to crawl on the floor in order to put the gun back in service. Fran is oblivious to his audience as he passionately assembles the weapon while completely blinded.

Masters did not play the combat soundtrack Friday during class; now all trainees hear the loud battle soundtrack. Some of the trainees are holding their hands over their ears. Perkins sits on the floor assembling and disassembling the fifty-caliber machine gun even after his fingers and hands are bleeding from handling the heavy and sometimes jagged pieces of metal. Sounds of anti-aircraft flak hitting the Plexiglas turrets, the aluminum bomb bay doors and the steel fuselage are clear in this recording. Sounds of the thump, thump, thump, thump of heavy machine gun fire hitting the steel surrounding the crew and 20mm cannon shots bursting inside create a clear picture in the minds of thirty young men. The vibration and sound effects hit home in the hearts and minds of these young boys as strongly as if they are in combat this very second. First Sergeant Masters is not watching Perkins now. He is confident that

Perkins will perform in combat. His eyes watch for visual signals in the eyes and posture of the other young men that Masters is sending into deadly combat.

No one flinches or looks away. These young boys have several things in common; they all volunteered for military service on December 8, 1941, one day after the Pearl Harbor attack. They all have a look of confidence and rock hard resolve. They are pulling for their classmate and possible shipmate Francis J. Perkins Jr. sitting blindfolded on the floor, crawling and clutching for parts. Every trainee is ready to jump in to help Perkins assemble and disassemble the fifty-caliber machine gun. Every young man with his eyes trained on Perkins is ready to trade his life for Perkins and each other when they go into battle.

The realistic sounds on the recording reveals the special look of the American fighting man. Hitler, Mussolini and Tojo, you are in for a big surprise. You underestimate the power of American determination. You underestimate the power of rock hard resolve. You underestimate the power of hope.

Finally, First Sergeant Masters calls, "Time," and Fran stops. Masters walks in front of Perkins, and turns off the sounds of battle. He looks out into the group of gawking armory students and loudly announces, "This trainee just set a camp record!"

The other trainees including Conley and Calhoun smile and applaud. Some men are shouting and whistling loudly. Trainee Fran Perkins' face turns red from embarrassment; however, this is just the opposite kind of embarrassment Fran experienced three days ago when he blew up out of frustration. Perkins is very proud of his achievement. Three days ago, he was a failure. Now he is a champion. Fran Perkins went from zero to hero. The first day of class, his fingers were shaking from fear. Now they are relaxed, calm, and confident. The machine guns are the same type Perkins, Conley and Calhoun will fire many times in their short, five-week training in Las Vegas. They will soon test their skills on these same guns in actual combat.

Masters' expression is grim and serious for his trainees. He never refers to any trainee by name or rank. That is his style. This keeps him from getting too involved with young boys and men who will die in combat over the skies of the Pacific, Atlantic, North Africa, Asia and Europe. He is determined to stay distant and professional at all times. He cannot allow trainees into his life. His job is to help boys fight like men. He needs to help each man find his combat face. However, in his heart, mind and soul, he is smiling for Fran. He knows Fran will not run from a fight. Perkins will find a way to win, regardless of the odds. He is just the kind of man who will hold up well in combat, just like the men applauding, whistling and cheering for him right now.

In 1942, over six hundred men attended the gunnery school in the desert of Las Vegas. Six hundred men completed First Sergeant Masters' Armory course and all six hundred moved on to the next course of Flexible Gunnery Training. The airfield became Nellis Air Field after World War II.

Successfully passing all courses in the Gunnery School Training Program, Perkins, Conley and Calhoun can earn their Gunner's Wings, just like pilots earning their wings after their intensive Flight School Training. There is no guarantee of getting Gunner's Wings as more intense and deadly training begins now.

Are Perkins, Conley and Calhoun ready for this challenge?

Chapter 6

Water Conley Water!

It is Monday morning and instead of ground machine gun training, the trainees receive crew training on a brand new B-24D aircraft. Out on the airfield the same aircraft that Perkins viewed in a picture when meeting with Major McIntosh stands before the "Flight." They are in awe of the wingspan and the overall size. In his excitement, Perkins wants to tell his two new shipmates everything McIntosh told him in confidence, but remembers the Major instructed him the information classifies as Top Secret. Fran will tell no one.

Today's training will give the crew a taste and feel of a real bombing mission. There are no active machine guns on the flight but the men will perform all of the other required duties. The purpose of the flight is to qualify the men before they are too deep into training. Not everyone in today's training will walk and work on a flying aircraft. Some may wash out because they are too afraid of heights or get sick on the bouncing bomber. It is better to find out sooner than later in real combat when lives are at stake.

The three trainees will fly with a pilot, co-pilot, bombardier, radioman and navigator. They will have an experienced flight engineer named Sergeant Seaman who will instruct and coach them on all of their responsibilities.

Sergeant Seaman

Sergeant Curt Seaman was born in Germany and his family immigrated to America during the Great Depression. The Depression was hard on the Seaman family living in Bremen, Germany. Hans Seaman, Curt's father, felt that his chances of employment would be better in America. Even though Sergeant Seaman grew up attending American schools, he retained a hard German accent and the other school kids bullied him, as World War I was fresh in their minds. Bullying is a national pastime for young boys.

Young Curt Seaman joined the Army and quickly earned the rank of Sergeant. He found his stride and his niche when he joined the Army Air Corps. He is an exceptional soldier and his peers, as well as the trainees, overlook his heritage and afford him deserved respect and admiration.

Seaman will have his hands full with these new trainees.

"Let's Bomb the Hell Out of Reno"

The mission is to bomb a deserted ghost town not far from Reno Air Field, Nevada. The B-24 will take off at Las Vegas Airfield, fly at 17,000 feet and circle the mountains near Lake Tahoe. Then they will quickly descend from 17,000 feet and attack from only two hundred feet off the ground.

The low-level flying gives the recruits a bird's eye view of a typical bombing run on an enemy naval ship or the Pacific Island ground targets. The American airmen call this tactic hedge hopping. The B-24D is perfect for hedgehopping. By flying in low-level bomber raids American bombing missions avoid radar controlled anti-aircraft guns and confound Japanese Zeros who patrol thousands of feet off the ground. The B-24s use their speed and stealth to complete these missions.

The mission will last five hours overall, including a real briefing at the end, so the three trainees will need to take copious mental notes.

As the crew climbs into the B-24, Calhoun jokes and says, "Let's go bomb the hell out of Reno." Then adds, "The plane is too heavy to lift off the ground." The copilot glares at Calhoun and orders him to shut up. Perkins and Conley look down at their shoes, trying not to laugh at the situation and to distance themselves from the bad boy.

73

This is an exciting flying adventure for the Flight of three. For the first time, they are actually flying in a bomber. They have been in the Air Corps for all of four months and the only time they flew was on the way here from their Advanced Airman Training in a C-47 Skytrain. The Skytrain is no pleasure craft, nor is the B-24.

The Pilot, Co-pilot, Bombardier, and Navigator have comfortable adjustable seats, not so for the rest of the crew. This bomber works for a living.

As the bomber takes off, Perkins watches the airfield fade away into the horizon. Below, the bustling machine gun firing lines give way to a barren desert. The sun is rising from the East and brilliant red and pink colors fill the sky in all directions. The Nevada desert resembles a giant sandbox, with rings of mountains off in the distance. If a desert carries the name Painted Desert, this is what it must resemble. Sky, rocks and sand bear a strong resemblance to painted colors on a canvas that change by the second as the aircraft soars upward.

Conley signs to the other boys that the customary nametags for the four officers, the pilot, co-pilot, navigator and bombardier have masking tape over them. It seems strange to the three trainees but this is the Army Air Corps and anything is possible.

Sergeant Seaman calls the three men to attention and motions for Private Larry Calhoun to follow him to the greenhouse that is located a few steps into the nose of the airplane. When it gets time for the bombing run, Larry Calhoun will have the best view in the house, as he assists the bombardier looking into the Norden Bombsight. Aware of this, Perkins whispers to Conley, "The joker is getting pretty great treatment." Conley nods in agreement.

Fran and Earl feel the large bomber leveling off at 9,000 feet of elevation. Sergeant Seaman issues both men oxygen suits and hoses and directs them to connect to the oxygen tanks. The bombardier is helping Larry Calhoun with the same task up in the greenhouse. Sergeant

Seaman next shows Conley his new home for the rest of the war located between the two rear rudders of the aircraft called the rear gun turret. Earl is going to be the tail gunner. Fran is getting that anxious feeling you get when you are trying to do well in a new job and you are just standing around doing nothing. An ambitious young man, he finds standing around doing nothing is not his forte. Finally, after about an hour, Sergeant Seaman helps Fran with his suit and gives him instruction on how to use the oxygen and the communication intercom connected by a wire to his clothing.

Claustrophobic

For the first time Fran experiences the thrill of climbing into the ball-turret that rests inside the belly of the B-24D Bomber and now he is operating the controls to lower the turret down beneath the plane!

Settling in, a feeling of claustrophobia floods every cell of Fran's body. He is barely five feet two inches tall and about 118 pounds; however, he feels like ten pounds of potatoes stuffed into a five-pound bag! Many anxious thoughts bombard his mind including, "I have to get out of here."

Then a little magic happens with a flashback of when he first met Elaine. They met at a Calumet High School football game a year earlier in Chicago on a beautiful Fall Saturday afternoon. Fran was wearing a large lion suit as the team mascot with a huge realistic looking lion's head. Elaine was with her best friends Marge and Sophie. Fran noticed how beautiful Elaine looked and wanted to get her attention, so he pretended to be claustrophobic inside the lion's head and marched up to Elaine standing between her two friends and beseeched her to help him out of the lion's head. Lady Elaine responded to Fran's begging and in front of her two giggling teenage friends, off goes his head (the lion's head). Fran begins laughing out loud with the clear images of their first meeting vivid in his mind.

6-1 Lady Elaine Birmingham

"What is going on down there in your turret?" Sergeant Curt Seaman hearing the laughter over the intercom worries that Fran has lost his mind in the tight confines.

Fran adjusts the intercom microphone over to where he can talk and confirms, "Everything's fine now, Sergeant. I'm okay."

Seaman then gives further instruction over the intercom about the hands on a clock. Gunners communicate the position of objects using the clock face as a parallel. The hands of a clock point toward objects and targets. Gunners use this method to communicate the relative positions of planes or other objects in their view. Trainees learn how to describe positions of enemy planes as they fly toward the bomber formation and as the planes are engaging in aerial combat. They learn to think, react and communicate to the other gunners quickly over the intercom. The targets, Japanese Zeros, fly over three hundred miles per hour and the B-24 flies over three hundred miles per hour as well. Combat is quick and deadly. It is imperative that all gunners in bubbles accurately communicate positions of enemy aircraft.

Sergeant Seaman calls out, "Tail gunner, what do you see at twelve o'clock high?"

Conley responds, "I see the sun."

Seaman calls, "Belly gunner, what do you see at 6 o'clock low?"

Perkins responds, "I see the ground."

Seaman calls out, "Nose gunner, what do you see at 2 o'clock high?"

Calhoun responds, "I see the hands of the clock."

Sergeant Seaman shakes his head with disapproval of Calhoun's wiseass remark and then cues the pilot. "Pilot and co-pilot, take us up to 17,000 feet.

"Tail gunner, belly gunner, and nose gunner, call out when you see patches of forest, other aircraft or water."

They all call back to Sergeant Seaman, "Yes, Flight Engineer."

As the B-24 flies closer to the practice range, aircraft are more numerous because Reno Airfield is not far away. The pilot swings to the Northwest to fly over Lake Tahoe, California, before heading back toward Nevada and completing the practice-bombing mission. Perkins and Conley are enjoying the ride. Conley is amazed how much he can see in all directions from his tail gunner position. Everything about the trip, other than the gunless flying carpet made of steel, is exhilarating.

The B-24 flies over Mt Whitney, which is the highest point in the United States at over 14,000 feet. Growing up in Illinois, flying over a mountain is another first for Perkins and the view from his Plexiglas turret is unmatched. Perkins rotates his turret up and down and from side to side to get better views. As the sun glistens on the snow, the scene is overwhelming. Crystalline ice, sculpted by nature fills his vision. Fran sees prisms of colored light everywhere as the sun dances off the ever-changing view. He now understands why Major McIntosh did such a sales job on him to become a ball-turret gunner. Riding in the Plexiglas turret below the belly of the airplane, Fran realizes that in all of his life, he will never see such a beautiful sight as Mt Whitney in all of her snowy grandeur.

Conley is equally impressed with his view and vows never to forget it. The mountain has a beautiful, yet relaxing quality. Calhoun is in the greenhouse and is sound asleep.

Suddenly Perkins yells over his microphone, "Water Conley Water. Water at 6 o'clock. Water Conley Water!" As Mt. Whitney fades in the background and the pilot swoops down over Lake Tahoe, an equally impressive emerald colored lake high up in the Sierra Mountains appears.

Conley yells back, "I see it, Belly Gunner. I see it!"

Sergeant Seaman hears the exchange and smiles to himself. Seaman remembers the first time he saw the Statue of Liberty in New York Harbor as a small child when his family emigrated from Germany. He understands the joyful and hopeful exchange between Perkins and Conley.

Perkins imagines Lady Elaine in the ball-turret with him. He relaxes in the tight confines of his ball-turret and allows himself to feel free at the same time. Riding under several tons of steel and aluminum, he realizes that in his position he is responsible for all of the lives on board. He vows to keep their safety first, no matter what the cost.

From Lake Tahoe, the B-24 descends quickly from 17,000 feet to just 200 feet above the target area. Fran feels he is riding on a long roller coaster. Our mighty B-24 dives just like a fighter plane coming in for a strafing run. It is amazing how the largest bomber on the planet, with four mighty engines and wings that spread to infinity, is able to maneuver this way. Larry, Fran, and Earl are truly impressed.

Up in the greenhouse in the nose of the bomber, Calhoun is awake and active as the nameless bombardier is flying the plane from his Norden Bombsight. The control of the flight of the plane transfers from the pilot and co-pilot, who sit behind and over the top of the nose of the B-24, to the bombardier located below in the nose.

The Norden Bombsight equipped in all of the new B-24s and B-17s is a crucial weapon in World War II. When bombers crack up in the air or crash land, the primary job of the remaining flyers on the plane is to throw the bombsight out the nearest window, bomb bay doors or exits. They need to make sure the enemy does not get it and reverse-engineer it for their own use.

Fran watches the target come up quickly. The target is a dilapidated pile of wood that once was a functioning bunkhouse for cowboys taming wild Mustang horses. Fran spies a large buckskin Mustang horse standing a good distance from a small field that is located near the target. The name Wildfire pops in his head and Fran hopes for Wildfire's safety, far away from the simulated war zone. Wildfire lowers his head to chomp more grass, uninterested in the noisy bomber overhead.

Fran's father, Francis Perkins Sr. told his sons how he saw many horses die in France during World War I. In fact, over seven million horses died in World War I. Cavalry troops fought among the new planes, tanks, artillery and poison gas of a new era in warfare. The brave and elegant warhorses never had a chance.

Suddenly a voice in Fran's ear shouts, "Bombs away!"

Two bombs drop from the open bomb bay doors and right past Perkins who is guarding the B-24's belly. Perkins sees two small explosions of real fire and smoke about fifty yards from the dilapidated bunkhouse. If these were two 500-pound bombs rather than the harmless training rounds, the bunkhouse and Wildfire would have been obliterated from the planet. The young trainees watch the target as the nameless, faceless B-24 begins a steep climb back to 17,000 feet.

Fran watches Wildfire racing over the sandy hills, tail high while the Liberator soars away. "Good boy. Stay far away from these bombers and you will be okay," Fran mumbles to himself. "I'll see you after the war, Wildfire, I promise."

Soon the bomber reaches an altitude of 17,100 feet. Pilots always go a little higher and then level off the plane by dropping it down one hundred feet to the proper altitude. This is a training mission and carried only two small training bombs. On combat missions, they will carry thousands of pounds of high explosives so if they reach 17,000 feet and level off from the climb, the plane may drop under the required altitude. By trial and error, they find leveling from a slightly higher altitude works best. This pilot feels one hundred feet is sufficient as the tactic keeps the heavy bomber flying on course.

"Retract your turret and report to the cabin," blares over the intercom.

Fran reaches over and struggles a bit to get the turret to retract. "It is not that easy," Fran thinks to himself, "But I'll get the hang of it."
Conley and Perkins report to the cabin. The B-24 is flying level now and is on automatic pilot. As a precaution, the nameless navigator is sitting in the pilot's seat. The pilot salutes both men and says, "Good job, men, on your first mission. Where is the other trainee? Go get him and bring him up here."

Fran and Earl look at each other and walk quickly in their bulky jumpsuits breathing rapidly through their oxygen masks. Instead of being up in the nose with the bombardier, Private Larry Calhoun is walking on the narrow catwalk spanning the large bomb bay doors beneath his feet. It is a difficult chore balancing and walking the narrow passageway while a bomber is bouncing along with the turbulence and

300-miles per hour speed. Perkins and Conley yell and wave at Calhoun to approach.

At that very moment, the large aluminum bomb bay doors accidently open. Calhoun loses his balance and falls off the catwalk. Perkins reaches out and grabs Calhoun by his right bicep. Perkins is small and wiry and his right hand operates like a vice-grip. Air rushes in quickly. Calhoun's oxygen mask falls through the open bomb bay doors, down toward the Nevada desert 17,000 feet below the bomber. Conley somehow balances himself on the catwalk and grabs the back of Calhoun's jacket and left bicep. Together Conley and Perkins are able to pull Calhoun down the narrow catwalk and out of the danger. Calhoun has no oxygen mask so Perkins removes his mask and gives Calhoun alternative puffs of oxygen.

Sergeant Seaman wrestles with the manual override controlling the bomb bay doors. Seaman closes the doors and all three trainees sit down on the bare fuselage floor between the bomb room and the cabin. The pilot and Sergeant Seaman are the first to administer aid to Calhoun. Seaman has an extra oxygen mask for Calhoun and helps him activate it. The mask is oversized, in fact gigantic, but Calhoun figures it out. The pilot asks if he is okay and in a state of terrified shock, Calhoun gives two thumbs up.

The unnamed pilot and the partially unnamed crew are experienced combat veterans. The Pilot is the captain of his ship and is the man responsible for every man's safety on his ship. He is the man who writes the letter back home to the next of kin. He is thankful that on all of his combat missions, he has never lost a man. He has never written that letter. Now on a relatively safe training mission he almost lost three men during a technological breakdown. He almost had to write three letters.

Both pilot and co-pilot share the blame for the incident and order the men to wait for instructions that must come from the officers or from Flight Engineer Sergeant Seaman before moving about in the aircraft. All three trainees nod their heads in acknowledgment.

It seems Calhoun is recovering quickly. He tells a joke inside his oxygen mask that only he hears. Now with the bomb bay doors secure, the pilot and co-pilot resume their positions at the controls and the three trainees settle down near the tail of the B-24 for the rest of the trip. Calhoun soon wanders off again and Perkins and Conley just shake their heads from side to side and laugh.

After the B-24 lands at Las Vegas, the crew needs to meet at the debriefing area. The pilot, co-pilot, bombardier and navigator walk towards the debriefing area at the end of the flight line with Calhoun, arm in arm with the pilot and co-pilot. Calhoun is telling some of his best jokes and the officers are howling with laughter. Since officers and enlisted men never, ever cavort, this seems stranger than the near death experience the three trainees faced just a few hours earlier. The officers part ways with Calhoun as they enter a small circular Quonset hut to debrief the mission, while Larry, Fran and Earl head back to their barracks. This is a mission for the books. Neither Perkins nor Conley are angry with Calhoun, but they are amazed that such a screw-up can be so likeable at the same time. That is until the next day, when all three train in aerial machine gun combat.

Tuesday morning the men shower to get ready to fire the big fifty-caliber machine guns from a firing line on the ground. As Calhoun takes off his shirt and grabs his towel and soap, Conley nudges Perkins and points at Calhoun's right bicep. There on his bicep are dark black and blue marks from when Perkins grabbed him, so clear that it resembles a permanent tattoo.

"Tattoos are only for swabbies," Conley laughs. "You know, (pause) Navy guys!"

The Flight

The three men, Perkins, Conley, and Calhoun make up a small training unit called a Flight. Usually a Flight consists of six to eight men, but for this trio, three seems to be the magic number. They were in a Flight of

82

three men back in Armorer Training and again they are in the same Flight during the active machine gun training.

The first training class takes place in a large room with tiny machine guns mounted facing tiny airplanes moving along a track. The tiny machineguns fire BBs and the target stand resembles an amusement park feature. The boys think that this will be fun! Anyone can fire a toy BB gun, but usually people shoot at fixed images of targets, not moving ones.

The purpose of the training is to teach the men how to lead the target. If they take aim directly at a moving target, it may be in their gun sight when they squeeze the trigger, but the target is moving while the BB or bullet is traveling and they end up shooting behind it. They have to learn how to lead a moving target so it flies right into the path of the bullet. Additionally, in space the bullet is dropping below the target over distance. The added force of gravity as you travel higher and higher above the ground adds to the shot difficulty.

Sergeant Masters explains, "Flying in a moving aircraft while shooting at moving targets adds another dimension of difficulty. The speed of the plane you are shooting at as well as the speed you are traveling must be taken into consideration. One aircraft will be flying faster or slower than you, so you must adjust your aim accordingly."

The simple amusement park set gives these trainees their first kills while learning how to lead an enemy target from a fixed position, not from an aerial position. Once the trainees are in the air, they will receive more training on air-to-air combat and targets moving alongside the aircraft. They will react to targets moving toward or away from them at varying speeds.
The men enjoy the first thrill of shooting something together as a team. The three-man Flight completes the training in an hour and all feel confident about moving up to the real machine guns after lunch.

Look at the Ducks

The men report to a Top-turret Shooting Range where they receive instructions and prepare to shoot at their targets. Earl Conley volunteers to go first and shoots the lights out of the target. He is motivated and completes his mission successfully. Next Fran Perkins, highly motivated as well, shows an equally impressive performance. He remembers everything Cleveland, Tennessee's Billy Lewis taught him back in Texas.

"I am glad we are shipmates," Conley says with a smile.

Now it is Larry Calhoun's turn. He takes aim and fires off a long blast. The target does not move. All of Calhoun's shots go wildly to the right. Conley points to the right and yells to Perkins, "Hey, look at the ducks!"

Once again, Calhoun is off doing his own thing. The instructor quickly commands Larry to stop firing. Instead of ordering him to shoot again at the real target, he tells Calhoun to sit over on a long bench that is nicknamed the bolo bench. The word "bolo" signifies missing targets completely. Calhoun sits all alone on the long bench. Luckily, the gaggle of geese flying far to the right of the firing line was able to maneuver out of the way safely from the Wildman's wayward shots. They will never fly over this course again.

Larry Calhoun is one of a kind. Wednesday brings on new challenges.

Calhoun's the Name

Wednesday morning the Flight of three trainees, along with about thirty others begin a day in the classroom for a class titled "Shooting the Angles." This is not a class about gambling, but rather about learning how to destroy moving targets in aerial combat. The class is all about mathematical theory, which excites Fran and Earl. However, Larry Calhoun has no interest in solving mathematical problems or using geometry and nods off to sleep several times during class. The only time Calhoun comes to life is when the instructor releases the men for a one-hour lunch to return precisely at 1300 hours for four more fun-filled hours of mathematical theory. Perkins and Conley go straight to the mess hall. Calhoun says he needs to take a "colossal dump" and goes back to the barracks. After lunch, Perkins and Conley get back to class and at precisely 1300 hours, the class begins, but Calhoun is missing. His seat is empty. Did he go AWOL or did he just fall asleep and fall into the latrine while taking his colossal dump?

The answer appears about three minutes past the hour, when Calhoun practically trips and falls down the stairs as he charges toward his desk reminding Perkins of the scarecrow character in the Wizard of Oz tripping down the Yellow Brick Road. The classroom of young trainees laughs and applauds at the performance. Ray Bolger, the actor, would be proud of Larry's imitation.

Calhoun apologizes for his tardiness and then accidently knocks over his desk as he falls forward to climb onto the seat as more laughter ensues from everyone except the instructor who just glares at the misfit. He has witnessed this type of behavior before in class. However, he never witnessed a Larry Calhoun.

As the math instructor directs the class to open their books, a sudden sound of gunfire explodes somewhere inside the building. The instructor yells for everyone to hit the deck and stay put! The entire group of unarmed trainees flattens on the floor. The instructor pulls his forty-five caliber Colt 1911 style pistol from his holster and cautiously heads up the flight of stairs toward the gunfire.

Another trainee takes charge of the men lying on the floor and radios for the Military Police. Six MPs join the instructor and slowly, cautiously move up the stairs. One MP climbs up on the roof; another MP standing just under the roof, reaches up and hands the MP bending over from the roof a Thompson submachine gun, also called a Tommy gun.

85

Water Conley Water

Two more men including the instructor cover the roof and one MP finds three bunches of firecrackers strung together on long fuses. Additional firecrackers are discovered in the ventilation ducts on the roof leading down to the classrooms directly over the mathematics classroom. The Captain in charge of the Military Police team orders the trainees to fall out on the street. All of the men comply and stand at attention with heightened awareness. Everyone is afraid to move. Within minutes, the Base Commander arrives to address the men.

"I am only going to ask you one time. Who is responsible for this disturbance? I want to know right now, who set off these firecrackers! How the hell do firecrackers get into a secured military base in the first place?"

No one moves for several minutes. Finally, a voice roars out loudly from the line as though a large amplifier is sending it through hidden loudspeakers.

"It's me, Sir!"

Private Larry Aloysius Calhoun III marches in parade drill form stopping in front of the commander, stomps his feet together at attention, renders a slow perfect military salute and shouts,

"Calhoun's the name!"

"Take this man into custody," shouts the commander to the six military policemen standing next to him. "Trainees, back to class." The students go back to class and the day finishes at 1700 hours.

Perkins and Conley arrive at the mess hall for dinner but neither is very hungry tonight. They feel bad for Calhoun. Even though he is a screw-up, he is part of their training Flight; he is one of the crew. Conley and Perkins invested emotional capital in the man and now he is gone forever.

"I miss him already," Perkins says to Conley. "He kept us laughing and made training fun."

"I guess that's why we're not supposed to get that close," Conley replies, "Can you imagine when one of our crew dies in combat? It has to be even worse than this."

"If we do die in combat, I hope we all get it at once. Then we don't have the pain and guilt of survival afterwards. I have two brothers in the war right now. I hope they make it home after the war."

Following moments of thoughtful silence, Fran adds, "Do you think they'll shoot Calhoun in front of a firing squad?"

"No, they'll probably just lock him up for a while and give him a dishonorable discharge from the Army Air Corps," Conley replies.

"He may even get some prison time at Fort Leavenworth in Kansas."

Air Superiority

The next day is a big day with live aerial combat training high over the Nevada desert and the surrounding national forests.

Conley and Perkins will take off from a runway at Las Vegas in a single engine two-seater airplane. The pilot sits in the front and controls the aircraft. The trainee sits facing the rear of the plane with a single fifty-caliber machine gun mounted on a tripod. Another small single engine plane tows the twenty-foot drone target across the desert skies. The drone target looks like a large cigar resembling something UFO witnesses draw on a pad of paper when they talk about viewing an Unidentified Flying Object. Since the cockpit is open without a seatbelt, each trainee needs to be careful not to fall out of the maneuvering aircraft.

Perkins volunteers to go first. Moving up to the small plane, he notices the pilot has a nametag that reads "Suicide" giving Perkins an ominous sense of foreboding. After almost falling to his death earlier this week with Larry Calhoun, Perkins wonders what lies ahead on this training mission, especially one piloted by "Suicide."

Diminutive Perkins struggles to climb into the plane safely with a parachute attached to his back and pants. The entire package keeps catching on the door as he tries to climb into the plane. From the crowd of Flights waiting to take their turn at shooting at the flying drone, he hears "Hey, your ass is dragging" and "Take a load off." Fran is embarrassed but finally makes it onto the plane as the jeers turn into cheers.

While the two-seater aircraft accelerates down the runway, Fran feels the rush of air flowing against his back. "This is going to be one wild ride," Perkins thinks to himself.

Once in the air, the plane levels off and Perkins sees an identical aircraft towing the large cigar shaped drone. He imagines the drone to be several Japanese Zero planes going after his B-24 Bomber. Fran takes care to lead the flying cigar with his aim. Suicide, the pilot, tells Private Perkins, "Fire when ready, trainee."

Perkins computes the speed, angle, direction and distance from the analytical side of his brain and sends one long, concentrated burst into the cigar with his fifty-caliber machine gun and evaporates the target. Suicide pays no attention to the shredding of the drone. He is watching ahead for other aircraft, as he is getting ready to land at the Las Vegas Airfield.

Disembarking the plane, the ground instructor congratulates Fran with a pat on the back and a hug! The instructor tells Fran this is the best shooting he has ever seen from any trainee. When Fran let go with that long burst, his computations on speed, angle, direction and distance were so exact that he destroyed the twenty-foot long cigar drone.

Nothing but rope dragging behind the tow plane is the only evidence that a twenty-foot long solid object was once connected to the tow craft, evidence of amazing shooting from an eighteen-year-old boy who never handled a gun until a few months ago. The praising instructor invites Fran to sit next to him as they watch the rest of the trainees, telling him that he will receive three stripes to wear on his shoulder for the rest of his tour.

Private Francis J. Perkins Jr. is now Staff Sergeant Francis J. Perkins Jr. and Fran is grinning from ear to ear. He cannot wait to get back to the barracks and write home to Elaine. She will be so happy for him. "Can't wait to see Conley shred the target. We make a great team."

Private Conley walks out to the flight line to climb inside the cockpit, but unlike Perkins who had so much trouble climbing in the plane with a load of parachute dragging down the back of his pants; Conley holds the parachute behind him to make onlookers think the parachute connects to his pants. He does not want to hear the ridicule and barbs from the other Flights waiting their turns. The parachute is detached from his back, only appearing to be connected. No one notices as Conley climbs aboard easily. He has no trouble taking his seat behind the pilot. The other Flights cheer Conley in approval of his flawless entry into the plane. Conley gives Suicide two thumbs up and off they go into the wild blue yonder.

This time Suicide takes a different route that flies him high over tall pine trees in the national forest. After hitting his target with the fifty-caliber machine gun, Conley imagining himself to be boxer and heavyweight champion Joe Louis, throws both arms up in the air, celebrating a hard fought win. Just then, Suicide banks the airplane and Conley empties from the aircraft high above the forest, plunging towards the ground nine thousand feet below.

Suicide has no clue that he lost the trainee until the plane lands, everyone runs out to the aircraft, and he turns to see an empty compartment. The faces of Fran and the instructor turn white in shock.

Water Conley Water

Fran cannot believe what he has just witnessed. Suicide dumped Conley somewhere over the state of Nevada.

Immediately several search planes, including Suicide with his training aircraft, warm up their planes to search the entire route for the last flight of Private Earl W. Conley.

Requiem

Back in the barracks, it is after 1700 hours and will be dark shortly. "I hope they find Conley's body for his family," Perkins laments. "This cannot be happening. I've lost two of my crew and we haven't even flown our first combat mission. We have not yet begun to fight. This just can't be happening," Perkins says repeatedly.

"Requiem aeternam dona eis, Domine," Fran hears in his mind from his Sundays as an altar boy at St. Margaret's Church in Chicago. The English translation from Latin means, "Eternal rest grant unto him, O Lord." Perkins kneels by his bunk, makes the sign of the cross and says the prayer in Latin softly so only he and God can hear it.

"I won't forget Conley but I hope I can forget feeling this way, someday. Until then I promise I will honor his memory. I'll just have to shoot down twice as many enemy planes."

Fran hears the door open. It is the base commander. "Mind if I come in, Private?" he asks.

"No Sir!" as Fran snaps to attention and gives the commander the best salute he can muster.

"Are you fit to pack up Private Conley's personal effects, son?"

"Yes Sir," Perkins replies sadly.

"Have you ever lost men before, Perkins?" the commander asks compassionately. Perkins raises the first two fingers of his right hand. In the 60s, it would have been the Peace Sign. In World War II, it meant "V" for Victory. For Perkins it means two. He lost Calhoun and Conley on two consecutive days. It is just not fair.

"Just put everything including his uniforms in these boxes," the commander continues. "For smaller items, use this small box. Then tape them shut and write your name over the back of the tape. I will write home to Private Conley's parents. I know it doesn't seem like much now but Private Earl W. Conley destroyed his target like you, and he is now a Staff Sergeant just like you. My aide will sew his new stripes on each of his uniforms to send home. Conley earned his gunner's wings, which will also be attached to his uniforms. I know his family will be sad, but they will also be proud. They should be proud."

The Base Commander salutes Perkins, does an about face and leaves the barracks. Fran wants to write back home and tell his parents of the events. He knows, however, this information is classified. Fran thinks about his family. "Jim and Bob know what I am going through. They have their own buddies to consider. I wonder how they handle this." This is a dark moment for Fran Perkins, the darkest moment of his young life. "I lose two of my crew before I see combat. I just cannot believe all of this stuff. Now there is only me. I wonder if I am next. Dad always says death comes in threes." Fran works slowly and meticulously to make sure Conley's family receives all of his personal effects.

Sunrise over Gunnery School

The next morning Fran awakes unrested. He is used to Conley's banter and humor before they turn in at lights out, as well as first thing in the morning. Fran watches the sunrise over the building. The Nevada sky seems darker than normal so Fran can go back to sleep for a few more minutes. Just then, he hears movement by the door. The door swings open with a bang and a dirty, bloodstained man appears with bandages covering his face.

Bandaged man yells loudly, "Water Conley Water!"

Perkins's face turns as white as a sheet. He blinks, swallows hard then recognizing the voice, returns the verbal volley crowing, "Calhoun's the name," just as loud as he can, mimicking Larry Calhoun's voice.

From under bandages that cover minor cuts and bruises is the familiar face of one Staff Sergeant Earl W. Conley. Perkins is elated, yet he thinks he must be dreaming. "How did you survive a fall of thousands of feet?" asks Perkins.

Conley answers, "After shooting my target I threw my arms up like Joe Louis when he wins a fight and the plane turned sharply and I fell out. The parachute was tied to one of my boots and I was able to get it attached as I was falling. I'll always keep it on next time. I didn't know how to navigate the parachute so I just closed my eyes and hoped for the best. I landed in a soft pile of dirt, dragging across the ground for a while but not before, I bounced from tree limb to tree limb in a forest of tall pine trees. My face hurts from the cuts but I'm okay. It feels like I shaved with a dull razor."

"How did you get back here?"

"After I landed I tried to get my bearings but I was in a canyon surrounded by huge pine trees. I couldn't figure out which way to go so I climbed up on a high point of rocks and then saw several campfires only a couple of football fields away. I zigzagged in and out of pine trees until I reached the first campfire. Three lumberjacks were sitting around the campfire drinking coffee. The oldest one in the group stood up and asked, 'Who the hell are you?' I told him 'I'm Private Conley and fell out of an airplane.' Since my parachute shredded on a large pine tree branch, it must have looked as though I fell out of the airplane without a parachute."I heard a voice in Spanish say 'Ave Maria!' almost as loud as Larry saying, 'Calhoun's the name.' The lumberjacks were spellbound as I told my story and they admitted to not hearing any gunfire all day or any airplanes for that matter.

"The large, grizzled lumberjack leader said, 'I got some bandages here. I'll clean ya up and take ya back in the truck, son. We should get to Las Vegas by early mornin'. I know where to find the airfield. I bet your unit has given you up fer dead.'"

Conley sent the three lumberjacks into stitches as they were cleaning him up using his humor and charm and threw in some patented Larry Calhoun material for good measure. As the truck left with Conley and the Foreman, the Spanish-speaking lumberjack yelled out, "Good luck, Ave Maria." Everyone laughed.

Conley added, "I arrived just a few minutes ago. I wanted to see you again before reporting back for duty."

"Let's go together to report to the Base Commander. I want to see his reaction when a ghost pays him a visit."

Perkins and Conley enter the commander's office to find the Base Commander pouring over maps of the aerial range and impact area. He has national forest maps on his desk with crayon markings on them. Perkins could not help himself as he reports to the Commander. "Staff Sergeant Perkins reporting with Staff Sergeant Conley's personal effects."

The Base Commander snaps his head up, bolts out of his chair and gives Conley a hug. The Base Commander forgets the decorum of his military rank for a moment out of relief for young Conley's safety. "I am damn glad and happy to see you, boy. I will get you to the aid station and make sure you are okay. Perkins, you can come as well. After that, Perkins, help Conley get his effects put back in his wall locker and footlocker. Get him something to eat. Report to the Officers Mess Tent. You two will be welcome there."

After the examination by the emergency room doctor on duty, both men feel very lucky to be allowed to eat in the Officers Mess Tent. Conley cleans up well after his death-defying miraculous experience falling out of an open cockpit of an airplane flying over 9,000 feet, bouncing like a pinball off tall pine trees into a pile of soft earth. No one ever finds the parachute Conley shredded as he bounced off the trees.

Perkins is glad his friend is okay and they will be in the same crew. It will not be long before they go on real combat missions together. They will ride into the history books soon in a battle called the Alamo in the Sky, the last flight of the **Daisy Mae**.

Chapter 7

Thumper

Since January, Perkins and Conley have been training in the Southern Arizona skies near Tucson with the other gunners with whom they are assigned as Crew #2 of the "A" Flight, 459th Bomb Squadron. In the beginning of April, excitement reigns as Crew #2 anticipates meeting their officers and their new home for the rest of the war, a huge B-24D Bomber with the 42nd Squadron 11th Bomb Group.

The 11th Bomb Group is in the Seventh Army Air Corps. The Seventh hails as the Hawaiian Air Force because it patrols the skies around Hawaii day and night. It also trains for offensive bombing runs over the Japanese bases located in the Gilbert and Marshall Islands of the South Pacific Ocean.

"It's great to finally finish training and get into World War II," says Perkins.

Conley agrees. "It has been a long time coming. For two months, we've had our orders and the names of our other crewmembers. I hope we meet our officers soon and I hope they're good."

Davis-Monthan Airfield

Now they are going to meet the men who will fly them to victory or defeat in the Pacific War.

At the Consolidated-Vultee factory in Fort Worth, Texas, a handsome, young Pilot Joseph A. Gall meets the other four officers who together will fly in a brand new B-24D Bomber, fresh off the assembly line.

Thumper

Gall is the son of a blacksmith growing up near Allentown, Pennsylvania. After high school, he worked at Mack's Trucks in Allentown, fixing all types of heavy vehicles. Mack's tools were ancient so young Joe Gall had to wrestle big trucks developing superior hand and arm strength. There were no power tools. As was the custom back then, on payday, Joe presented all of his pay to his father. In return, Joe received an allowance just as many other men did at that time, giving all to the family. The Great Depression is fresh in the hearts and minds of these young men, who were children during the depression and suddenly adults during a great war. Gall entered the Army Air Corps in 1940.

Standing and waiting for authorization along with Gall are Co-pilot Flight Officer John N. Van Horn, Navigator 2nd Lt. Benjamin I. Weiss, and Bombardier 2nd Lt. Myron W. Jensen. All four young men are trying to restrain the thrill of being real live Army Air Corps Aviators. On the outside, they are all business-like but on the inside, they are jumping out of their skin in anticipation of flying into combat. Long months of training in simulations are over. Now they will fly to Davis-Monthan Airfield near Tucson, Arizona and pick up the enlisted men who will protect the bomber in the air.

"What are we going to call our bomber?" Van Horn asks Lt. Gall.

"I don't know yet. Let's wait until we pick up the gunners in Arizona."

"I hope they're good," Lt. Jensen remarks.

Weiss nods his head in agreement. It is April 2, 1943 and is the official beginning of the war for the four young officers. Pilot Joe Gall is just twenty-three years old and is the oldest in the group. Today they will ride off into history with their brand new bomber.

An officer greets the four-man bomber team and points at two long stripes of paint leading out to hangers located to the North and to the East of the main building. A long green stripe heads to the hangar to the North and a long pink stripe leads to the hangar to the East. Both of the

Thumper

stripes resemble chalk foul lines in a professional baseball stadium. Each stripe is six inches wide and seems to stretch to infinity, pointing at the massive hangars.

"Who is the pilot," the young officer asks and all four crewmembers raise their hands. After all, all four of these men are qualified pilots.

Bombardiers and Navigators also go to flight school as many times pilots and co-pilots receive wounds or die during frontal assaults by enemy fighter planes. The Navigator and Bombardier, as well as the Co-pilot, need to be ready to step in and save the rest of the crew.

"Okay, wise guys, who is the guy designated as the real pilot?" Lt. Joe Gall smiles and nods.

"You will receive your orders when you follow either one of the chalk marks. The pink line will lead you to a brand new B-24D flying off to one theatre of war and the green chalk mark will take you off to a different theatre of war.

"Every mission you fly is top secret including this one. I have no information as to which colors go to which war fronts. I do not have a top-secret clearance. The only thing I know is an officer will be waiting at the end of your yellow brick road to give you the written orders from Headquarters and your brand new B-24D Liberator. Now pick a color and fly off to victory."

Gall quickly makes his first decision as Pilot. "Let's go down the green road."

Weiss jumps in and pushes himself in front of the Co-pilot Van Horn. The two young men fake trading Joe Louis punches and all are laughing as they enter the hangar and gaze at their new bomber for the first time.

Thumper

"She is beautiful," says Bombardier Lt Jensen. "I can't wait to get into her greenhouse," referring to the Plexiglas covering the nose of the aircraft.

A young officer hands Gall a clipboard with just two words on the cover sheet of many pages. Kualoa, Hawaii is where Gall and his crew will fly after picking up their gunners in Arizona.

Kualoa is a secret base housing the 42nd Squadron of the 11th Bomb Group. Their mission is to protect the Hawaiian Islands from invasion by the Japanese and destroy the Japanese Empire moving a forward bomber line all the way from Hawaii and Australia to Japan.

If Gall chose the pink stripe rather than the green one, he would have flown to North Africa to help Patton beat the Desert Fox, General Rommel, and eventually attack Sicily, Italy and Germany. Gall did not care which theatre he chose. He wanted to help win the war as quickly as possible and he vowed to do the best job he could.

All four pilots decide to take turns flying the bomber once it is in the air. A B-24 is difficult to fly because it is slow to respond to the controls and almost seems like it goes where it wants to rather than where you want it to go. The pilots learned how to fly the bomber in simulated situations so they understand what to do. It will take a while to master the ship's idiosyncrasies.

The new bomber is working perfectly. Each crewmember has a chance to take the controls under the watchful eye of Lt. Joe Gall who is responsible for the lives of his crew and he does not take his role lightly.

Gall at the stick of the new Liberator approaches Davis-Monthan Airfield a few hours later and lightly touches down dead center. The four officers climb out.

Thumper

The Cast and Crew of Lt. Joseph A. Gall's Big Brown Bomber:

- 1st Lt. Joseph A. Gall, Pilot
- Flight Officer John N. Van Horn, Co-Pilot
- 2nd Lt. Benjamin I. Weiss, Navigator
- 2nd Lt. Myron W. Jensen, Bombardier
- T.Sgt. Arvid B Ambur, Flight Engineer and Waist Gunner
- T.Sgt. George Hutman, Top-Turret Gunner and Assistant Flight Engineer
- S.Sgt. Robert L. Patterson, Radioman and Waist Gunner
- S.Sgt. Francis J. Perkins Jr. Armorer and Ball-turret Gunner
- S.Sgt. Robert "Snuffy" Storts, Nose Gunner
- S.Sgt. Earl W. Conley, Tail Gunner

Gall introduces the officers to the enlisted men. Technical Sergeant Arvid B. Ambur introduces the enlisted men, including Perkins and Conley to the officers.

Arvid B. Ambur is a farm boy from Presho, South Dakota. Farming and ranching is in his blood. He ranches as well as farms and raised a prize steer while still in high school. He is the link between enlisted men and officers. Being the Flight Engineer, he relays all information about the operation and conditions of the aircraft to the Pilot, Co-pilot, Navigator and Bombardier. Arvid needs to know the aircraft inside and out and understand the enlisted men, the gunners, inside and out.

He and Technical Sergeant George Hutman, who is Arvid's backup flight engineer, are also the medics. Most of their medical training involves stopping the bleeding, protecting the wound and administering doses of morphine for pain. The flight engineers are the only crewmembers who receive this type of emergency medical training. The bombers flying over the Pacific Ocean will be in the air for eight or nine straight hours. When a man gets hurt over the target, he could easily bleed to death in the four hours it takes to get back to base or die from shock.

Thumper

Thumper is Born

The young men fly to Sacramento, California where their B-24 is transformed into the "D" model by installing a nose-turret for Snuffy Storts, and a ball-turret for Fran Perkins. Perkins requests permission from his new pilot, Joe Gall, to watch the work on the new B-24. Gall understands Perkins' interest in big machines as young Gall worked on big machines at Mack's Truck Garage, just a few years earlier.

The rest of the crew hitches a ride to downtown Sacramento and settles in a restaurant/bar. An older man walks up to the group of nine airmen and asks if they just brought in a new bomber. Gall answers, "Yes." The older man asks, "What is the name of your bomber?" Navigator Benjamin I. Weiss replies, "B-24." All the men laugh. Joe Gall tells the older man they have not considered a name yet and have no artwork on the bomber. The older man tells the group he is a Walt Disney artist. He adds that he drew all of the characters including Bambi and Thumper for the colorful movie hit, Bambi. "Would you give me the privilege of painting "Thumper" on the nose of your aircraft?"

All of the men nod their approval unanimously as the crew supports the name. This makes Gall's decision on a name very easy. Gall thinks, "**Thumper** is the bomber that is taking us into World War II. I hope she is a good ship."

When the unnamed artist finishes his work, the airmen marvel when they view **Thumper** for the first time. The nose artwork looks professional, as it truly is. "**Thumper** it is," remarks Ben Weiss. "She will lead us into battle and carry us safely home." All of the men nod their approval and climb aboard.

Flight Engineer Sergeant Arvid Ambur turns each propeller according to the Air Corps Operation Manual for a B-24D Liberator and the Number Three Engine begins to fire up, followed by Number Four, Number Two and Number One. With all engines fired up to 2500 RPM, the flight engineer returns to his station on the aircraft and Pilot Joe Gall begins the roll call. Everyone is at their battle stations and calls in their position, including the co-pilot, John Van Horn, even though he sits inches away from Pilot Joe Gall. They follow this sequence in every mission forward.

They leave from Sacramento, California and stop at San Francisco briefly to gas up and meet up with the rendezvousing airplanes that will fly with them to the Territory of the Hawaiian Islands.

Fran Perkins and Earl Conley move back by the tail and take turns watching out the rear gun turret. Lt. Joe Gall calls for Perkins to take his battle station in the ball-turret. Fran enthusiastically says, "Yes sir!" He climbs into the turret inside the plane and operates the controls to move the turret underneath **Thumper**'s soft aluminum belly. It's official! Fran is protecting his brand new B-24D Liberator and her crew from the enemy. He watches outside for any sign of other aircraft or ships. Fran consults the flashcards he carries from gunnery school that will help him identify enemy aircraft.

As he swivels the turret to face toward **Thumper**'s nose, he takes time to enjoy looking at the Pacific Ocean for the first time. He gazes at the countless whitecaps and wonders how he will find stranded aircrews bobbing among the whitecaps in the busy ocean. The life rafts are tiny in comparison to the huge waves.

Gall informs the men they will be flying at twenty thousand feet and instructs them to put on their cold weather gear, as they will need their oxygen masks and cold weather gear to breathe and operate as this altitude. As soon as they level off from 20,100 feet to 20,000 feet, Pilot Joe Gall calls Perkins over the intercom and says, "Belly Gunner, test your guns."

For every young man, firing the fifty-caliber machine guns is noisy and fun. This is the most exciting moment for Perkins and the rest of the gunners as each get the order from their new boss, Pilot Lt. Gall.

Thumper

Fran and the gunners on the other ships in formation communicate by flashing Morse code using small rectangular lights connected to each gun position by a wire. This way the crews can converse with men on other ships in the formation. The signal lights are the bomber crew's social media and keep the men sharp in using their Morse code when they enter air combat.

For the first time in his life, Perkins sees the awe-inspiring sight of Diamond Head, a large rock formation on Oahu. As discussed in his history class in high school, Perkins knows that Diamond Head was the landmark for which invading Japanese were looking when they bombed Pearl Harbor and the airfield at Hickam. Gall takes **Thumper** down to one thousand feet and heads toward Kualoa Air Field on the other side of the island. Fishing boats, hula girls and beaches grow larger with the descent. Gall instructs Perkins to retract his gun turret inside the belly and the other gunners to get into position to land.

Landing on Kualoa

Nobody prepared Gall for landing at Kualoa Airfield on the island of Oahu.

The airfield hides on a beach on the other side of some sharp mountain cliffs with the runway cutting across a road. When airplanes are landing or taking off, the road closes temporarily, leaving no alternative routes for automobile drivers. Fortunately, because of gas rationing in territories like the Hawaiian Islands, not many people are driving automobiles.

The sun is beginning to set and the gunners begin to nod off as the pilot, co-pilot, navigator and bombardier are doing just fine at the controls. Suddenly, the gunners are shocked back to attention. "What is that awful sound!" they think in unison. "Are we crashing?"

Gall and Van Horn at the controls have no idea what is going on. **Thumper** touches down on the steel plank runway at Kualoa and the ship shakes, rattles and rolls down the runway. No one warned the pilots about the ungodly loud noise they would experience landing on the island. No one told them that their bones would rattle with each simple takeoff and landing. They see headlights of automobiles waiting for them to land. There is ocean behind them. There is ocean ahead of them. There is ocean on three sides of the airstrip. A sharp mountainous cliff glares at them from the landside of Kualoa.

Steel planking covers the surface of the runway resembling a steel pontoon bridge spanning the airbase across the sandy beach. The steel pontoon bridge is made of several sections bolted together. When an airplane takes off or lands, the noise and vibration inside the plane is horrendous. It sounds and feels as if the entire airplane is falling apart.

This is the perfect place to test a pilot's nerves. It is also an impossible place for the Japanese to attack.

Hey Dude, Where's My Bomber?

Feet finally on solid ground, ears still ringing, the officers head over to the officer's tent, the enlisted men to their tents.

The four officers share one large tent and there are two other tents to house the remaining six gunners. They decide to sleep three to a tent. Perkins, Conley and Ambur share one tent and Storts, Patterson and Hutman share the other enlisted men's tent.

The four officers report to the Base Commander and he instructs the men to eat and then turn in for the night. He adds that after **Thumper** fuels, a second crew is taking her out on a night patrol. **Thumper** will be in the air from 1900 hours until 0400 hours. After **Thumper** lands, Gall and his crew will begin their mission at 0800 hours and fly until 1700 hours. The mission will be typical, including searching for enemy planes, surface ships and submarines. They will take several loops around the island of Oahu as they get used to their brand new home in the skies for the rest of the war.

Thumper

The B-24 Bombers assigned to the 42nd squadron never rest. Neither do her crews. This is the modus operandi for the Seventh Air Corps, as well as the other units of the United States Army Air Corps assigned to dismantle the Empire of Japan.

Thumper takes off with her substitute crew at 1900 hours and at exactly 2000 hours, the control tower loses contact with **Thumper**. The aircraft must have quietly gone down at sea. Two destroyers anchored at Pearl Harbor and two PT Boats begin a search. It is now around 2030 in military time on April 3, 1943. **Thumper** and her crew of ten men are lost forever. Naval search planes go out in the morning but find no wreckage of the aircraft or her men.

At 2100 hours, Bombardier Lt. Jensen goes into the enlisted men's tents and requests that the men meet outside the tent in ten minutes. Perkins, Ambur and Conley are in a deep discussion about the last baseball season, when they quickly put on their fatigues and meet with Jensen, Weiss, Van Horn and Gall.

Lt. Joseph Gall announces, "Men, **Thumper** and her crew are missing. Tomorrow morning at 0800 hours, we will meet to wait for a new bomber for our next assignment. We will be here at Hickam until they find another B-24 for us."

Fran, standing at attention while receiving orders from Lt. Gall, feels as if someone just punched him hard in the stomach. "This is the worst news possible. I met **Thumper** when they were still building her. I spent all day watching them install my ball-turret and Snuffy Stort's nose-turret. What happened to the crew? I wonder if they felt anything when they died. I hope the guys did not feel anything," Perkins laments. "That's the way I want to go when my time comes."

Conley, Ambur and the rest of the crew had similar thoughts as Perkins, but no one ever talked about **Thumper** again. This is a silent tribute to ten young men. They died quickly and quietly for their country.

Thumper

Hickam Field

For several days, Perkins, Conley, Ambur, and the rest of the crew fall out in formation each morning at 0700 hours and then they are on their own until 1700 hours. During the day, they clean up the barracks and then walk around the base or hitch a ride into town. This part of the War is boring for all of the men. They worked hard in training for a long time, only to become spectators in World War II. Now, boredom becomes a new enemy and none of the officers or the enlisted men ever received training for boredom. At night, the endless boredom continues until **Thumper**'s former crew receives a special invitation to an entertainment event held Saturday night on base. The unsigned invitation creates curiosity among the crew. Every man will have to attend.

A little more than a year earlier, Hickam burned on December 7, 1941 and there was little chance of any entertainment. Now every weekend, entertainment flies in from California. Tonight is a real treat because an orchestra with the big band sound of the 40s is performing. Also on the marquee is a women's vocal group that sounds exactly like the Andrews Sisters. They will play the rousing song, "Boogie Woogie Bugle Boy of Company B." to a large, howling, appreciative group of young airmen.

The opening act is a comedian named Bolo Bob. It is April of 1943 and a large tent complete with its own beer garden stands waiting for the 500 or more GIs looking for fun in the middle of World War II.

Bolo Bob

The Master of Ceremonies jumps up on the stage, grabs the microphone and says, "We have so much entertainment tonight. We'll proceed from act to act with a short introduction.

"Our opening act is one of a kind. He is one of us. Get ready for some fifty-caliber humor from one of our very own, or maybe he is not one of our very own. Hell, I don't know. Bolo Bob wrote this introduction, not me. Don't blame me if this character falls flat on his face. That's his trademark by the way, falling flat on his face. If he does fall on his face, I'll need two airmen to come to the rescue. Straight out of his straitjacket and right into the 7th Army Air Corps at Hickam Field, I am happy to present... Bolo Bob!"

Perkins grabs an empty chair next to Conley. All of the other enlisted men of **Thumper**'s former crew are standing together and facing the large stage. Several rows in front sit all the officers of the crew. The officers do not mingle with the enlisted men.

"I hope this is good," Perkins says to Conley. "Comedy seems so hard when everyone wants to see the USO girls and dance to the music. A mechanic told me today that the orchestra is great. They have a trumpet player who sounds just like Harry James."

A long snare drum rolls in the background and Polynesian drums pound while Bolo Bob comes out on stage dressed in an Air Corps uniform with Staff Sergeant's stripes on his sleeves. He wears an oversized airman's oxygen mask on his face. It is gargantuan. The crowd howls at the sight. Two scantily clad Hawaiian girls, dressed in their native Hawaiian costume, wiggle, jiggle and giggle across the broad stage to the sounds of the jungle drums and music in the background.

With their lovely hula hands, both girls are motioning for Bolo Bob to take off his oxygen mask so they can plant kisses on his face. Fran, Conley and his crewmates join in on the cheers to "take it off, take it off, take it all off." The officers sitting several rows in front of their gunners put aside their military decorum and yell, "Take it off, take it off, take it all off." The wounded from nearby hospitals sit in wheelchairs on either side of the stage. They smile through their bandages, laugh, applaud loudly and yell, "Take it off, take it off, and take it all off."

The two hula girls are now standing in front of Bolo Bob's body and begin to remove the gargantuan oxygen mask. As Bolo Bob reveals his

106

face, from twenty tables back, Perkins and Conley gasp together at the sight. They both turn facing each other and shout loudly, "Calhoun's the name, Calhoun's the name!"

"I thought he was shot before a firing squad," says Perkins. "Or at least booted from the Army Air Corps with a dishonorable discharge!"

Instead, Larry found his way back on his feet with no help necessary from Perkins or Conley. His show is unbelievable. When you think of Bob Hope, Jack Benny, Bing Crosby and all of the comedians entertaining troops, Larry Calhoun is in the same ballpark. Perkins and Conley laugh and listen to Bolo Bob, also known as Larry Aloysius Calhoun III, as he keeps five hundred men in stitches for over an hour and a half.

No one wants him to leave and Larry has several encores. Even the great orchestra and dancing girls remain in dressing rooms as Larry holds the audience spellbound, laughing and in the palm of his hand. Larry Calhoun is a wild shot with a fifty-caliber machine gun, but every single joke tonight is a fifty-caliber bull's-eye. The expression, "he had them rolling in the aisles," describes Larry tonight. Young men who were on bombing missions earlier in the day are falling and rolling on the floor laughing. One Sergeant from the next table quickly runs to the restroom as he laughs so hard he wet his pants.

Several times Perkins and Conley look at each other and smile. Both men never thought much about saving Larry's life from a free fall at 17,000 feet to the Nevada desert floor below. After all, he was a shipmate on a bomber and that was their job. Shipmates put other's lives before their own. Think of a firefighter going into a burning building to save a trapped and frightened child. These young fighting men have the same stuff. Perkins and Conley instinctively are ready to trade their lives to save others and each other. They represent the heart and soul of every American fighting man during World War II.

Thumper

Larry Calhoun finds the best possible way he can serve his country. In place of bullets and bombs, Larry Calhoun fights World War II with humor and hope.

There is a hush in the show as Bolo Bob marches in true military style off the stage to the audience floor. You now hear a soft military tattoo on a snare drum. Wally Soffer, a jazz drummer from Chicago, is lightly rolling his sticks. Two hula girls hold their fingers in front of their lips making repeated loud "shish" sounds directed at howling GIs. Conley is laughing at the group table and telling a crewmember sitting opposite of Perkins some of Bob's punchlines again. Both Perkins and the other crewmembers laugh at the way Conley does a perfect imitation of Bolo Bob. After all, Conley has heard Bolo's voice many times before the show when Bob was Private Larry Calhoun.

Suddenly, the only people who are laughing and talking are **Thumper**'s former crew at the table. Fran punches Earl in the arm, during mid joke. Two feet away from their table, standing at attention, facing Perkins and Conley is none other than Bolo Bob, the entertainer, also known as Larry Calhoun, the aerial combat trainee extraordinaire.

Larry yells out, "Ten hut!" in such a loud voice it seems to have come from hidden loudspeakers. Five hundred men including all of the officers in the front rows jump to their feet, as if General MacArthur and Admiral Nimitz are walking into the venue. Only those wounded warriors in wheelchairs remain seated. They, too, master their best military salutes. Larry begins a long, slow, sweeping, ceremonial salute. Generals and Presidents receive this type of salute during burial ceremonies at Arlington National Cemetery. He then shouts out in an equally impressive voice, "Thank you two gentlemen for saving my life!"

Both Conley and Perkins are waiting for a punchline that never comes.

Larry then yells out, "Order arms!

Thumper

Slowly and in grand military ceremonial form, he returns his salute and his arm to his side. Five hundred men are saluting and no one knows why. One drunk pilot at another table yells loudly, "Bolo Bob salutes enlisted men!" Everyone, including the stuffy officers sitting up front laugh hysterically at the remark.

Everyone, except Perkins and Conley, thinks this as part of a funny bit, mocking the military. The only men who are silent in the entire building are Perkins, and Conley. They own a secret they are willing to take to the grave for this wonderful tribute. Calhoun marches quickly back to his stage, sometimes skipping and falling like Ray Bolger's character in the Wizard of Oz as the hula girls and backup band are singing, "Follow the Yellow Brick Road."

Five hundred men laugh their approval. They have no idea of what is going on and what the exchange really means to a couple of nineteen-year-old kids on the threshold of the biggest battle of their lives.

Fran, always analytical, wonders how Calhoun found him and Earl Conley. The staging was perfect. "Larry had to rehearse," wonders Perkins. However, this is Larry Calhoun. Calhoun is a master of improvisation. He has a way of avoiding death and making fast friends in the process. His talent is as vast as the Pacific Ocean and as naturally beautiful as the early winter snows on Mt McKinley. Calhoun found his greatness in a way that serves all the brave men and women of the Armed Forces. Larry Aloysius Calhoun III is a master of comedy and a master of men.

Fran wonders if he should ever receive a medal for bravery, it could never top the unique and private tribute hiding in plain sight of five hundred other men who never had a clue what was going on.

Funny material for many that Saturday night is a lesson in hope for two young men, who will face the fight of their lives in just two months. They are going to need all the hope they can muster.

Thumper

"Now we need a bomber, says Conley"

"Yes we do, Conley," Perkins smiles, "Yes we do."

Chapter 8

Meet the Daisy Mae

It is the Sunday after running into Larry Calhoun. Perkins and Conley appreciate their brand new day. Lt Gall sends Jensen and Weiss to give the men the good news. They found a new ship!

This ship is not brand new. It has been through hell.
It does not have the new bomber smell.
It does not have the new bomber feel.
It does have the new bomber sound.
It does have some flaws.
It does have something **Thumper** did not have.
It does have a heart and a soul.

Standing on the tarmac, the crew hears "This is it," from Navigator Ben Weiss as he looks at the bomber from the driver's side of the aircraft. Weiss, Gall, Jensen and Van Horn walk around to the passenger's side of the Liberator and Jensen says, "Yes, this is it! Meet the **Daisy Mae**," pointing at the image of a young woman posing with one hand over her head waving hello or goodbye. The **Daisy Mae** image sits underneath the window on the co-pilot's side of the plane, Flight Officer John Van Horn's side of the B-24 Liberator.

Van Horn adds, "She won't run from a fight," while putting his finger in a bullet hole below **Daisy Mae**'s armpit and wiggling it around a bit.

Gall orders the rest of the crew to climb inside the aircraft while Flight Engineer Arvid Ambur turns the propellers and Van Horn ignites the number three engine after the sixth turn.

April of 1943

At this very moment, World War II is on full throttle impacting every country. The only large-scale escape of Allied prisoners-of-war from the Japanese in the Pacific takes place when ten American POWs and two Filipino prisoners break out of the Davao Penal Colony on the island of Mindanao in the Philippines Islands. The Japanese Army swiftly overran the island nation immediately after the infamous Pearl Harbor attack. Major General Jonathan Wainwright surrendered over 75,000 Allied Forces to the invading Japanese. Now early in April of 1943, several Americans escape from prison and are the first to break the news to the world of the infamous Bataan Death March and other atrocities committed by the Japanese Empire.

On the other side of the world, the Americans are fighting in Tunisia, North Africa. This is exactly where Gall, Van Horn, Weiss and Jensen would have been flying and fighting had they followed the pink line back at the B-24 factory in Fort Worth, Texas.

In Europe, Allied bombing raids are reaching Berlin, Germany, and the Russians are protecting their homeland and defeating the Axis Powers with stunning victories.

It is a long war and there are several turning points giving the Allies momentum and hope. The island of Guadalcanal is not the exception. The Japanese discover the true grit of the American soldier. They continue to test the young men and ultimately retreat in disbelief. After World War II, Japanese call Guadalcanal, "Japan's Graveyard."

First Mission

The first mission for Gall's crew is to fly over and around Guadalcanal taking pictures of the islands and flying all the way to the famous channel where small, quick moving enemy transport ships try to shoot the gap and supply Japanese ground forces on Guadalcanal.

The Americans called these ships the Tokyo Express. For six months, the Japanese fought against highly committed Marine and Army personnel before abandoning the island just two months earlier in February of 1943. It was hard for the Japanese to stomach defeat, especially to the Americans who they considered a sub-human species. The Japanese Army had smothered most of Asia in easy battles in Manchuria, China and the Philippines. How could these undisciplined and unprincipled Americans defeat them?

Just as the Battle of Midway in which Major Perry McIntosh flew his B-17, became a turning point in the war at sea, Guadalcanal proved the same in the ground war. The marines exude determination and hope, as they understand without a shred of doubt that they will beat the Japanese, one-on-one. Most of the Japanese senior officers now understand they will lose the War against America. The Japanese are more determined to fight and die for every inch of property among the hundreds of conquered islands forming their perimeter around Japan. They will not die easy.

Even after giving up the Guadalcanal Island, they did not leave gracefully. Some of the Japanese stayed behind, living in the bug-infested and crocodile-inhabited thick jungle that covered most of the island. There were over 2500 square miles of jungle on Guadalcanal. It was an easy place to hide in the daytime and a scary place at night.

The sounds of the night are eerie. Sometimes Japanese soldiers will come into the camp at night and make scary sounds. In broken English, the American forces will hear Japanese soldiers call over loud speakers, "Tonight you will die the death of dogs." Sometimes they shoot at the parked aircraft. The Japanese soldiers only move at night. They crawl very slowly through the jungle to the flight line on Henderson Field to climb inside the resting airships and slit the throats of sleeping flyers inside. Sometimes they stick their heads through the trap door and throw hand grenades inside to blow up the plane.

Gall asks two volunteers to protect the aircraft at night. Perkins and Conley volunteer for the job. Perkins once again forgets the advice his father gave him before joining the Air Corps. A Marine Captain instructs Perkins and Conley how they need to defend the aircraft at night saying, "Always keep watching the point of entry. If one man falls asleep, wake him up. Leave one point of entry open to make it easy for a Jap to stick his head in and then blow it off. If you leave a door open, they will think it is a trap. It is a trap. I hope that they will move on to the next bomber or just go back into the jungle. It is best for both of you can stay awake all night. The sounds in the night are scary enough with biting bugs and man-eating crocodiles. They get even scarier than the Japanese soldiers you face.

"Are you good shots with those things?" the Marine Captain questions. Perkins and Conley each hold two weapons. One is a 45-caliber Tommy gun and the other a 45-caliber 1911 style pistol.

"Yes Sir!" Perkins and Conley shout out.

"That's good," says the Captain. "Keep your weapons loaded with safeties off. You will need to act quickly if you spot a head pop up through the open door. One more thing, men. Do not leave your airplane for any reason until the marines sweep the area at first light. Also, if you do shoot at the enemy, do not follow him outside. Other enemy soldiers may be lying in wait. We find that they remove most of the bodies of their fallen during the night to demoralize your efforts and convince you of poor marksmanship skills. Do you have any questions?"

Both men look at the Marine Captain and then Lt. Gall and reply, "No Sir."

Gall and the Marine Captain, both exclaim, "Carry on, men, that is all." All exit except Perkins and Conley. Flight Engineer Sergeant Arvid Ambur pops his head back into the **Daisy Mae** and asks, "Do you need any help? Do you want me to stay with you?"

Perkins and Conley assure Ambur they will be fine. "We worked together before. We can handle it, thank you." says Perkins.

Ambur leaves the plane and heads for the tent housing the enlisted men who play cards to stay distracted from the fear of attack with a counteroffensive by the jungle-based Japanese.

In the **Daisy Mae**, Perkins and Conley finish cleaning their weapons and lock rounds in their chambers. They are ready. The time goes by very slowly. They do not hear any more sounds of civilization. Both men hear only the sounds of the fright-filled jungle. They move far away from each other to guard more of the bomber. It is too hard and noisy to walk, so they crawl on their bellies. Only ten minutes pass and Earl breaks the silence.

Earl asks, "What time is it, Fran?"

"Ten minutes after you asked me last time."

There is a long pause in the darkness. Then Fran hears a lone voice. "And what time was it ten minutes ago?"

Fran says nothing, but his body shakes as he tries to hold back laughter.

The harder Fran tries to suppress a laugh, the harder it is for him to do so. His body begins to shake uncontrollably, reminding Fran of all of the crazy stuff Larry Calhoun put them through when Larry was getting into trouble. Now, hopelessly attempting to suppress laughter, Fran is shaking and rolling on the floor of the mighty air fortress. He is just a nineteen-year-old boy on an adventure.

Just as Fran quiets his body and mind, Conley begins again.

"What are you doing over there in the dark, Perkins?" chortles Conley.

Perkins holds both hands over his mouth and his mind fills with funny images. He does not want to laugh but the funny images push out any hint of the actual danger he faces. Images of Larry Calhoun the soldier and Larry Calhoun as Bolo Bob the entertainer flood his consciousness.

Conley is laughing now and both act like teenage girls at a slumber party rather than the trained killers they pretend to be. **Daisy Mae** herself seems to join in on the fun as the vibrating noise inside the hollow tube blares out like Calhoun's booming stage voice. **Daisy Mae** likes her boys who guard her day and night.

The noise is getting so loud now with rolling soldiers and vibrating tons of aluminum and steel, that the Japanese hiding along the field must be confused.

With tears of laughter rolling down his face, Fran whispers through a laugh, "Water Conley Water."

Conley responds loudly with the familiar comeback, "Calhoun's the name." The retorts become a trademark for these boys at least for the first mission. Afterward, World War II becomes much more serious for these young men.

Less than fifty yards away, a Japanese soldier is low crawling through the jungle and now spots the image of the **Daisy Mae** clearly in view. The soldier has a handgun drawn and a grenade ready on his belt. He crawls slowly and confidently toward the large bomber. Suddenly, twin fifty-caliber machine guns open up from the top-turret of the bomber parked behind and in line with the **Daisy Mae**. Occasionally the men guarding the bombers from the inside will fire their guns into the jungle along the runway to scare away or kill the enemy lurking nearby.

Conley and Perkins immediately turn off the funny button and grab their guns, training them on the trap door. If any enemy soldiers pop in, they will pay the consequences.

The top-turret fires several hundred rounds into the nearby jungle. There are no sounds of any return fire. It is an overcast night so no moon or stars appear overhead as Perkins looks out the rear-turret for a moment. "I can't see a thing," says Perkins. "I smell the jungle and see a cloud of gunpowder from the top-turret of the bomber parked behind us."

It gets quiet again and the jungle begins with the now familiar sounds of creepy, scary things. There are bats, rats and flying fox that make noise and there are over sixty-nine species of birds on Guadalcanal that seem to compete at the same time, singing or squawking at night.

Perkins and Conley see a helmet appear at the trapdoor. Both men fire their 1911 style 45 pistols at the invader. There is no return fire. A few bullets ricochet around the interior of the **Daisy Mae**, settling in something soft.

"I got 'em," says Perkins.

"No, I got 'em," says Conley.

"Quiet Conley, I'm going out the trapdoor to find the body and then we'll see who got him."

"You can't go out the trap door! Remember we have to stay in the bomber until given the all clear by the marines after first light. Marines'll shoot at anything that moves out there. That anything is you."

Perkins ignores Conley's warning, slowly and quietly crawling on his belly toward the trap door. By now, both Conley and Perkins know the ship in total darkness after crawling through the fuselage several times through the night. They have memorized every nook and cranny of the **Daisy Mae**. Perkins is crawling like the native reptiles that are slithering through the jungle. He is holding his breath as he closes in on the open hatch, just inches in front of him. He takes a deep breath and holds it.

117

Just as Fran aims his pistol out the hatch, Conley yells in a booming voice, "What are you doing over there in the dark, Perkins?"

Fran's body jumps forward from the shock of hearing Conley's voice and he almost falls through the open hatch. He fumbles his pistol but catches it before it falls outside the bomber in enemy territory. Perkins catches a glimpse of the outside and does not see an enemy soldier's body on the ground. Could he and Conley have missed their target, or was the target an apparition born out of fear and isolation?

Not a peep comes from Conley lurking in the darkness. Perkins does not hear Conley, but feels the floor of the Liberator vibrate and shake from the uncontrollable laughter coming from the seldom serious, Earl W. Conley. "Conley, stop laughing!" Perkins demands in a whisper. Both of the young men break out laughing and **Daisy Mae** is vibrating too. The crew and the ship are laughing in the face of serious peril. They are two nineteen-year-old kids on a dangerous mission. They are on an adventure.

Now the night passes swiftly. More birds screech and sing from the jungle as the sun shoots through the rear-turret where Perkins and Conley are now resting. They decide to put distance between them and the forward hatch. A marine on patrol is walking next to the rear-turret and he sees Perkins and Conley through the glass. "It's all clear, airmen," the young marine corporal shouts. Perkins and Conley crawl through the hatch and see no sign of the man or apparition they shot at a few long hours before.

Lt Gall and Flight Officer Van Horn, along with Bombardier Lt. Jensen and Navigator Lt. Weiss, approach the B-24. Conley and Perkins render their best military salutes and Lt. Gall asks the men if they had any trouble.

"We did, Sir," says Perkins confidently. "A Japanese soldier popped his head through the front hatch and I got him."

"No, I got him, Sir," corrects Conley.

"No, I got him," Perkins says once more, loudly.

"That will be enough men, you both got him. Report to the mess tent and get some breakfast. You both were through an ordeal last night."

"Wait a minute," Van Horn yells out his window in the co-pilot's seat. "I want to speak to Perkins and Conley right away." Perkins and Conley as well as the officers, board quickly.

Van Horn stands behind the co-pilot's seat and wiggles his index finger in a new bullet hole and a 45-caliber bullet resting in the hole.

"Look at this," Van Horn shouts, seemingly agitated. "Who shot my chair?"

Perkins and Conley both snap to attention for Flight Officer John Van Horn. Conley looks Van Horn dead straight in the eye, points to Perkins and says, "He got 'em, Sir."

Van Horn cannot maintain his officer posture and begins laughing like hell. The other officers try to keep it in but the pressure from four laugh-restrained officers and two enlisted men are enough to allow **Daisy Mae** to join with her vibrating action.

Gall covers his mouth as he orders Perkins and Conley off the plane. "To the mess hall right now and get some breakfast. That's an order!"

The marines on patrol are walking close enough to hear officers and men actually laughing together. The squad leader turns to his men and says, "The pilots just came from the mess hall. Murphy must have used diesel fuel again to clean the breakfast coffee pot."

As soon as the enlisted men leave for the mess tent, Weiss, Gall, Van Horn and Jensen turn to each other and have a laugh of their own.

119

Jensen declares, "There is no way I would stay on board at night. I was scared enough in our quarters last night being inside a protective ring of over a thousand marines." Van Horn echoes Jensen's statement.

Lt. Gall decides, "We will make the rest of crew take over for our trip back to Hawaii for Perkins and Conley since they didn't get any sleep. We will be flying over a ton of ocean all the way back. We will receive orders shortly for a mission with the entire 42nd Squadron. I wonder where we are going next."

Flying the Friendly Skies

Back to Oahu, Hawaii, Gall is true to his word, Conley and Perkins sleep while Radioman Patterson crawls into the ball-turret and the Flight Engineer Ambur and Bombardier Jensen take turns in the tail turret.

Bombardier Jensen is the Armorer and Ordnance Officer on the plane. In Bombardier School, Jensen had to qualify on all gun positions on heavy bombers. He enjoys his trip back to Hawaii and even hopes he has a chance to shoot at enemy aircraft on the way back.

After touching down in Hawaii, the bombers of the 42nd Squadron prepare for the big mission. They will be setting up a temporary base on an island named Funafuti. The airships of the 42nd Squadron take off in Hawaii and head for Canton Island; after refueling at Canton Island they will fly another seven hundred miles to Funafuti.

Funafuti lies in the South Pacific Ocean, thousands of miles South and West of Hawaii. Funafuti is a remote base in position for the Allies to attack the Solomon Islands held by the Japanese, as well as defend Australia, which is under a bombing attack right now. Australia serves as General MacArthur's headquarters from where he leads the Allied Forces in Asia, South East Asia, the Pacific Islands, and Alaska.

Over the intercom Gall orders, "Battle stations," so Perkins, Conley, Ambur and the rest of the crew watch the beautiful Pacific Ocean and perfect blue skies for the next several hours from their stations. It is like flying the entire length of the United States except that you have no features, only ocean below you.

When Perkins cranks his turret outside the Liberator, he has a hard time getting his bearings as the sea and the sky blend into one color. Due to a lack of features below, he wonders how Navigator Ben Weiss knows exactly where he is. Perkins feels he has the best crew in the Air Corps and is lucky to be here. He remembers his conversation with Major McIntosh, a hero of the Battle of Midway. "I hope we get to fly a mission from Midway so I can see what he saw. It sounds like it is beautiful there," he thinks to himself.

Both Fran Perkins and Earl Conley are awe struck as they view a sky filled with B-24 Liberators. There are twenty-four large four-engine airplanes with ten-man crews on each. Two hundred and forty airmen and several photographers flying en masse to Funafuti.

Fran pulls out a letter from Elaine, his Lady Elaine. This is the best time for him to focus on letters from home because being surrounded with nine other brothers so much of the time leaves little true privacy. In Elaine's letter, she talks about early spring in Chicago, Illinois. She said the White Sox should have a great year this year. Luke Appling, the star shortstop for the White Sox is considering going into the Army to help end the War. Appling is Fran's favorite baseball player and he does not want him to leave baseball. "I hope he stays put," Fran says to himself, listening to his words bounce back to him while rotating in his bubble. "There is nothing out here except water, clouds and sky. He'll miss the lush green grass and his fans at Comiskey Park."

Conley is back in his rear-turret, also feeling disconnected from reality. Earl knows that thinking about home is good up to a point and "then you just remember what you would do over again if you could go back," he thinks to himself.

The trip is uneventful, as the bomber-filled sky is getting smaller, as some bombers have already landed. Gall circles his Liberator over the island shaped like a pork chop, which is Canton Island. In 1938, Pan American Airlines built an airport and a runway on the flat hunk of coral rock sitting in the middle of the ocean. These days, Japanese submarines shell the island but their larger ships consider it too far out of the way to bother it.

The stop at Canton Island is just long enough for the bombers to refuel and off they go to Funafuti. Perkins watches the island fade underneath him as Gall levels off the **Daisy Mae**. Looking at the pork chop island below, Fran begins to get hungry. He takes a nap in his turret and dreams about eating pork chops. "I hope we get to Funafuti soon and they have pork chops for dinner."

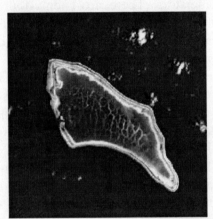

8-1 Canton Island, Fran's Pork Chop

The Funafuti Food Flight of Forty-three

Funafuti is located almost at the 180th Meridian Longitude, the International Date Line. The shortest distance in real miles, when flying between Funafuti and England is to navigate on the 180th Meridian that turns into Zero on the other side of the Earth. Pilots fly due North to Alaska or South over the South Pole and follow the 180th Meridian to

Greenwich, England. They do not have to fly to Hawaii and across the Pacific Ocean to America and then over the Atlantic. If you dig deep enough in the coral reef known as Funafuti, you will end up in Africa or Europe. This is the place where most of the other B-24s are flying and fighting. Some of the B-24s in the 42nd Squadron will soon fly an important mission in Europe. Even though we need more bombers to defeat the Japanese right here at Funafuti, the Air Corps prioritizes the missions around the World that need the most immediate attention. The short-handed American airmen fighting in the Pacific feel they are fighting with one hand tied behind their backs. At the same time, the men commit to do their jobs. They will fly, fight and trade their lives for the other strangers wearing the same uniform. It is their nature.

It is a long flight from Canton Island to Funafuti. Fran is still amazed at how long these bombers can fly without refueling. Gall calls Perkins through his headset and orders him to retract his turret into the belly. Perkins joins Radioman Patterson, Flight Engineer Ambur, Nose Gunner Storts, and Tail Gunner Conley and all sit on the floor for a short game of poker.

As they approach their new temporary base, Gall orders the men to their battle stations except for Perkins who is to keep his ball-turret retracted and safe inside the aircraft while they are circling Funafuti. Perkins sticks his head out the open left waist gun window and says, "This island isn't much to look at. It looks like a lasso thrown across the water. It's very thin with ocean around the outside and a large lagoon on the inside."

Once on the ground the men find their tents and it is time for lunch. Perkins, Conley, Ambur, Storts, Wyckoff and Patterson head for the mess tent. Perkins says, "I hope they have pork chops." Conley wants pork chops too. Ambur, the official farm boy who raises prize steers says, "You can give me a big South Dakota beef steak anytime."

Inside the mess tent, dozens of marines are eating, but they are eating hardtack.

Hardtack is a mixture of flour, water and salt and tastes like a cracker. Soldiers, sailors and marines can carry it with them in battle and do not have to preserve it. Every fighting force around the world, including the Japanese Army, eats hardtack also called sea biscuit.

Perkins, Conly, Ambur, Storts, Wyckoff and Patterson almost wretch at the sight. They cannot believe this is all they get after flying halfway across the world from Hawaii. However, as starved as they are, they join in with the marines and make the best of it.

"I wish Larry Calhoun was here," Perkins says. "He would know how to make me forget about my pork chops. You know, Conley, Calhoun found a way to serve our country without firing a gun. If he did fire a gun, he would shoot and miss at the ducks. He would sit on the bolo bench and become Bolo Bob."

Soon Conley begins telling Larry Calhoun stories and the men at the table, including the marines are in stitches. More marines and airmen gather around the table as Conley does his best imitation of Calhoun, remembering verbatim the stories Larry told in Gunnery School.

Hardtack and sea biscuits taste better now.

"Calhoun's the name."

The officers meet with Marine Command in a tent adjacent to the mess tent and find out that the supply ship bringing in food for Funafuti is still at sea. It has been a month since the marines had a good meal.

Later in the afternoon, Bombardier Jensen tracks down the rest of the crew in their tent, sporting a wide grin. "We'll have food in just two days. Several B-24s are heading back down from Hawaii loaded with food. The General has a soft spot for you gunners as well as the thousands of marines guarding the airfield."

"They won't even have to cook it," says Perkins; "Just stick it in my ear."

Waiting two days for a good meal is rough but at least now, there is hope. Hope is a good thing.

While off duty, the enlisted men swim together in the shallow waters ringing the island. With the average temperatures around 85 degrees all year, swimming is the best way to exercise and relax. Perkins loves the warm waters off the coast of Funafuti. It feels like taking a warm bath. The Pacific makes him forget about missing home and forget about the War. In the peaceful tropical waters, he can live in the moment; however, the men are wary of the sharks that live in the area. When sharks appear, the men swim toward a rock formation a short distance from the beach and wait for danger to swim away. In recreation, airmen are able to do that, but in battle, they will always go to their assigned targets, fighting their way to the target and fighting their way back home.

"Water Conley Water" Once Again

One morning as Conley is walking out near the lagoon, Perkins arrives with several water canteens slung around his neck. With his 5'2" frame, the canteens surround his whole body.

"What's that for?" Conley inquires.

"Water Conley water," Perkins smiles. "We're flying a mission today and you and I have the job of filling canteens for everyone on the crew."

"You must have picked the short straw," Conley quips.

"Yeah, I always get the short end of the stick," Perkins laughs. "I have two older brothers to contend with and have to be the big brother for my two baby brothers. You have nothing on the ribbing I take at home, Conley."

"Where do we go for the water? Where do we enter the lagoon?"

"We have to go past the marines posted over there," Perkins says as he points toward the village.

A marine sergeant posted by the gate sees the airmen, smiles and asks, "Sergeant Hardtack and Sergeant Seabiscuit, where do you think you're going?"

"We received orders to fill these canteens for our crew," Perkins replies.

"You need to go back and get your service guns. You have to walk through the village to get to the water supply, and these people are cannibals. They will kill you and eat you," the big marine sergeant instructs. "We found dead Japanese bones laying around in their village. They killed a couple of us marines, but they didn't like the meat. They said US Marines are too tough."

Not understanding if the guards are kidding or not, both Perkins and Conley sling Thompson submachine guns around their shoulders and strap on their 45-caliber pistols. With all of the weight, they decide to make several trips past the guards, through the village and then past the man-eating denizens of Funafuti.

The two gun-toting water bearers walk past several native men standing outside their huts. They are large men of Samoan ancestry. Every one of them is well over six feet tall. Back in the 1940s, not very many Americans were over six feet tall. Conley and Perkins feel giants surround them. None of the men smile at them. Their bodies feature tattoos and open cuts. They wear bones through their noses and some wear entire vests made of bones. The bones look human. All of the villagers appear angry, very angry. What was once a beautiful island paradise with trees in every direction is now an airfield with hundreds of trees bulldozed down to make way for World War II. Perkins and Conley notice Japanese helmets, uniforms and rifles thrown in a pile along the narrow road. "I wonder if these guys are really cannibals,"

Perkins whispers to Conley. Conley nudges Perkins to stop talking. "Just look straight ahead and focus on the water," Conley says, "just focus on the water."

"I can't help it, Earl. I was looking at the biggest cannibal and I think he had a cartoon tattooed on his big belly."

Earl says, "What did the cartoon look like?

"There was a picture of a GI looking over a wall, and it said, Kilroy was here."

Both men go into hysterics as they go back and forth all morning filling canteens.

8-2 Kilroy was here. Famous in WWII

Five trips to the water fountain were enough. Both Conley and Perkins hope all of the other shipmates get a chance next time to fill the water canteens. As Conley and Perkins walk past the marine sentries and back to the flight line, they hear the echo of laughter coming from the marines behind them.

"Shit heels!" Perkins mumbles to Conley.

Other Liberators are circling Funafuti and landing as Perkins and Conley load **Daisy Mae** with their canteens. The circling planes are bringing real food from Hawaii. As the planes land, marines are cheering as if the group just bombed Tokyo. Marines like to eat and from now on, they will have plenty. The bombers filled their cavernous bomb bay area with food for one thousand marines and almost three hundred Air Corps crew and mechanics. In just a few days, the scheduled food ship will also arrive and everyone will have plenty to eat. Marines and bomber crews load up jeeps and other service vehicles and hurry to the mess tent. Everyone is happy.

While Fran loads several boxes of canned corn onto the back of a jeep, one carton breaks and out spills several cans. The box is marked Monsanto, DeKalb, Illinois. Fran smiles and wonders if the corn came from the Nelson farm. He remembers seeing tall corn for the first time when he fought the "Battle of the Beans," a few months earlier in basic training. Perkins tells Arvid Ambur that if he makes it through the war alive, he wants to move out of the dangerous city into the country. "I love that tall corn in Northern Illinois," he says. "When I have kids, I want them to grow up appreciating the beautiful farmland of the Midwest and the mountains like we saw near Reno, Nevada."

Arvid replies, "If you ever get to Presho, South Dakota, stop by. Presho is a beautiful little town, just like the farm country around DeKalb, Illinois. I'll show you some real ranching to go along with your farming. I've been farming and ranching all of my life."

Fran and Arvid grunt as they lift the heavy box onto the back end of a jeep. "Arvid, you remind me of another guy who's not afraid of work," remembering his Basic Training friend John Paul Olsen.

"I hope he is okay," Perkins murmurs softly. "I hope they all are okay.

128

Chapter 9

Missions of the **Daisy Mae**

From late April until late May most of the missions are either submarine patrol or standard "Y" formation searches for missing airmen or sailors at sea.

What no one knew at the time was General MacArthur shared the Command with Admiral Nimitz. They wanted the Seventh Air Corps to patrol from the Aleutian Islands off the coast of Alaska all the way down to the South Pacific. This took them right up to MacArthur's headquarters in Brisbane, Australia. The Japanese were faking attacks from Alaska down through Canada and south from there. Since the Liberator was born to handle long ocean flights, most of the B-17s left for the European and North African fronts. This meant that new pilots trained in the operation of the B-24 like Gall, Weiss, Van Horn and Jensen, were now responsible for more long distance flying then they ever imagined.

Flying over the ocean for long periods is nerve wracking. Gall sees this as an opportunity to train all of his pilots to take a turn in his pilot's seat on the **Daisy Mae**. Many times Bombardier Jensen and Navigator Weiss take over in the cabin. This is great training for the backup team as it gives them the kind of experience needed in case Gall and Van Horn die in combat, giving the rest of the crew has a fighting chance to survive with Jensen and Weiss at the helm.

Gall and Van Horn enjoy the break. Even though it is a boring stretch in the war for these young men, Japan tracks many of these bombers by radar and knows these flying warriors never sleep. As soon as **Daisy Mae** lands, another crew spends the day with her. The only break she gets is when an engine breaks down or other maintenance is required. The brave and industrious mechanics on these remote islands make sure the bombers are ready for battle. The mechanics are nameless, faceless heroes, vital to winning World War II.

Strange Field Landings

May 26, 1943 from 2230 to 0245

The **Daisy Mae** is on a night mission, testing the pilots in what they call strange field landings. There are four airfields from which Gall and crew will be landing and taking off in the dark including Kahuku, Hickam, Wheeler, and Mokuleia Airfields. Some of these fields are remote and dark at night and some like Wheeler and Hickam are in well-lit areas of Oahu. Even on training missions like these, all four officers aboard the **Daisy Mae** must keep alert at all times. Many airmen have crashed and died on practice runs just like these. In fact, most men from this squadron of twenty-four bombers lose their lives with no bullets fired. The B-24 Liberator is subject to pilot error as well as the fact that sometimes it just leaves the sky for no apparent reason.

The four officers on board **Daisy Mae** are vigilant and the other six enlisted men do their jobs but would prefer to be in combat because they need to complete 40 combat missions to go home. The patrols on which they are in search-mode do not count toward their 40 missions.

Takeoff at 2230

It is late Wednesday night and the crew seems half-asleep as they enter the Liberator. They think they will be napping in between take offs and landings, but Lt. Gall has other plans. As the aircraft takes off and Gall has sufficient altitude, Perkins hears Gall's voice in his headset. "Belly gunner, lower your turret." Then nose gunner Snuffy Storts hears Gall's order to take his battle station in the nose. Storts found a soft corner to lay down but he moves to his battle station quickly. Flight Engineer Ambur and Radioman Patterson move to their battle stations near the

130

waist windows. Conley is ready at his post in the rear-turret. All of the gunners are in position.

Gall has an idea to keep the men in training mode. He knows he has a talented Navigator in Lt. Weiss. Gall will exploit Weiss' talent during the boring exercise to keep his men sharp, engaged and combat ready. "Ben, I have an idea. The moon and stars are bright tonight and all of our airfields are on the coast of Oahu. As we face the dark over the ocean, why not test our gunner communication skills over the water. We'll have each gunner call out the position of the moon, stars, and planets. Ben, can you describe to the men some of the star formations and planets you see and have the gunners call out those positions as well?"

"Sure, Joe, that'll be fun," Weiss replies.

The next voice over the ship's interphone is Navigator Ben Weiss. Weiss begins with the moon. He says the moon is an enemy Betty Bomber, and starts his training game with the nose. Nose Gunner Storts sees the moon first and says, "Betty Bomber at eleven o'clock. Take it right side gunner." Right side Waist Gunner Ambur spots the moon and calls out to the tail gunner, Conley. "Tail Gunner, Betty Bomber at eleven o'clock high."

Navigator Weiss sees a familiar planet in the lower horizon. This is far off and very hard to see. He describes Jupiter at the very end of the horizon of the Hawaiian skies and calls Jupiter a Zero. Perkins in the ball-turret excitedly shouts, "Zero at five o'clock low. Tail Gunner, get ready." Conley squints, spots the far off planet and says, "I am ready for it. It's out of range now and is disappearing over the horizon."

Pilot Joe Gall calls for Perkins to retract the ball-turret and the crew prepares for landing. The **Daisy Mae** lands perfectly and softly, dead center on the runway. This becomes Gall's trademark in World War II. Every time he lands any of the aircraft he flies, the landing is soft and dead center. His crews always appreciate Gall's flying skill.

Once the crew is on the ground at Kahuku Airfield, they take a short break and get ready to take off again to another strange airfield. Even though it is after midnight now, the men seem energized as they talk to each other on the ground. Ben is standing in the cabin directly behind Pilot Gall and Co-pilot Van Horn. "The gunners are our shooting stars," the Navigator says with a grin. Gall and Van Horn nod their agreement.

On the ground Gall, Van Horn, Weiss, and Jensen are walking together to get a quick bite to eat. "Good job, Ben," Gall smiles at Weiss. "I feel safe with our gunners. I hope we don't let them down."

"The men feel the same way toward you, Joe. When we get into battle, I feel safe with the gunners we have. We're very lucky." Jensen and Van Horn smile and nod in agreement.

Bombers, Submarines and Zamperini

May 27, 1943

After retiring to their barracks, Perkins awakens in the afternoon after just a few hours of sleep. The schedule is hard on the body and mind. Sometimes airmen fly a mission beginning in the early morning and sometimes they begin late at night. Fran is too tired and worn out to sleep, so he gets a cup of coffee and walks out to the flight line.

A mechanic recognizes Fran as one of the crew on the **Daisy Mae** and explains why the big bomber is gone. He tells Fran that the bomber is on a search mission in standard "Y" formation to find Lt. Corpening with the 380th Bomb Group, 530th Squadron. On May 26, while the **Daisy Mae** practiced shooting the stars, Lt. Corpening was lost at sea flying a B-24D, serial number 42-40519.

Flying from Hickam Air Field on Oahu, Corpening needed to refuel at Canton Island, Fran's giant pork chop at sea, just as the **Daisy Mae** did last month when arriving at Funafuti. Instead of going to Funafuti, Lt.

Corpening headed to Amberley Airfield in Australia. The Liberator never reached Canton Island, which was the first leg of the journey.

Fran spills out his coffee cup as he hears the news on the flight line with the mechanic. The **Daisy Mae** is off to find Lt. Corpening with the Green Hornet, a rickety plane not suitable for combat. Pilot Lt. Phillips took the Green Hornet as only other bomber ready to find Corpening's aircraft #519, a B-24D Liberator.

Fran runs back to tell his shipmates the bad news from the mechanic on the flight line. He knows the Green Hornet is a mess and wonders if **Daisy Mae** will be ready after flying all night on their training mission. Fran is upset about the missing Liberator flown by Lt. Corpening. More importantly, his thoughts are on **Daisy Mae**. Perkins is very fond of the Big Girl and is afraid she will be lost at sea as well. He runs back to his tent just in time to see the whole crew waiting for him.

Gall announces, "This morning we found out a Liberator is lost at sea. Lt. Phillips took the **Green Hornet** while Lt. Deasy took our bomber to search between here and Palmyra Island. I know how fond you are of our assigned ship, the **Daisy Mae**. I am too. Our ship is in the hands of Lt. Joe Deasy, an excellent pilot, and his crew from the **Dogpatch Express** and is bound to find the lost Liberator. Especially with **Daisy Mae** showing him where to go. Lt. Weiss can vouch for the fact that **Daisy Mae** does some of the flying and navigating by herself."

"She has a heart and a soul," adds Weiss. "She can handle anything."

Fran feels dejected but has confidence in any ship assigned. "Lt. Gall is the best pilot in the whole damned Air Corps and my shipmates are the best crew. We'll be okay," Perkins thinks to himself.

The days and nights are tough on Gall and his shipmates. Even though Gall is a quick study, each bomber displays its own quirks. All of the pilots on board make sure they know each substitute bomber inside and out. Gall makes sure each crewmember is cross-trained on each bomber.

Cabin in the Sky flown by Lt. Storm continues the search for Lt. Corpening and crew downed before reaching Palmyra Island. Lt. Phillips along with his Bombardier Louis Zamperini and the other eight shipmates of the **Green Hornet** go missing. Twenty airmen are now missing at sea and none because of any combat with the enemy. The new enemy of the squadron is the long stretch of barren sea, a quiet killer of the young men of the Seventh Army Air Corps. The Seventh Army Air Corps cannot afford to lose any bombers while one of the largest naval fleets and armies in the world is still in business.

Lt. Storm flying the bomber called **Cabin in the Sky** is heading on the same course Lt. Corpening and Lt. Phillips before him were heading. Their goal is to reach Palmyra Island because neither Corpening nor Phillips ever made it to that point and Phillips never made it to Canton. Now a Deasy-flown **Daisy Mae** is hoping to find survivors and other rescuers that are out to find and save the 20 missing men.

May 31, 1943 at 1600 Hours

Lt. Smith landed twelve hours earlier and reported that in the moonlight, he saw wreckage consistent with the food boxes carried by Corpening and Phillips on their bombers. Lt. Smith circled many times and called the Navy to investigate. There were also many fish swimming around the boxes. It was dark at the time, however; the swimmers appeared to be sharks. After debriefing on the flight Lt. Smith tells Lt. Gall, "You and your crew will be taking refueled Bomber **Cabin in the Sky** to continue the search." Gall cannot wait for the opportunity. It will be dark through most of the search, but he knows his crew is up to the task. Twenty men's lives depend on old **Cabin in the Sky**.

The ship takes off at 1600 hours and is up in the air quickly. Gall takes the ship below 8,000 feet so the crew will have greater vision. Gall is counting on Storts in the nose, Conley in the tail and Perkins in the ball-turret to find the missing men or at least the wreckage of the ships. Aircraft **Cabin in the Sky** is flying by instruments or automatic pilot for most of the flight while all of the pilots, except for Navigator Weiss, are watching out the waist gun windows in earnest.

Nose Gunner Storts watches out his turret and has nothing to report. Flying from 1600 hours until 0330 hours, the men are weary. It is close to the end of the shift and it is hard for the men to stay alert. The darkness seems to get darker.

The one common element driving the men is saving any survivors at sea. Lt. Jensen looks out the right waist window. He catches a glimpse of something moving on the surface. The island of Oahu is near on the horizon. Gall and Van Horn pass the binoculars between each other watching for any evidence of a crash in the ocean from the left waist gunner window.

Bombardier Jensen calls to Navigator Weiss to resume control of the aircraft. Gall and Van Horn run to the cabin to take over from the Navigator and Jensen runs to his bombardier position in the nose. "Get ready," Jensen says. "I spot an enemy submarine off the right side of the bomber. I can see two to three feet of the conning tower." Weiss turns control over to the Norden Bombsight and Flight Engineer Ambur makes sure the depth charges are armed.

"We have us a submarine!" shouts Jensen. Wyckoff immediately radios a report of the submarine sighting to the base.

Bomber Pilot Gall and Co-pilot Van Horn quickly climb into their seats. They are spectators now as Lt. Jensen has full control of **Cabin in the Sky** and is making a bomb run with depth charges armed and ready. They are about twenty-six miles from Kaena Point, which is the westernmost tip of Oahu in the Territory of Hawaii.

The ball-turret guns swing around. After cocking his machine guns in the ball-turret, Perkins sounds over the intercom, "I see whales down below." Lt. Jensen readies the release of depth charges. Instead of the submarine conning tower, he viewed a few moments ago; Jensen now only sees pods of humpback whales. They are swimming, breaching, and calling as only whales do.

Now Conley, Ambur, Storts, Wyckoff, and the pilots see them as well. Wyckoff handling the radio for Patterson calls Gall over the intercom and asks if he should radio in that they didn't see the submarine after all.

"No," Gall says, "Let's just say that we don't see any more evidence of submarines. There is a naval patrol boat in the area. Maybe he will find submarines on his patrol."

The rest of the crew relaxes, as they will be landing in just 30 minutes. During the briefing after they land at 0330 hours in the wee morning, they report the depth charge bombing run and terminating the run after finding no more trace of submarines or other targets. There is nothing ever reported about the whales, however, the whales allow the men to relax at their battle stations and take a break from the stress of war. They are relieved as well. The men begin to laugh at the excitement of readying for battle only to find frolicking whales. Lt. Jensen exhales and relaxes for the first time all night.

It is a long night for the crew of **Cabin in the Sky**, but in the end, they find no bombers, no submarines and no Zamperini.

Gall's Bomber Crashes

The only missions they seem to draw are search missions in standard "Y" formation or training missions. They are always watching for enemy submarines, surface ships and planes, and usually they find none. Japan wants to catch the Seventh Air Corps napping.

On all of the ships Gall and Van Horn fly, they make sure there is no napping during the missions. The officers instill a sense of duty in every gunner and officer in their command. All of these men are ready to trade their lives for each other as they fly through the Pacific skies, every night and every day. All of the men under Gall's command understand it.

Japanese agents posing as bar girls in Honolulu and other places frequented by flyers get information back to their handlers by short wave radio. Gall instructs each shipmate on the importance of never talking about missions to anyone, even if that person wears a uniform. Gall and Van Horn want to give their bombers and crew a fighting chance to win the war and go home.

On the night of June 24, 1943, the men will take off for another routine training mission.

The **Daisy Mae** is flying another mission so Gall and crew are flying a brand new ship, called **Tail Wind**.

The B-24D Liberator Bomber has four enormous engines. Pilot Gall sits in the left front seat, just like where the driver sits in an American automobile. Then he looks out his left window and further down the wing at the furthest engine, the outboard engine number one. The number two engine would be the inboard engine, the one nearest him.

Co-pilot Van Horn sits in the right hand front seat. When he turns his head to the right and looks at the inboard engine nearest him, he sees the number three engine. He then looks further down the wing at the furthest engine, the number four being the outboard engine.

The Flight Engineer, Technical Sergeant Arvid Ambur, the old-timer on board at the ripe age of twenty-four, will begin his duties outside of the aircraft, first giving the propellers six turns each with the engines turned off to get the oil lubricant flowing in each engine. The flight engineer will then signal the co-pilot to flick the ignition switch to start the number three engine.

Tonight Co-pilot Van Horn tries something to help improve the morale of the men. Van Horn opens his side window and cheerfully reminds Ambur, "Six good turns, Ambur, six good turns!"

Top-Turret Gunner Wyckoff and Radioman Patterson burst out laughing. They know Flight Engineer Ambur needs no reminder how to do his job. Ambur stands back from the dolly holding the fire extinguisher, suddenly looking confused, "What?" Van Horn repeats his order with a huge grin, "Six good turns, Ambur, six good turns." Now Ambur is laughing uncontrollably, body shaking as he processes the joke. The officer/co-pilot finds a way to ignite the crew with humor. Still laughing, Ambur signals the co-pilot to start the engine.

Van Horn flicks the ignition switch for the number three engine nearest his window and the propeller starts revolving faster and faster. Amber moving to the number four engine, he hears Van Horn repeat, "Six good turns, Ambur, six good turns." It is a long walk from wing tip to wing tip on the monster-size bomber, as Ambur walks around the nose to the number two engine and gives the props six good turns, then to number one engine.

The sequence is always the same all the time. The flight engineer begins with number three engine then goes to the number four engine, across the front of the aircraft to the number two engine and then number one engine. It is imperative that the pilot, co-pilot and flight engineer remain alert and focused, and be extremely careful during the routine startup because many flight engineers have lost their lives walking toward the wrong engine when either the pilot or co-pilot flipped the starter switch for that engine.

One reason they always start with the number three engine is that it is the most important engine on the aircraft. It controls the hydraulic fluid pumps that operate the flaps, ailerons, rudders, and brakes. Hydraulic systems control all of the vital functions of the aircraft. If the number three engine is out, the aircraft will never leave the ground. If the number three engine fails while in flight, it would be almost impossible to land. You can think of the number three engine as the heart of the B-24 and the hydraulic fluid as its blood. If the number three does not start, that is the end of the mission for that B-24. On bombing runs that span eight or nine hours with only the point of origination as an acceptable place to land, several bombers turn back on every single mission. It is better to turn back while they have their landing strip in sight than several hours out to sea where the odds of rescue are slim to none. Even if the number three engine works fine, other mechanical breakdowns can happen on these long dangerous missions.

Now that Flight Engineer Ambur is finished and taking his battle station, Gall throttles number one and two engines to 2500 rpm while the still smiling Van Horn is goosing the three and four engines to 2500 rpm.

Word of the joke passes quickly to Conley and Perkins sitting in the rear of the mighty, steel air fortress. "The officers are brothers just like us gunners," Patterson tells Perkins.

Tail Wind lifts off with no problems. As usual in all of the other missions, Gall circles the airfield and he salutes the men on the ground as he drops his wing to turn to the left. Van Horn facing Gall looks past Gall down the wing and past the number one engine. He, too, salutes the brave men and women who work to protect the ship and protect our freedom.

Perkins is down in his turret, looking for enemy subs, sailors, and survivors. The moon is bright tonight and he is reading a letter from his Lady Elaine. Elaine talks about how much she misses him. She tells Fran she is keeping a list of all of the duty stations that she deduces from the postage stamps on his envelopes. She will not mention them in the letter in order to keep the information out of enemy hands. Elaine writes about a movie, "Riding High," that she saw with her friends Marge and Sophie, starring Dorothy Lamour and Dick Powell. It is a love story about a girl wanting to start nightclub act in the old West. Dick Powell plays a prospector hunting for gold. Dorothy Lamour is a singer trying to make a name for herself in the West. Fran reads the ten-page letter and feels he is sitting right next to Elaine, holding her hand in a movie theatre.

The moonlight is dancing inside the Plexiglas ball-turret and the four engines are humming but all Fran hears is the quiet of sailing through the air at the speed two hundred fifty miles per hour. When Fran closes his eyes, he can feel Elaine's tiny hand in his, instead of the massive, cold fifty-caliber machine guns. This is a special, magical time for Fran and from now on, he vows to bring Elaine's letters with him on every mission. He will tuck them in his boots to keep them out of the way when operating the turret.

The night is quiet. Almost too quiet.

Suddenly there is an explosion that rocks the ship. The shock waves come from the number three engine, just below Co-pilot Van Horn. Fran swings the ball-turret around so he can see. Gall calls Fran on the headset in a calm voice, "Belly gunner, crank your turret back in the belly and report to me in the cabin." After retracting the turret, Fran jumps out of his tiny home and races to the cabin.

"We have a mayday, Perkins. Grab the radio and call Barking Sands." Gall instructs Perkins what to say and they set up a crash landing at Barking Sands Airfield located on the tiny Hawaiian Island of Kauai. "Perkins, the number three engine controlling all of our hydraulics blew up. The landing gear is shot, and the backup mechanical system is not functioning. We cannot lower our landing gear. We are going into Barking Sands on our belly."

Perkins gets no reply from Barking Sands. Either the communications are shot or someone is asleep at the switch at the airfield. Without clearance from Barking Sands, Gall has no idea where to land. He feels that landing on a runway, even a dark one, gives him better odds of survival than trying to land in the choppy water off shore. The many large rocks near the shore that obstruct a safe landing on the water will crush **Tail Wind** and the men inside.

"Our only hope of survival is to land dead center on a dark runway. No hydraulics means no brakes. I hope they have no aircraft on the runway or we will be plowing through them at over 200 miles per hour. Strap yourself in, Perkins. We're going in for a bumpy ride."

Unafraid Fran buckles up at the radioman position behind the Pilot, knowing that Gall can get them down safely. It is still quiet in the rest of the ship. No one needs to worry. Gall and Van Horn control the aircraft. Gall is worried but has confidence in his skills. Van Horn, Jensen, and Weiss are all in the cabin helping Gall with the landing. Due to the lack of hydraulics because of the failure of the number three engine, there are no brakes. Tail Wind will have to find another way to stop on the runway in the dark.

Gall reduces his airspeed until they go into a stall and Navigator Weiss calculates the best angle to land. In the end, they find themselves guessing, as there are no lights illuminating the runway. With no landing gear, Tail Wind comes down hard. Huge sparks now illuminate the runway. Gall notices he is dead center. He and Weiss guessed correctly. After a long thirty seconds on her belly, the aircraft skids to a stop. Some of the men dozing in the back of the plane wake up but by the time they are fully alert Tail Wind is sitting still, dead center in the middle of the runway with the number three engine smoking. A fire engine resting at the end of the runway is on the way to put out the flames.

The pilots feel lucky. They are very lucky. The crew walks away from the crash landing with ship and shipmates intact.

As Perkins walks to the escape hatch, something falls on the floor inside Tail Wind. Behind him, Top-Turret Gunner Wyckoff picks up the wad of paper that fell from Fran's boot. He looks inside and grins at the signature, "Love Elaine."

"Conley tells me of the Knights of the Round Table and Lady Elaine. Rogue, is this scroll from the famous Lady Elaine, we beseech?"

Fran's red face is noticeable and thoughts of his older brothers kidding him and saying the same things to him about Elaine make him smile. "Yes, she is the fairest in the land," Perkins laughs. "Wyckoff, you have nothing on my older brothers. They can cut me to the bone with their comments. Teasing is an art form in the Perkins household."

"Here is your scroll, m'lord. After you," says Wyckoff as he follows Perkins off the smoking hot Tail Wind with her number three engine still burning. Wyckoff adds, "Part of my job description will be watching your boots when you climb out of the turret. I know how important it is to have letters from home. Your letters from Elaine are always so thick they are easy to spot, even on this huge bomber."

"Thank you, brother Wyckoff. You're just like my brother Bob. In fact, brother Bob is a top-turret gunner and assistant flight engineer, just like you."

"He must be the smartest, bravest and handsomest knight on his crew," says Wyckoff.

"Yes. He is, Thom, he is!"

Gall and the rest of the crew wait for a flight back to the Island of Oahu. At night, they listen to the jungle birds on Barking Sands Airfield on the Island of Kauai. They remember the scary night at Guadalcanal. The crew finds an empty barracks and the entire crew beds down for the rest of the night. The men will await rescue in the morning and will ferry back to Oahu to wait for the orders for their next mission. Tail Wind undergoes repair and will soon live to fight again.

Bombing Nauru

Just two days later Gall and the boys will see combat. The long, lonely days and nights on their sea search missions are behind them, at least for today. Instead of looking for phantoms, Perkins, Conley and the other gunners will be finding real targets.

Nauru is a small island nation that Germany controlled during World War I. They found huge resources of phosphates, the same phosphates used in the manufacture of gunpowder. The Grey Geese are going to bomb the phosphate factories on the island. The ships will take off from Canton Island, Fran's giant pork chop, bomb Nauru and then fly on to their forward base at Funafuti.

The mission begins in the morning and then ends in the afternoon. The mission includes B-24 Bombers from the 98th, 26th, 42nd and the 431st squadrons. Canton Island is ready with a full squadron of twenty-four Liberators going after the largest phosphate plant in the world.

From the tarmac, the bombers taxi to the runway, lining up in single file. The first heavy bomber takes off and immediately crashes at sea. The bomb load on the B-24 is just too heavy and the plane cannot get any lift. The crew of the **Daisy Mae** views the fire as they begin to creep up into position. The second and third plane just barely make if off the island but **Daisy Mae**, the fourth in line does not budge. There are nineteen bombers directly behind Gall's ship. The **Daisy Mae** is defiantly blocking the path of the other bombers on the airstrip. What is wrong?

Navigator Weiss directs the officers' attention to a windsock by the control tower. The sock is not moving. The normal constant gale of wind that blows into the face of the bombers is non-existent. Gall calls the control tower to report the lack of a headwind. The heavy bombers need that wind in their face to get enough lift to raise the ships into the sky.

There is chatter back and forth over the radio with the tower, resulting in an order to stand down and wait for the wind to pick up. Usually that would be early afternoon. Lt. Jensen goes to the back of the plane where the men are getting ready for takeoff. "We will not lift off until there is sufficient wind to get us up in the air. That's why Lt. Gall is going nowhere for the moment."

Perkins is very upset and questions Lt. Jensen. "Can Lt. Gall get in trouble for not lifting off now?"

Lt. Jensen answers, "I don't think so. He may have saved the lives of two hundred men as well as a large inventory of these rare and expensive bombers. They have plenty of these bombers fighting the Germans from bases in England, but we don't have many covering the entire Pacific and Indian Oceans. The crews come here faster than the bombers. We are expendable. The bombers are not. The first three bombers had photographers on them. Therefore, the first bomber had eleven men in her crew today. Lt. Gall requests that you bow your heads in prayer for these fine men." Ambur says a few words in prayer and all heads bow in unison. The shipmates know that with no headwind, there is little chance for a successful take off. The **Daisy Mae,** as well as all of the bombers on the mission, is loaded down with the largest bomb load a B-24 can carry. When there is no breeze for takeoff, the airmen give it the term 'dead air'. Today, dead air kills a crew of eleven young heroes.

Lt. Gall calls the crew on their headsets and orders, "Men, leave the ship now and be back at 1700 hours. It will still be daylight over the target. That is all."

Later there is more wind, however, not the gale you need to get maximum lift to launch a heavy bomber. The **Daisy Mae** grunts, groans, struggles and lifts off. The crew holds their breath until the Liberator levels off.

As the ship circles Canton Island, the crew looks out the windows and watches the fire still burning in the shallow waters right off shore. Perkins whispers to himself "Requiem aeternam dona eis, Domine" which means eternal rest grant unto them, O Lord.

Perkins and Conley watch out the right waist window and salute the crew and the burning plane. With real combat a part of their daily lives, the humorous banter between Perkins and Conley is gone. The familiar "Water Conley Water," with the response, "Calhoun's the name," vanishes. These young warriors are serious all of the time. The weight of the War rests on these young soldiers and they think more of their loved ones back home.

Fran thinks of Elaine, his special Lady Elaine. He pulls a letter out of his boot. This letter is from Mae Birmingham, Elaine's Mother. Mae focuses on what fighting men actually need to hear. She addresses Fran's heart and his soul. Mae writes in a voice that sounds familiar and safe. He wonders how she knows so much about how he is feeling. He never writes about how he feels to Elaine. Mae just seems to know exactly what to say to these young men in times of stress and danger.

Men on the massive airships never talk about their feelings. It would be a sign of weakness. These warriors need to stay strong at all times. Watching the flames on the B-24 below, Fran needs to read the encouragement and support of Mae. While Mae is very religious, the words talk in a voice that includes everyone, even if they have no religious leanings. Her messages are universal. In fact, Fran shares his letters from Mae with Thom, Arvid, Earl, and his other brothers that fly the not so friendly skies.

She always signs her letters, "To my favorite Son, Mom." By signing it, "Mom" the other men can feel like their own mothers are writing these letters.

Although Fran is only her daughter's boyfriend, the positive messages she writes makes him feel like her son. Fran's biological mother cannot write because of a stroke at the age of 26 that robbed her of the use of her right side. Now Mae Birmingham is a quiet and encouraging mother to Fran and his shipmates. In a way Mae seems to be the voice of the **Daisy Mae** herself, positive and encouraging to shipmates all. Mae Birmingham and **Daisy Mae** are coaching and coaxing the men to victory.

Back in Evergreen Park, Mae will be rising in the morning and driving in rivets at the Ford Aircraft Engine Manufacturing Plant in Chicago all day. Mae works fulltime at the Plant and Clarence works part-time at the plant during the hours he is not on his regular CTA job. In letters her favorite son, Fran, refers to Mae Birmingham as Rosie the Riveter, after the woman plastered on magazine covers posing with a flexed bicep and rivet gun.

Fran hands Mae's letter to Thom and watches out the waist window.

As the planes are lining up in the air to form their attack formation, Conley sees a flash of light out the rear-turret. The eighth bomber taking off from Canton Island also crashes into the ocean. Fran crawls out to the rear-turret and Conley moves toward the fuselage as Perkins looks at the flames. Without saying a word to Conley, Perkins brushes past and then climbs into his ball-turret. He remembers to stuff a recent letter from Elaine into one of his boots and lowers the turret outside. He is in position to do his job. His job is to guard the belly of his favorite ship, the **Daisy Mae**. Fran's job is to protect the ship and protect the crew.

About a half hour into the mission, Conley walks up to the cabin on a break and overhears a conversation between Gall and Van Horn. A third B-24 Bomber and crew are missing after takeoff from Canton Island.

Over the Target

About eighty miles from Nauru, Perkins hears Gall's voice over his headset. "Belly gunner, test fire your guns." Fran aims down at the sea to make sure he does not hit any of the remaining twenty-one bombers in formation. Instead of Fran's patented long burst, he shoots just two quick bursts of about ten rounds each from his twin fifty-caliber guns. The top-turret, rear-turret and nose-turret gunners all take practice shots. Flight Engineer Ambur and Radioman Patterson also let go with bursts from the waist gunner or side gunner positions.

Perkins is looking down watching the trail of bullets speeding toward the ocean when he spots three Japanese Zeros below. "Three Zekes at five o'clock low!" Perkins shouts excitedly over the interphone. Fran lets out with a long burst. He is slightly out of range and he watches the drop and drift of the tracer rounds to adjust his aim.

The three Zeros or Zekes, as the gunners call them, move out of range. Next the Zeros head toward the nose; however, Nose Gunner Snuffy Storts opens up on all three. They turn quickly away from the always-accurate nose gunner. All three Zeros remain out of range but now it is clear that the enemy is testing to see how to attack these new B-24Ds.

Last April, the crew flew in their new B-24 Bomber to the airfield in Sacramento, California. Mechanics installed a ball-turret for Fran Perkins and a nose-turret for Snuffy Storts. They converted a B-24 to a B-24D to give it protection from assaults from beneath the bomber and from the front of the bomber. The three Zeros needed to verify the version of bomber they are facing in this attack. Fran saw for the first time how fast the Zeros move in the sky. They were like fish swimming in the ocean, smooth and fast. The fighter pilots knew exactly where they were going and how to get out of trouble quickly.

Engaging the enemy in the air is much more difficult than shooting at targets on a range, Perkins thinks and he vows to get them next time. After the brief foreplay with the Zeros, the bombers near the phosphate production center and the mines on Nauru.

9-1 B-24 Bomber over Nauru

Gall transfers control of the bomber to Bombardier Jensen to take **Daisy Mae** over the target. Enemy anti-aircraft fire is hitting the Big Girl from below. The Japanese anti-aircraft gunners hit their targets with every shot. The ship rocks and bounces and the crew is worried. They hope they will not blow up from the accurate shooting below. Softball size projectiles hit, penetrate or bounce off the **Daisy Mae**. Each one makes a loud thud. Some explode on contact. Crouching over the Norden Bombsight, Jensen lines up the target with the cross hairs, squeezes the plunger and finally the crew hears, "Bombs away!" Eight 500-pound general-purpose bombs leave the open doors. Ten stomachs react to the feeling of instantly bouncing up a couple of hundred feet from the recoil of losing four thousand pounds in a few seconds.

Perkins, Conley and Storts watch for the bomb bursts below. Large fires and a huge black cloud form from the burning gunpowder. All eight bombs hit their target. Lt. Jensen keeps watching through his Norden Bombsight. He is satisfied with his mission completed. With a smile on his face, he transfers control back to the cabin. Perkins, Conley, Storts, Ambur and the rest of the crew now know how it feels to be in combat. Their faces are grim on the way home to the forward airfield. The adrenalin high submits to battle fatigue. The excitement of facing an enemy intent to kill dulls to the reality of war.

After the short ride to Funafuti, some of the men inspect the damage from anti-aircraft fire but most go directly to their quarters. Perkins touches a patch of wounded metal sticking out of **Daisy**'s belly near his ball-turret. He marvels at the deadly accuracy of such a large projectile, hurled thousands of feet in the air at a target moving hundreds of miles per hour. How lucky he was! Perkins walks like a zombie until Top-Turret Gunner Wyckoff taps him on the back of his shoulder, hands him a wad of paper and says, "Your letters from Lady Elaine and from Mother Mae"

"Thanks, Brother Thomas." Perkins replies with eyes unseeing. Wyckoff refolds the letters and stuffs them back into Fran's boots. Fran feels the sting of battle. It was scary as hell, not fun.

148

More Combat Missions

Missions blur in memory as every day and every night the men go on sorties. One evening the ship is patrolling the sea. The next morning, they go on a bombing run to some far off island. One damn island after another becomes the unofficial slogan of the 11th Bomb Group. From Alaska down to Australia and every patch of ocean in between, the men engage in combat. Every night and every day the crew moves from one bomber to the next. Sometimes they fly **Daisy Mae** but most of the time in June and July of 1943, they do not. Names like Scholar, Deasy, Schmidt, Cason, Stay, Thompson, Boyd and even Colonel Holzapfel take the yoke of the **Daisy Mae** during this time. Every morning, Fran inspects **Daisy Mae** when she is in his area and every day he finds more evidence that she has been in battle. When Fran sees the Big Girl, he touches the precious metal container that houses the heart and soul of the 42nd Squadron hoping that either he or **Daisy Mae** will make it through the War. It will be fine if they make it together. However, always analytical, Fran knows they will not. They are both tired and want to go home, however neither complains.

Every morning Fran, Earl, Arvid, Robert Patterson, Snuffy Storts and Thomas Wyckoff notice personal effects packed up quickly and sealed in boxes in every air base they sleep. All the other squadrons of the 11th Bomb Group and the rest of the Seventh Army Air Corps lose valuable young men and valuable Liberators. Each time Fran witnesses the silent events, he remembers in Gunnery School packing up Earl Conley's effects. Fran understands other crews are going through that pain right now. Fran got Conley back. These other men are not coming back to their crews who are their new brothers in World War II.

For these young men of World War II, there is no time and there is no relief. There is no hope.

Chapter 10

Mischief and Duty

You might watch movies or read comics about **Superman, The Green Hornet, Thumper, Dog Patch,** or **Daisy Mae**. You might smile when you remember images or memories attached to these names. I have different memories. When I see those names, I think about a squadron of twenty-four B-24 Liberator Bombers in the 42nd Squadron 11th Bomb Group 7th Army Air Corps.

In the summer of 1943, they protected our nation against a Japanese invasion and led a forward advance in the fight on the Pacific Front during World War II. I see brave Airmen from the Seventh Army Air Corps and brave United States Marines and Sailors fighting together as a team in a determined struggle to win World War II and find a way to transform fear into hope.

All ships are grounded by orders July 21, 1943. The Seventh Army Air Corps sends orders to land all ships and stay put awaiting further orders. There is something mysterious going on. Has the War ended? Did we win or did we lose?

The crew of the **Daisy Mae** land at Kahuku Airfield on the Island of Oahu. Upon landing, Lt. Gall gives orders to the men to remain nearby because on Friday July 23, 1943, they will be going on a special mission. For the first and last time ever, the enlisted men disobey orders and hitch rides to Honolulu to spend some time at the bar. They deserve a good drink or two.

Fran carries a gut feeling this will be his last mission. He and his shipmates skirted death for a long time over large stretches of water. Fran wishes Elaine was here. He has not seen or talked to Elaine for many long months. He thinks about all of the wonderful letters from

Elaine, Mom, also known as Mae, and his brothers Jim and Bob. He is lonely and at a breaking point. He keeps his feelings to himself because he is a team player as Major McIntosh pointed out back in Advanced Airman Training. Fran will not pester his brothers with his own problems. He is the protector of the **Daisy Mae**. He is **Daisy Mae**'s Knight of the Round Table, exactly as he is Lady Elaine Birmingham's when he is back in Washington Heights and Evergreen Park. Tonight he will enjoy one last time in Honolulu, Hawaii.

This is the first time under Gall's command the boys become mischievous. After all, they are just boys and young men. Each man strikes out on his own personal mission. The mission would make Larry Calhoun proud. They spend much of the night at bars in Honolulu. The next morning the men head back to Kahuku by hitching rides all the way back to the base. They are going to arrive late for the mission. The exhausted airmen left their 'A game' back in Honolulu.

The men stumble into Kahuku Airfield and find fourteen bombers on the field with engines revving up, filling every available piece of tarmac and runway. All of the bombers are spinning blades. That is all except **Daisy Mae**.

Daisy Mae is just sitting still alongside the runway, innocently polishing her nails or brushing her hair, while a red-faced Lt. Gall is talking to the control tower from the pilot's seat. He is talking to a superior officer who can bust him down to buck private and put him on permanent potato peeling detail.

"Where are my men?" a frustrated pilot hears a voice screaming inside his head.

Gall covers for his missing men by saying there is a problem with one of the engines. Van Horn suggests Gall tell the tower something ridiculous like his "flux capacitor isn't fluxing." The tower stops the chatter for several long minutes. The **Daisy Mae** is holding up an important combat mission. Finally, after a long period of silence, the word comes down over the radio that **Daisy Mae** is scratched from the mission. The crew will mount up ship #165 instead.

The team is not on the playing field.

Lt. Gall does not want to leave the **Daisy Mae** because the whole squadron will see just Gall, Weiss, Jensen and Van Horn leave their aircraft to board another. They will see a four-man crew enter a ten-man bomber. Imagine the response of the other pilots in the other bombers. Imagine the response of superior officers after the incident on Nauru, when Gall held up the squadron on a bombing raid.

How mortifying!

Perkins, Conley, Ambur and the rest of the enlisted men are running toward the flight line. They quickly climb into the **Daisy Mae**, only to find the officers missing!

Gall, Van Horn, Weiss and Jensen have exited the aircraft, worried about walking across the flight line to take control of #165. They are hiding under **Daisy Mae**'s twin rudders in the rear of the aircraft. Lt. Jensen spots the wayward boys running toward the plane and the officers quickly climb back into the **Daisy Mae**.

Gall races to the cabin and quickly radios the tower saying that his Flight Engineer solved the mechanical problem and all is ready for flight. Perkins, Conley, Patterson, Wyckoff, and Storts sport their best poker faces as Lt. Jensen goes to the rear of the ship to question the men while Ambur assumes position outside the ship at the number three engine.

At the same time, fourteen bombers with engines revving at 2500 rpm are waiting as Flight Engineer Ambur is standing in front of **Daisy Mae**'s number three engine with a fire extinguisher resting on the dolly. The officers are angry with the enlisted men. Flight Officer Van Horn pops his window open and hangs his head out the window in his usual friendly manner.

He yells out to Flight Engineer Ambur, "Six good turns, Ambur...Six good turns!"

Van Horn flicks on the ignition for engine number three and then Ambur dutifully marches to the number four. After another six good turns, Van Horn flicks on the number four and Ambur takes the long walk over to the number two engine directly outside Gall's window.

Van Horn smiles at the visibly angry Gall and says, "You understand that we trust our lives to these men." Gall laughs and his stress begins to subside. Gall knows he commands the best crew in the Army Air Corps and feels for the men after these many months of solitude and danger. Gall shakes his head from side to side as if he understands and then opens his window as Ambur is watching and waiting with his dollied extinguisher handy.

For the first time in history, Gall repeats Van Horn's jest, "Six good turns, Ambur...six good turns."

Ambur smiles back and all is well. "Yes Sir!" Ambur says laughing aloud.

Gall is laughing now. He holds no malice for his mischievous crew. Sitting next to Gall, Van Horn continues, "The men needed some relief last night. All of the missions with no time off take its toll. Flying over these long barren stretches of ocean with nothing but sky and water to view will drive any man to drink."

Gall replies, "I understand. You, Ben, Myron down in the greenhouse, and me all owe our lives to the gunners. We have to maintain our military decorum and I understand why from a command perspective. However, these are fellows just like us. We are in a fight for survival in the skies. They just snapped a little bit."

Navigator Weiss remarks, "When I hear how the plane is covered by the turret gunners over the intercom, I feel safe up here. Perkins, Conley, Storts and Wyckoff have eyes like hawks. Their communication with each other over the interphone sounds as efficient as the baseball infield of Tinker to Evers to Chance. I love how they track and pass the Zeros around the plane as if they are passing the ball around the infield."

Joe flicks on the number two engine. Arvid Ambur walks down the line near the end of the wing and then gives the number one engine's props six good turns. Finally, all engines are starting and the last man, Flight Engineer Ambur, takes his place with the rest of the crew inside their favorite home in the skies, the **Daisy Mae**.

"Where are we headed?" Perkins asks Ambur with Conley standing nearby.

"We are headed for Midway," Ambur replies while watching the fuel gauges. "We are headed for Midway."

Fran's glum attitude gives way to excitement. Perkins remembers his conversation with a hero from Midway, Major Perry McIntosh. He closes his eyes and remembers the top-secret information about the capabilities of the B-24D Liberator. He also remembers how McIntosh wished Fran would see the beautiful Eastern Island of Midway. Fran remembers every word.

"I remember my last takeoff from the Midway. First, you are watching the pavement on the ground and the horizon off in the distance. The engine starts and you move quickly down the runway and finally you feel the wheels leave the ground from beneath you. Then you feel a sense of freedom only felt by the birds that have been here long before man. You look down when you reach the water and see hundreds of fish near the shore in the clear shallow waters. You can see ten to twenty feet below the surface on a clear day.

"It is an incredible feeling. I am certain your travels will take you to Midway. It is our last line of defense before Hawaii, Hickam Field and Pearl Harbor. I hope you will be able to enjoy the journey."

Perkins remembers asking McIntosh, "Do you think I'll ever fly a plane?"

"Yes, you will someday," McIntosh replies. "However until that day, your mission is to protect the Big Brown Bomber and every man in your crew. Someday you will fly a plane at Midway."

Flight from Kahuku to Midway

The massive fleet of Liberators takes off from Kahuku and Fran crawls inside his belly turret and cranks it down below the **Daisy Mae**. Inside the bubble, he becomes anxious to see Midway for the first time. Fran promises to remember everything about it, in case he ever runs into Major Perry McIntosh again. As Fran swings his guns around to watch the air armada behind him, he wonders what dangers lie ahead. Deep down he knows that this is the last time he will see Kahuku. This is the same airfield where he spotted the breaching whales. Fran is beginning mission number thirteen with **Daisy Mae**. Will thirteen be his lucky number?

He will find out shortly.

It is a short flight of only two hours. After usually being in the air for four to eight hours, this flight seems like a pleasure trip. Fran cruises in the belly turret, looking down at the ocean below and the beautiful Pacific sky above. He hears Gall's voice over his headset. "Retract your turret. We will be landing in fifteen minutes."

Earl Conley greets him as he climbs out of his turret. "Fran, I hear we are going on a combat mission tomorrow. We have a briefing tomorrow at noon. It should be a good one." Fran and Earl make small talk as they gaze out the right side waist gunner window.

The **Daisy Mae** circles the Midway Islands and Fran looks down at the Eastern Island, the island from which they will begin their next combat mission. If they are successful, they will end their mission on this island.

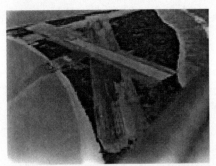

10-1 Eastern Island of Midway

The Battle of Midway represents the greatest military defeat in the history of Japan's Navy. The Japanese lost face when they gave up so much to the Americans. Everything the Japanese accomplished with their Pearl Harbor victory is forever reversed. The top military leaders of Japan knew they had lost the war. They had picked on the wrong country.

Perkins, Conley, Ambur and the boys flew their first mission to Canton Island in April. While they were in the air, Admiral Yamamoto, the architect of the Pearl Harbor Attack, was ambushed by our P-38 Lightning fighter planes over the Solomon Islands. Six of the eight battleships sunk at Pearl Harbor are now back in service. Only the Battleships Arizona and Oklahoma rest on the harbor's floor. The Japanese victories are fewer in memory. They must find a major victory and that victory could materialize with another attack on Midway and Pearl Harbor.

The Japanese wanted the island as badly as they wanted Hawaii. Midway is only two hours away from Diamond Head, the prominent landmark feature on the Island of Oahu. If they invade and occupy Midway, they have an airbase from which to launch attacks against Pearl

Harbor and Hickam Field. If they invade Hawaii, they will be able to attack the mainland of the United States daily. They will win the war against America.

Painted on an archway at Midway is the motto of the Marine Unit guarding it. The message is clear. "Hold Midway until Hell freezes over." The marines guarding Midway commit to never letting a single Japanese soldier the opportunity to walk on Midway's shores.

Briefing on Midway

On Friday July 23, 1943, it is time for the next mission's briefing. Perkins, Ambur, Conley, Storts, Wyckoff, and Patterson sit together for the briefing. Outside the window, Perkins notices all of the albatrosses clustered together. "I wonder if those are enemy agents," Fran wisecracks to the boys.

"They are certainly big enough," Earl remarks.

A first sergeant commands loudly, "Ten hut!" The squadron snaps to attention. During the briefing, the officers sit in the front and the gunners sit in rows behind their pilots. It is important that all of the pilots know every detail while the gunners already know what they need to do.

The Backstory of Wake Island, the Alamo of the Pacific

The Commander takes a pointer and begins a short history lesson of both Midway, the point of departure and return, as well as the target area, Wake Island, the Alamo of the Pacific.

"Midway is located equidistant from California to Japan, perfect for a great military base for Japan as an attack launch point for an American invasion. Better to serve as an American base launch point for an attack on Japan. Midway was the scene of an unbelievable victory for the Allies in the war. The American Air and Naval Forces destroyed four of six aircraft carriers that carried out the gruesome Pearl Harbor attack only six months ago. While the Japanese carrier fighter planes were out looking for the American fleet and bombing Midway, our forces destroyed all of their aircraft carriers. The remaining Japanese planes had to ditch in the Pacific Ocean, taking many of the best Japanese pilots and aircraft out of the war. This represented the greatest naval defeat of the Imperial Japanese Navy since the 1500s.

"On December 7, 1941, the same day Japanese warplanes were attacking Pearl Harbor in Hawaii; the Japanese fleet invaded the American base at Wake Island. A tiny unit of marines and sailors held off the mighty Japanese fleet for several days before the enemy finally conquered the island in late December. The marine unit, short on soldiers, outgunned by the Imperialist Japanese Navy, and without hope, gave it their all to buy time for the American forces struck down by the Pearl Harbor attack.

"There was a famous newspaper illustration shown prior to the invasion during the Christmas Season of 1941 in newspapers around the world. The illustration shows Santa Claus reading letters from children requesting toys for Christmas." The Mission Commander's voice softens a bit as he says, "Santa Claus reads a letter that says just four words, 'Send me more Japs.' The Commander of the Naval and Marine Forces on Wake Island, Commander Winfield S. Cunningham, signed the letter. He is saying that his tiny band of warriors is ready to take on every soldier Japan can send on the invasion. Cunningham received his Christmas gift when the Japanese finally were successful, killing or capturing the remaining marines.

"For thirteen days, these brave marines and sailors held out against the mightiest naval fleet in history. They held out for thirteen days, just as the defenders of the Alamo did against the mighty Mexican Army almost a hundred years ago in Texas. They sent our men in chains on prison ships to Japan on December 23, 1941 just two weeks after the Pearl Harbor attack.

"The reports of the heroism on Wake Island by the tiny band of determined marines gave hope and inspiration to the American forces serving on all fronts, just as the sacrifice of the men at the Alamo brought hope to Sam Houston and the Texans. The Texans needed time for their forces to train and deploy for combat. The Battle of Wake Island brought hope to all fighting men in the Pacific.

"Hope is always a good thing...and hope never dies."

In July of 1943, the Japanese have a garrison of troops, ships and planes within four hours airtime of Midway Island and may stage another attack on the Hawaiian Islands and then the United States, if they are able to build up their forces on Wake Island. The mission is to eliminate that fear for all of the islanders and all Americans.

"Our mission, men, is to bomb Wake Island. Wake Island is the Alamo of the Pacific."

The Commander goes on to explain how the attack is not just some misdirection run while the other bombers in the Seventh Army Air Corps are moving the bomber line closer to Japan. The Air Corps' bomber line, followed by the marines' island hopping, is making strides to keep the Japanese on the defensive. "We do not want any more invasions on territories by the Empire of Japan. You are the men who defended America; now you are the men who are liberating the Islands."

The weather officer takes over and talks about a storm blocking the path of the bomber raid. "You will be heading into a tropical storm pattern about 100 miles out and it will continue until you reach your targets at Wake Island. From about one hour into your flight until about eighty miles from Peacock Point, you will be flying your bombers through a watery hell. For two hours or more in each direction, the storm will test your flying skills. The storm is your enemy, so prepare for that enemy. The B-24 Liberator will handle the storm. You, pilots and navigators have a history of navigating through this many times before during the day and night missions you carry out across the Pacific. The enemy forces will never expect a bombing mission with a storm like this going on. By the time they see the Grey Geese insignia on your tail, you'll be dropping bombs and heading home. Home is back here at Midway."

Perkins, Conley, Ambur and the rest of the gunners go to their quarters and talk about the upcoming mission. "What do you think, guys, are we going to make it back alive?" asks Perkins.

"Sure we are," Conley responds. "The hard part is flying through the storm. Wake Island is just a submarine base. I doubt if they can shoot us down. They are not expecting planes heading through a storm like this."

"I heard some radio chatter about Zeros from the Black Dragon Squadron flying to Wake, but they should be gone by now," Patterson adds.

Wyckoff speculates, "Even if they are there, they may not have time to get up in the air. We could destroy them with the explosions on their airfield."

Storts asserts, "I can handle the fighter planes. I'm worried about the storm. They say this is going to be the worst tropical storm in over ten years."

Ambur wisely cuts in, "I vote for getting a good meal and some rest tonight. We'll be up early for the raid."

Perkins jests, "You get some rest, Grandpa. I'm going swimming."

Ambur jokes, "I should take you over my knee and spank you, Perkins. Your mother never taught you to respect your elders."

The other men laugh at Ambur's remark. He's the oldest man on the **Daisy Mae**, a whopping twenty-four years old, even older than the four officers on board. He knows this is good-natured jesting from one of his younger brothers.

160

Mischief and Duty

These men enjoy a bond so tight that is difficult to understand, not biologically connected but connected by spirit. Knowing that any one of these brothers in battle may give his life to save yours is humbling. Back in training when Perkins and Conley saved Larry Calhoun from falling to his death, all three men could have perished. Neither Perkins nor Conley gave one thought of watching the event or being a bystander. They jumped into action with both boots on. They know unconsciously that the man standing next to them will gladly volunteer for the honor of keeping the continuum of life moving forward.

It is ironic that the horrors of war accentuate brotherly love.

The Ole Swimming Hole

Fran goes back to his tent, changes into his swimming trunks and heads toward the beach. Fran sees a large stretch of sand at the end of the runway. "Now for some fun," Fran thinks to himself.

"Where are you going?" sounds a marine sergeant wearing full combat gear and an M1 Carbine pointing in Fran's direction.

"I'm going to take a swim in the ocean," Perkins shouts back.

"No, you're not, cowgirl," replies the sergeant. "The beach you're looking at is mined. We put hundreds of anti-personnel land mines in the sand in order to stop the Japanese when they try to invade the island. Even if you could go swimming, there are schools of sharks everywhere around the island. They're extremely aggressive and would love for you to jump right in so they can have a snack."

"Thanks for the advice, Sergeant. There'll be no swimming for me today."

Disappointed Fran walks back toward his tent, thinking about Funafuti and the warm, clear waters with an occasional shark. Then he thinks of all the times he spent with his older brothers, Jim and Bob, swimming in Lake Michigan in Chicago.

"I wonder if I'll ever see them again. It's been a long time since December 8, 1941 when we all enlisted together. It's almost two years, but it seems a lifetime. Now I have new brothers. We're going into battle tomorrow morning. We've been so lucky so far, but I've got a bad feeling about this. Almost like when I see someone's personal effects being packed up."

Chapter 11

The Alamo in the Sky

It is Saturday morning, July 24, 1943. Just as December 7, 1941 is the anniversary of the Pearl Harbor attack, July 24, 1943 marks a personal Day of Infamy for these brave men from the United States Army Air Corps.

Chicago, Illinois

In Evergreen Park, Illinois, a Southwest Chicago suburb, young Elaine Birmingham begins her morning writing letters to her boyfriend, young Fran Perkins. Elaine is leaving later this morning to join her friends, Marge and Sophie, on a bus ride to Chicago to spend a day at the movies. They are excited to see a new motion picture titled, *Cabin in the Sky*, a film based on the Broadway show with the same title. She is very excited about the music because she is taking voice lessons at DePaul University while attending Calumet High School. Her goal is to become a famous opera star. Elaine loves great music and great musical performances.

Whenever Marge and Sophie want to have a girl's night out, Elaine enjoys being included and has a great time. Growing up as a single child, Elaine finds comfort in being with her friends. Elaine is very pretty and she turns down dates often. Her mother, Mae, explains to Elaine the difficulty young men have with talking to young women. "Girls and boys are not the same," Mae says, "You must be careful to understand their feelings. You never want to hurt a boy's feelings." Elaine always tells the young men, "My boyfriend is overseas and I am waiting for him. Thank you anyway."

Arriving at the movie theater in Chicago, Elaine, Marge and Sophie find great seats near the center of the theatre. Marge begins telling a story

163

about her boyfriend while a newsreel, narrated by Ed Herlihy, plays on the screen. The newsreel features Allied gains in the European battlefront during the week. As Herlihy reports on the current bombing campaign by the US Eighth Army Air Corps and the Royal Air Force over Hamburg, Germany, sixteen-year-old Elaine tries to focus on Marge's story. During Marge's relationship story, Elaine keeps one ear trained on Ed Herlihy because Fran's brother, Robert "Bob" Perkins, is in the US Eighth Army Air Corps.

When a Bugs Bunny cartoon begins, Elaine's focus shifts back to her friends. The three girls are not quite ready to think about the war going on around them. They are just high school kids and have the usual problems girls face in spite of a World War II. It is summer vacation from school and the girls take the time to catch up on their social lives.

Clarence and Mae, to Fran known as Rosie the Riveter, left earlier this morning to their jobs at the Ford Plant in Chicago to build bomber engines, like the ones that carry Fran and his shipmates today.

DeKalb, Illinois

Deuce and Jacob Nelson have a large buffet breakfast, then accompanied by Jacob's wife Tina, they go out and work on the tractor out in the now famous bean field.

Tina asks, "Do you remember a year ago when we had so much trouble with the tractor?"

Jacob replies, with a good pat on the back for Deuce, "Our nephew and handyman, Deuce, took good care of us with Captain Korn and the US Army. I'm glad we are so blessed. Just the sight of all of those troops out on the road coming to attention and then working all night to get the job done, was sure powerful. I wonder if the men are still with us."

Deuce says, "Tomorrow when we go to church, let's say a prayer for those boys. By now, all of those men are deployed in combat around the world."

Jacob looks at Tina and Deuce and says, "There is no better church than right here with our soybeans to humble us in thanksgiving prayer."

On this warm Saturday morning Jacob, Tina and Deuce are standing at the site where the Battle of the Beans was fought and won. They look out across the bean fields and tall cornfields beyond, remembering and praying for the young men who gave them the wonderful gift of hope.

San Diego, California

It is morning in San Diego, as Molly thinks about her upcoming week at the Liberator plant. She is getting more and more headaches at night resulting from the vivid nightmares that haunt her now. Each time she sees a ball-turret gunner surrounded by fire, bullets and bombs. Molly closes her eyes and hopes the young airman will survive the attack. After her nightmares, it takes her hours to get back to sleep.

Molly is determined to shake her troubles away and focus on the moment. She does not want her headaches and nightmares to affect her family. Molly is getting ready to take Mom and children for a fun day at the beach. She recently located a small beach absent of tanks and soldiers. It feels more like a peaceful United States. She wants everyone to enjoy the clear Pacific waters on a warm, sunny, summer day.

Midway Island

In the early morning, the crew sits together at breakfast in the mess hall. The men are not paying much attention to their meal as their thoughts are on the battle they will face today. After breakfast, Fran, Earl and Arvid clean their weapons. Each will carry a Colt 1911 style pistol and a Thompson submachine gun. Each man wonders, "If I get shot down

165

over Wake Island, and somehow survive, will I be able to shoot the enemy at close range?" They understand that the Japanese will torture and kill them if found alive.

These men make a pact that if they are forced to land in Japanese territory; they will use their Colts and their Tommy Guns to kill each other after taking out as many of the enemy as possible. Fran states, "I refuse to allow the Japanese the satisfaction of torturing Americans. They won't take me alive." All agree. They will not suffer like the brave men who recently escaped a Japanese prison and told the world about the Bataan Death March.

The crew of the **Daisy Mae** will die with dignity.

Crew of the **Daisy Mae** on July 24, 1943

Here is a list of the flight crew of the **Daisy Mae**, B-24D Liberator Bomber on July 24, 1943. Remember these heroes:

- 1st Lt. Joseph A. Gall, Pilot
- Flight Officer John N. Van Horn, Co-Pilot
- 2nd Lt. Benjamin I. Weiss, Navigator
- 2nd Lt. Myron W. Jensen, Bombardier
- T.Sgt. Arvid B Ambur, Flight Engineer and Waist Gunner
- T.Sgt. Thomas Wyckoff, Top-Turret Gunner & Assistant Engineer
- S.Sgt. Robert L. Patterson, Radioman and Waist Gunner
- S.Sgt. Francis J. Perkins Jr. Ball Turret Gunner & Armorer
- S.Sgt. Robert "Snuffy" Storts, Nose Gunner
- S.Sgt. Earl W. Conley, Tail Gunner
- S.Sgt. Joseph "Pop" Evans, Photographer

The Alamo in the Sky

The Mission on July 24, 1943

The mission beginning on this date is supposed to be a two-day bombing attack. They will strike the airfields and barracks on July 24, return to Midway and then on Monday Morning, finish the job. Photographers will take hundreds of pictures of Wake Island. The purpose is to see if Wake Island is building a new submarine base that would deploy their submarines to Midway and to Pearl Harbor to sink American ships, and launch an invasion of the Hawaiian Islands.

The bombers today are reaching out over one thousand miles away. They are sending fourteen bombers, although only ten actually get up in the air because of mechanical problems that ground four heavy bombers. Over the target, the Japanese Zero fighter planes will be flying and shooting at speeds exceeding 300 miles per hour, firing both machine guns and cannons with deadly accuracy.

Today all of the men will converse through an intercom system and shout out the enemy fighter locations to direct the other gunners. They will pass the enemy from one turret position to another. Each man knows where his fields of fire begin and end. They know and respect every shipmate's abilities and recognize their voices over the intercom. The gunners help each other during these deadly duels in the skies. These brave men have flown many missions and this is number thirteen while flying the **Daisy Mae**. It is a very tight and professional unit. It is hard to believe these men range from only eighteen to twenty-four years in age.

Marines stand alongside the small air base at the Eastern Island of Midway silently watching the launching of ten heavy bombers, seven of which are from the Grey Geese Bomb Group and three from the 416th Bomb Group.

When Army Air Corps crews lose gunners in battle, these same marines confidently jump at the chance to help. On the morning of July 24, over 200 United States Marines line up to replace the one tail gunner needed on a B-24 Bomber when the gunner had a hospital emergency and could not go on the raid. Experienced marines often ride shotgun, operating any one of the seven gun positions on these mighty air fortresses.

Marines and sailors on Midway unite and wish to avenge the famous attack on Pearl Harbor. Additionally, they want to avenge the invasion of Wake Island on December 7, 1941.

Hold Midway Until Hell Freezes Over
- The motto of the 6th Defense/AAA Battalion, First Marine Division

The airmen want revenge for the destruction of their 11th Bomb Group on Hickam Air Base during the deadly Pearl Harbor attack and also want to avenge the death of the beloved Commander of the Seventh Army Air Corps, General Tinker, who died after piloting the lead bomber in the first air mission over Wake Island a year earlier. Tinker's bomber was lost at sea. The Navy never found any sign of wreckage. Tinker was the first U.S. General killed in World War II, and in the bravest tradition was leading the rest of his troops into battle. Tinker reasoned that if he was ordering his men to fight and die for their country, it was only right that he lead them in combat. His lead bomber never made it to Wake Island and his remains are lost forever.

The marines in the Pacific, respected General Tinker as he was made of the same stuff as any marine rifleman. General Tinker was the first Native American to reach the rank of General in all of the United States Armed Forces. Many Native Americans served with the marines including the famous Code Talkers. They were very proud of the fact that one of their own was able to reach the top position in the Armed Forces while no Native Americans had the right to vote yet. The right to vote happens in another four years in 1947, the same year the Army Air Corps became a separate branch of service called the United States Air Force. General Tinker flew every airplane that the Army Air Corps had to offer. He was not a desk jockey. He learned to fly and fight very well. Leading his troops into battle is a trait going back to our founding fathers such as General George Washington, as well as the leaders of his own Native Nation.

"6 Good Turns, Ambur, 6 Good Turns"

The **Daisy Mae** has gone into battle many times before. She carried many Grey Geese pilots during World War II. They included names like Gall, Phillips, Smith, Scholar, Stay, Deasy, and many others. Many times **Daisy Mae** spent sixteen hours a day in the air flown by two different crews. She loves her crews and now it is time to fight.

Just before 0800 hours, Co-pilot John Van Horn, hands Pilot Joe Gall his clipboard to begin the flight check and Flight Engineer Arvid Ambur prepares to spin the blades.

Ambur is standing outside across from Van Horn's number three engine and gives the co-pilot a hand sign. At the ripe old age of twenty-four, Ambur musters up enough strength in his rickety old bones to turn the big props. Grandpa readies to give the propellers six turns each with the engines turned off, in order to get the oil lubricant flowing into each engine. Van Horn looks out of his side window and cheerfully reminds Ambur, "Six good turns, Ambur, six good turns." Ambur then signals Van Horn to flip the switches of **Daisy Mae**'s engines one last time. Van Horn pushes the ignition switch for the number three engine and the propeller starts revolving faster and faster.

The mighty engines hum now and Ambur puts away his dollied extinguisher and climbs aboard to join the crew that will ride and fight one more time before riding off into history. Ambur is satisfied that **Daisy Mae** is ready for war.

All engines running, Gall announces over the intercom these two words, "Checking in." One at a time, the eleven-man crew checks in.

Van Horn begins with "Co-pilot checking in."
Ben Weiss adds, "Navigator checking in."

From the nose, we hear Myron Jensen, "Bombardier checking in."
Snuffy Storts continues, "Nose Gunner checking in."
Robert Patterson, "Radioman and Waist Gunner checking in."
Arvid Ambur, "Flight Engineer and Waist Gunner checking in."
Fran Perkins, "Ball-turret Gunner checking in."
Thom Wyckoff, "Top-Turret Gunner and Assistant Flight Engineer checking in."
Earl Conley, "Tail Gunner checking in."
Finally, the voice of the Aerial Photographer Joseph "Pop" Evans joining them on the mission, "Aerial Photographer checking in."

After accounting for everyone onboard Gall and Van Horn go down their official checklist and make sure all tasks are completed. The flaps, brakes, and communications are 'a go'. The bombs and ammo are on board and the **Daisy Mae** is ready for action. Cartoonist Al Capp's rendition of one of his characters, **Daisy Mae**, is rolling down the tarmac toward the runway, the same tarmac and runway Major McIntosh piloted his B-17 Bomber during the Battle of Midway about one year earlier.

The Last Mission Takes Off on Midway Island

"Off we go into the wild blue yonder, climbing high into the sun"
– From the United States Air Force Hymn

The bombers take off at 0800 hours for what should be an eight-hour mission. They will climb to 17,500 feet, drop down 500 feet and level off at an altitude of 17,000 feet. They will fly four hours over open sea, make their bomb runs, complete a "U" Turn and then fly four hours back to Midway Island. There will be no fighter plane protection today because the fighters' range is too short to protect the lumbering giants.

If any of the bombers go down in the ocean today, there will be no one to rescue them. The B-24 bomber is not a pleasure yacht. It is not sea-worthy. It could crash into a million pieces upon hitting the ocean. Once it touches water, it will sink like a brick to the bottom of the sea in about four short minutes.

Daisy Mae's crewmembers are concentrating on their jobs. They have worked side-by-side on the plane for thirteen missions and on other bombers for many more. Gall cross trains each crewmember, so in combat, one can quickly take over another man's station should he go down.

The Deadly Storm

As the Brown Bomber streaks down the Eastern Island of Midway runway at ninety-five miles per hour, Gall watches the gauges to make sure he lifts off at 140 miles per hour. The runway at Midway is built for fighter planes that do not require much runway for takeoff; therefore, each take off by the bomb-laden bombers is a narrow miss of hitting the ocean just beyond the short airstrip. The weather this morning is a little wet but visibility is good. The crew is resting at their battle stations, wondering what resistance they will face once reaching Wake Island.

As the plane takes off, it heads directly over the archway that sports the famous Marine Motto, "Hold Midway Until Hell Freezes Over."

As the plane climbs higher in the air, Perkins moves to the left waist gunner window. Looking at the ocean below he remarks to Ambur, "The Pacific Ocean is as blue and clear as I imagined it. I can see twenty feet below the surface and see sharks and fish below."

Arvid returns with, "I hope you are able to use your talent to see the Zeros below when we reach Wake Island."

"You just keep those engines going. I won't let anyone hurt the Big Girl." Fran pats the retracted ball-turret sitting a few feet away from the window.

Ambur says, "The Brown Bomber, right Fran?"

"Right, Arvid," with Perkins demonstrating a left jab, "The Brown Bomber."

About an hour out to sea, the air armada runs into the monstrous storm. Each B-24 weighs over 56,000 pounds fully loaded, yet the ships toss and jerk like corks in the water and each shipmate braces himself for a wild ride. Radio silence is the order of the day to prevent enemy ships discovering the surprise attack, however, unknown to all of the shipmates, Japanese submarines lurk in the flight path ready to warn the Japanese garrison on Wake Island. As the crew members look out their turrets and windows, all they see are thick clouds, lightning and rain. Gall and Van Horn strain their eyes to see any sign of the other bombers in the formation. No windshield wipers are installed on the B-24 so the pilots have to stick their heads out their side windows fumbling with oxygen masks. It would be easy to collide with other bombers in the group. Van Horn remembers the briefing they received back in Hawaii last night when the Weather Officer briefed them that the largest, most violent tropical storm may await them. The clouds will clear up by the time they reach Wake Island. Van Horn looks at Gall and just shakes his head and rolls his eyes as the **Daisy Mae** pitches and bounces among the thick clouds. Van Horn knows what Gall is thinking. When most of the time, weather predictions were one hundred percent wrong, why today are the predictions on target?

This is a fierce tropical storm. In fact, it is the worst tropical storm in over ten years. Looking out from the inside of the ship was like when you take your automobile into one of those automatic car washes. The water is coming from all angles, you cannot see out straight ahead until the water sprays are behind you, and the boys have their heads out the side windows.

The bombers are flying through the blinding elements trying to keep a tight formation without colliding into each other and at the same time maintaining radio silence. Belly Gunner Perkins weaves his way through the bobbing bomber up to the cabin and approaches Gall and Van Horn.

"Sir, request permission to climb into the ball-turret and lower it below the plane to visually spot the other bombers and call out through the intercom system to help you stay clear of the other bombers in formation."

All of his shipmates know of Fran's exceptional eyesight and depth perception. They had encouraged him to volunteer for the task concerned that the storm is getting worse.

Gall tells Perkins they must keep radio silence and intercom silence until they reach their targets at Wake Island. Van Horn adds, "If we drop the turret down right now, we may bump into **Cabin in the Sky**, another B-24 in the formation. We can't see through these dense clouds and heavy rain, but we're pretty sure she's down there."

All of the available pilots on board, Gall and Van Horn at the controls and Navigator Weiss and Bombardier Jensen huddle in the cabin keeping their eyes trained out the side windows as well as the windshield to maintain a comfortable distance from the other planes in formation.

Lt. Gall orders Fran, "Keep watching out either of the waist windows and run up here if you see other bombers getting too close."

"Yes Sir," Fran says as he retreats near the left waist window.

Back in the rear of **Daisy Mae**, Tail Gunner Conley squints out his rear-turret hoping another Liberator will not ride up and collide. "I don't want **Cabin in the Sky** to become Cabin up My Ass," Conley says nervously laughing to himself.

Nose Gunner Storts, down in the greenhouse below the cabin, is looking in all directions hoping he will not view other bombers in formation veering off course right into the **Daisy Mae**. Snuffy is confident in the **Daisy Mae** and her crew to stay on course, but does not know what to expect from the other planes in formation. Occasionally Flight Engineer

Ambur asks Storts if he needs a break. Storts remains in the greenhouse. "I will not abandon my post," Storts tells Ambur. So now, both Ambur and Storts watch and comment on what they were seeing together.

Patterson, Wyckoff, Ambur, Conley, Storts, Perkins and Pop Evans look out every window and turret hoping they can make it through the horrendous storm. With so much focus on the storm and the constant pitching and rocking, no one is thinking about other real dangers that lurk ahead.

Minutes seem like hours and hours seem like days as the **Daisy Mae** lumbers through the water-laden skies. Thunder, lightning and pouring rain beat up the ship. This bomber and the other bombers crawl through one of the worst tropical storms on record in the vast Pacific Ocean. Every time lightning flares outside, all of the crewmembers strain their eyes frantically to see the familiar outlines of the accompanying B-24s.

One at a time, five bombers in the attack formation turn back because of mechanical failure, pilot error, or just the will to survive. It is better to turn back early in the mission as your odds of crashing and being found alive, if you have to ditch, decrease dramatically for each mile further away from your base when your bomber goes down. It is almost impossible to navigate with accuracy under these conditions, but Navigator Ben Weiss is up to the task. He uses every available resource. The skillful navigator uses every technique he has ever learned in class or on other missions, making up stuff when he cannot remember. Weiss is focused on the job at hand and he is determined to get the **Daisy Mae** safely to and from the targets. He is determined to complete the mission come hell and high water.

Even with zero visibility in the middle of an unfriendly ocean, Gall is optimistic. The crew is aggressive not passive. They are scurrying around the aircraft doing their jobs to the best of their abilities. Everyone has his game face on as the life or death battle has already begun. All of the gunners keep at their battle stations with eyes trained outside and squinting in order to keep safe from the possibility of collision with the other bombers in the squadron. They do not realize yet how many bombers are still with them. Since visibility is zero, in their minds it is possible that the **Daisy Mae** is alone and lost with thousands of miles of ocean beneath her.

General Tinker disappeared on his mission to Wake Island. General Tinker was an expert at flying everything the Army Air Corps flew. It is not out of the realm of possibilities that twenty-three-year-old Gall may find the same fate soon.

Then again, Gall exudes optimism and hope.

Blue Skies, Blue Seas and Red Blood

"Here they come zooming to meet our thunder. At 'em boys, Give her the gun!"

—*From the United States Air Force Hymn*

About four hours into the trip, the bombers come out of the clouds as they near Wake Island and the sky clears.

"There it is!" shouts Snuffy in the nose-turret. Perkins immediately climbs into the ball-turret cranks it down beneath the belly of the bomber and swings the guns around to align with the bomber's nose, "I see it straight ahead."
Now Gall and Van Horn spot the bomber squadron in formation for the first time in almost four hours. "We are still second in formation." Van Horn says excitedly, "Good job, Joe."

Captain Jesse Stay pilots **Doity Goity**, which is the lead bomber. He flew **Daisy Mae** on a mission about two weeks ago. **Doity** and **Daisy** are friends.

Things are looking much better now. In the clear blue sky with Wake Island dead ahead, Van Horn and Gall smile at each other and take their first deep breaths in four hours.

175

Van Horn says, "We finally made it to our target. How Ben found this damn island is beyond me. The worst now is over. Let's go hit our targets and get out of here."

In the early afternoon only five bombers, **Doity Goity, Daisy Mae, Cabin in the Sky, Wicked Witch**, and **Sky Demon** are present and accounted for as they reach their rally position near Peacock Point. The other five bombers turned back along the way and are at Midway right now.

Tail Gunner Conley waves at **Cabin in the Sky** right behind. He can see the broad smiles in **Cabin in the Sky**'s greenhouse as the nose gunner waves back and the bombardier hunches over his Norden Bombsight, taking the controls from his pilot.

The small coral atoll called Wake Island is within sight.

Wake Island resembles a sprung paper clip from the air. Imagine a small paper clip stretched out and floating on a lake while you are swimming. How these fine pilots and navigators find these needles in haystacks is beyond comprehension!

Lt. Stay in **Doity Goity** leads the bombing run and the four bombers trail in a tight formation. They are about eighty miles from their target.

These B-24D Bombers can fly up to 307 miles per hour with a full bomb load, as they did on this infamous day. On the other side, the Japanese Zero can shoot and fly at speeds up to 320 miles per hour. At 17,000 feet above land or sea, these foes will engage in aerial combat while racing across the sky at over 300 miles per hour.

Fran is looking down at the ocean when he hears Gall's voice, "Belly gunner test your guns." Getting ready to shoot, Fran Perkins remembers his Gunnery School training in the Nevada desert. He thinks about the long burst of fifty-caliber fire that evaporated his cigar-shaped target. Fran remembers how the instructor complimented him on his accurate

176

shooting and promoted him to Sergeant. The next day Fran could barely lift the fountain pen he used for Elaine's letters. His arms were still vibrating and his hands shaky. It still excites Fran to remember that day. No sooner does Perkins clear his head after his two ten-round bursts of machine gun fire then he sees a single Japanese Zero fighter plane flying the length of the bomber squadron. Adrenalin fills his body and his flight or fight switch activates and he chooses "Fight." The enemy Zero leader makes a sharp bank and joins three more of his friends. Excitedly, Fran shouts into his microphone, "We have Zeros out of the sun at ten o'clock." Conley yells from the tail gunner position, "I count between twenty-eight and thirty Zeros. They are coming in at ten o'clock and at two o'clock."

In addition, there is a large bi-plane, possibly coordinating the Zeros in their battle to shoot down the invading bombers or coordinating anti-aircraft guns on the island lying in wait. There are two levels of Zeros zigzagging through the bomber formation in a coordinated figure eight pattern.

The leader and his three friends are attacking **Daisy Mae**'s soft belly. A long while back Major Perry McIntosh told Fran his job as ball-turret gunner is protecting the B-24's soft aluminum belly. Fran points his twin fifty-caliber machine guns at the first plane and repeats his performance of several months earlier in that Nevada desert. Perkins opens up and lays on those twin fifties for a long burst. Fran yells into the microphone, "Now there are twenty-seven." The first four Zeros attack the **Daisy Mae** in single file. Perkins shreds the first two zeros sending them into the sea and remaining bullets from the blast tear into the two remaining Zeros in the group. The battle is on and everything is happening quickly and simultaneously.

As the second Zero shatters, bullets and cannon shots rip through Fran's turret. The front sight on Fran's twin fifties smashes into his forehead. Instantly a blinded Perkins falls back in the turret. Shrapnel flies into his face and in his legs. From a gigantic hole in the ball-turret, Perkins feels intense pain as the cold air is racing in at over 300 miles per hour at an altitude of 17,000 feet.

In the nose, Snuffy Storts meets two Zeros and they quickly turn away from his deadly shooting. Radioman Robert Patterson is firing with his right-waist gun and Arvid quickly runs to help the aerial photographer, who falls from bullets penetrating the **Daisy Mae**.

When the Japanese made their first attack just a few seconds earlier, Aerial Photographer Pop Evans was raising his camera to his shoulder just as bullets from the second enemy plane that Fran just blasted strikes him down. As Evans lay dying, Arvid Ambur comes over to render first aid. Pop Evans realizes that the flight engineer needs to save the bomber, fix the plane and shoot at the enemy through the waist gun window. Staff Sergeant Joseph P. Evans, in his last act of heroism, waves off the approaching flight engineer wanting to take care of him. Pop knows that every able-bodied crewmember is needed to fight off the enemy. They need to keep the dying ship and crew airborne. Pop knows life is expendable. He knows he must pay life forward.

Arvid immediately jumps to help the remaining gunners. Arvid lets fly with a few bursts of fifty-caliber machine gun fire when the ship falls silent for a few moments. The enemy planes are attacking other bombers in the formation.

The Bombardier

Bombardier Lt. Myron Jensen is readying the Norden Bombsight. He senses he is missing some of his gunners just from the enormous amount of bullets and cannon holes in the greenhouse. Without communications in the ship he runs up to the cabin to see his flight engineer and waist gunner, Robert Patterson, carry the limp body of the aerial photographer to the rear of the bomber.

"Where are all of my gunners?" Jensen quizzes Ambur.

"Perkins is dead in the belly and I'm trying to fix communications and hydraulics at the same time. If I don't fix hydraulics we won't be able to fly the plane."

"I'll take care of one of the waist gun positions and Radioman Patterson will take the other. We cannot do anything about the ball-turret. First, I have to tell Navigator Weiss to take us to the target." Jensen quickly runs to the cabin.

"How come you are not in the nose?" Gall says to his bombardier.

"I need Ben to take us to target. Perkins is dead in the belly and Ambur is fixing our hydraulic systems. Our communications including our radio are gone!

Gall orders, "Ben, take us to target and bomb the hell out of the enemy. Jensen, shoot those bastards out of the sky!"

Van Horn adds, "Everybody's doing their jobs. We trained for this scenario. I hope Perkins is just wounded and we can get him out of there before we land."

Jensen quickly grabs the vacant machine gun in the left waist gun position. He readies his ammo belt and pulls back on the bolt. He watches for Zeros and spots one in his range. Jensen fires away with two quick bursts. The waist gunners have a shorter time to respond and limited range of fire because they do not want to shoot holes through their own wings. Two or three quick bursts fly from Jensen and from an enemy Zero. Jensen gets hit two or three times and goes down from the gunfire exchange.

Ambur races over from his leaky hydraulic lines and begins to work on Jensen, bandaging his wounds and giving him morphine.

Bullets are hitting and puncturing the **Daisy Mae**'s skin, the situation desperate.

Patterson turns around from his right-waist gunner position opposite Jensen and helps Ambur carry Jensen to the back. Ambur and Patterson hear Conley's fifty-calibers spitting lead at his attackers.

When Arvid returns to the left waist gun position, he sees that Jensen's watch had been fused to the bolt, jamming its ability to operate. Using his armorer school training, Ambur quickly and calmly removes the watch and restores the gun to fighting condition. As Arvid shoots bursts of fifty-caliber bullets toward the invaders, out of a corner of his eye he spots a fire near the fuel cells located inside the wings. The extinguishers will not reach the troubled area; therefore, Arvid after getting permission from Gall, stuffs the crew's flight jackets in the burning space trying to put it out.

The Tail Gunner

When Fran took out the first two Zeros, Conley could see numbers three and four bank quickly to the right and limp back toward Wake Island. Both planes were hit and smoking.

"You got 'em, Fran," Conley whispers to himself, "You got em. You took four Zeros off the battlefield. You were born to be a ball-turret gunner, my friend."

Conley now turns his attention to the bomber directly behind him as Zeros are attacking it viciously. Conley is vicious in his response.

One of the gunners on Lt. Cason's bomber **Cabin in the Sky** smokes a Zero and the fighter plane veers into one of **Cabin the Sky's** twin tail rudders taking off one of the rudders. The Big Brown Bomber spirals downward in a deadly spin to the sea far below.

"Come on, jump out of the plane!" Conley shouts in desperation as the wounded plane is spiraling downward. Conley is ready to count the parachutes from the falling bomber, but he sees none. He watches bursts of machine gun fire coming from **Cabin in the Sky** and views the scene all the way down to the sea.

"Poor bastards," Conley laments. "At least it is over for them. They must have had a pact like us. The enemy will never take any of us alive."

Cabin in the Sky explodes in a collision with the Pacific Ocean. The heroes of **Cabin in the Sky** kept fighting the enemy planes in a desperate struggle to help their brothers above; knowing they all would be dead within seconds. Eleven crewmembers including some of the best airmen assigned to the famous Grey Geese are gone in seconds. Like the **Daisy Mae** and Captain Stay's **Doity Goity** in the lead, it carries an extra man, an aerial photographer.

Conley thinks aloud, "I need more ammo but I'll have to get up and get it myself." Tail Gunner Conley is now tightrope walking on the catwalk above the open bomb bay doors, repeating Calhoun's stunt. "Fran and I know what it's like when those doors open. We grabbed Larry Calhoun that day with those aluminum doors flapping in the breeze," Conley thinks to himself.

Earl is racing back for more ammo belts, seeing bullet holes appear above, below, and on both sides of the rear-turret, but fortunately, Conley was too busy shooting at enemy fighters and thinking about his friends to realize the near hits. Right now Earl Conley is too busy saving his ship to think about his own personal safety.

The Flight Engineer

Flight Engineer Arvid Ambur is busy trying to keep the engines going and repairing shot up hydraulic lines. Hydraulic fluid is spraying all over the cabin and washing across the outside of the plane. The hydraulic lines and pumps are toast and the radio and interphone are fried. He tries to fix the communications interphone system and finds it blown beyond repair.

The Alamo in the Sky

Ambur, in addition to fixing the ship while it is airborne, is the only trained medic on the flight. He repairs men and machines with equal dexterity. Right now, he needs the skills of a surgeon for the wounded while repairing a giant aircraft at 17,000 feet and dodging flaming machine gun bullets at the same time. Quite a juggling act but on this day, Technical Sergeant Arvid B. Ambur is up to the job.

The Gunners

The gunners on the **Daisy Mae** have no communication as the battle rages on. Breathing through their clumsy oxygen masks with umbilical cords of oxygen attached to tanks located in the wings, moving, thinking and fighting for their lives is difficult. The gunners' playful banter passing enemy planes from turret to turret and gunner to gunner is vanished in the face of grave danger. The intercom, their communication lifeline, is deadly quiet. The only sounds heard are the rapid machine gun firing of all of the guns minus the ball-turret and left waist gun. The other turret gunners and the waist gunners feel like they are fighting alone, isolated without communications.

The Navigator

When Bombardier Jensen volunteered to reinforce the gunners, Navigator Benjamin Weiss became the bombardier. He is a trained backup bombardier so he is very familiar with the Norden Bombsight. He also knows the mission and the targets on the Wake Island Airfield.

Weiss hunches over the Norden Bomb Sight and now is flying the plane. "I feel sorry for Joe Gall," Ben thinks to himself as he lines up the target. "He loves being in control and now him and John can only watch the action."

Nose Gunner Snuffy Storts is directly in front of Ben in the greenhouse and firing in long bursts at the annoying and deadly Zeros.

The Alamo in the Sky

Daisy Mae is flying over Wake and engaging anti-aircraft fire from the ground. The Zeros regroup in the air but stay out of range of their own anti-aircraft guns. They will soon be able to intercept the bombers again, knowing the bombers will make a U-turn after depositing their bombs on the target below.

The Top-Turret Gunner

Technical Sergeant Thomas Wyckoff is blasting away at the enemy from the top-turret. One moment he is firing toward attackers in the nose and another moment, he is swinging his turret around and covering Conley in the rear. The only break he gets is when Ben is taking **Daisy Mae** over her Wake Island target and the Zeros retreat to safety in the sky.

"I hope Ben gets those bombs on target," Thom thinks to himself. "We have to accomplish our mission."

Over the Target

Reaching their targets on Wake Island, Weiss, the backup bombardier, located in the greenhouse in the front of the aircraft and below the pilot's cabin, readies the Norden Bombsight. As the **Daisy Mae** arrives over the target, a runway on Wake Island, there is a loud explosion just above the number two engine, the inboard engine, directly to the left of Pilot Lt. Gall. The bomber received a hit from accurate, enemy anti-aircraft batteries located below.

Daisy Mae is over the target. Anti-personnel bombs drop; each bomb capable of covering over one-hundred yards with smaller exploding "balls of bombs" located in each bombshell. These are designed to inflict heavy losses on ground personnel. Today the Japanese have a two-hour warning the bombers are coming and soldiers are tucked safely in their underground bunkers. The warning came from the radar of two submarines located between Midway and Wake Island, while the bombers were heading to the target through the monstrous storm.

Below the Bomber

Below the bomber in the destroyed ball-turret, Fran is struggling to see and shoot his machine guns. Blinded from the front gun sight impacted between his eyes, he knows the damaged, protruded ball-turret full of holes is slowing the ship down, leaving it an easy target for the pursuing enemy fighters. He knows that after the turret received those hard hits, it would never be able to retract back into the belly of the aircraft where it is stored before and after combat. If his turret will not retract and the **Daisy Mae** has to ditch at sea or land on a runway, Perkins will be crushed, as he lay helpless below the belly of the **Daisy Mae** in his claustrophobic test tube. Fran knows that if the plane ditches at sea or reaches an airfield, Gall and Van Horn will need to make a decision to belly land and crush their gunner. All these men try to stay distant; however, all know they are brothers. Fran knows the guilt held by the surviving pilots, Conley and the rest of the crew would be unbearable.

Fran hears the thud, thud, thud sounds of machine gun bullets striking the **Daisy Mae**. Occasionally he hears the Zero cannon shots penetrating and exploding inside. He knows every five shots contain a phosphorous tipped tracer round that helps the enemy adjust their aim. As the flaming rounds rip through the **Daisy Mae**, they start fires all over the ship. **Daisy Mae** and her crew are now in serious peril.

Fran can tell the ship is over the target because he feels the concussion of the anti-aircraft flak hitting the **Daisy Mae** and flying metal is hitting Fran and his damaged turret at the same time.

He feels useless and only a liability for the remaining ship and crew. He thinks about unhooking from the safety strap and falling into the sea 17,000 feet below. "I am blind, maybe dying," Perkins thinks to himself. "How can I possibly help my crew fight off the enemy? I'm useless to the crew. I need to get out of here quickly and save my ship. My friends, my brothers on the ship, will never need to bear the guilt of my death if I unhook and fall into the sea now. It'll be a swift and easy death. I know every one of my brothers would do this for me if I was the pilot and they were the belly gunners."

"I have to help save my ship!"

Time Stands Still

As Fran is thinking of unhooking, calmness overcomes him. All the noise of the battle silences. It becomes deathly quiet. Perkins hears a clear voice inside his head. Softly the voice says just five words.

"It is not your time."

Fran questions his mind for a bit. The analytical part of Fran's brain is working to put this into a logical frame. The voice interrupts again more insistent this time.

"It is not your time!"

Fran feels some broken pieces of his damaged guns fall into his lap. In his blind condition, he recognizes the machine gun parts by his sense of touch and by his new heightened sense of sound. Bolt, barrel, cover plate, lever, slag, spring, pin and stud fall one at a time right next to his right side. He remembers they fall in the exact same order as Sergeant Masters' opening lecture in Armorer School.

He laughs to himself making his body shake and head pound with pain. "I can't shoot anyway with all of these broken parts, but I sure know how to repair these guns quickly with a dark hood over my head. Now my blind eyes are my hood. I can still help my brothers in the ship. That bastard, Masters," Perkins, thinks to himself. "Now I understand why Masters had me fix those guns with a hood over my head. It makes sense. Conley and I slithered like reptiles through the **Daisy Mae** one scary night on Guadalcanal," Perkins thinks at that moment. "Maybe I can slither back and forth through **Daisy Mae** now and keep all of the guns firing. Major McIntosh was right. I was born to be a ball-turret

185

gunner. I was born for this very moment. I'm going to DO my job and help my shipmates."

An idea hits him. In order to get back into the belly of the ship, he needs to rotate his shattered guns, point them down toward the ocean, and then attempt to retract the ball-turret back into the belly of the ship. If in his blind, weak condition, he points the guns in the wrong direction, he will fall to the ocean below to his death. In the added dimension of flying through the air, it is difficult to feel which way is up and which way is down unless you can fix your attention on the earth or island below. However, Fran is blind and has to guess what direction he is facing.

Bombs Away!

Fran feels the anti-aircraft flak hit the plane and suddenly he loses his balance as the bombs leave the bomb bay doors next to him and the **Daisy Mae** recoils two hundred feet with her sudden weight loss. "There it is! I have it! I know where I am," he thinks, as he is given a sense of direction.

Time Moves on Again

Now the enemy gun batteries below are creating an uproar. Anti-aircraft shell bursting is getting louder and louder. After he was able to move the turret levers twice to the right then twice to the left, Fran is able to retract the damaged turret and climb inside the **Daisy Mae**. He remembers the people who installed turrets back in Sacramento, California. They did a great job. Maybe they saved his life. Despite being blind with shrapnel embedded in his legs, he is able to stand briefly on his weakened and shaky legs facing the cabin once inside the belly.

Inside the belly of the **Daisy Mae**, Flight Engineer Ambur, genuine farm boy and whiz kid, is fixing everything almost as fast and the Japanese are destroying it.

186

Time Stands Still Again

Seeing Perkins' bloody face, Ambur summons Radioman Patterson to help Perkins to the back with the wounded Lt. Jensen and Sergeant Evans. After Navigator Weiss yells "Bombs Away," he passes the controls back to Gall and then runs to the rear of the bomber to help save lives. Patterson is nursing wounds in his leg from the battle. He has a few large hunks of metal sticking out of his leg, but he puts the wounds out of his mind and helps his blind friend to the back with the other wounded men, while Thomas climbs down from the Top-Turret to get more ammo. Thom knows that after the Brown Bomber does the U-turn, the Zeros will pounce on **Daisy Mae** and fight until the ship is destroyed or out of range.

As Thomas grabs Fran's right arm he and Patterson notice a burning wad of paper stuck to the bottom of Fran's boot. He stomps on the wad of paper to put the fire out, just as Patterson says, "Get that fire out. Oh, wait! Is that a letter from Mom or Lady Elaine?"

Thom responds, "No, these are installation instructions for Fran's guns. Wait, here is a note tucked inside. It's not from Mom or Lady Elaine. A lefty wrote this. It says, 'Angels are flying with you now.'

Molly Alphabet's note, the one she wrote for the Ball-turret Gunners and taped to the instructions on the gun mounts, finds its way to a ball-turret gunner who needs it in a desperate battle. Molly, her team and thousands of workers in the Consolidated Plant back in San Diego, are with the men and the machine in spirit. The fruit of their labor is battling toe to toe with the enemy from Japan.

Patterson announces, "We are going to need some angels to get us out of here."

"Come on, Fran," Wyckoff says smiling. "Shuffle those feet, you slacker. You can rest in the back, sweetheart."

Fran is in shock but is able to shuffle his feet enough with the help of Wyckoff and Patterson to get to a place to lie down and have Patterson attend to his wounds. Navigator Weiss is helping downed Myron Jensen and Pop Evans.

Chapter 12

The Battle to Return Home

The Zeros are swarming upon them like angry bees. At least fifteen Zeros are chasing and shooting at the retreating bomber, firing while flying at speeds over 300 miles per hour. After the U-turn the wounded ship flies back through the gauntlet. The **Daisy Mae** can no longer keep up with the other bombers trying to get out of range and back home to Midway Island. The number two engine is fried and B-24s do not fare well on three or fewer engines.

Wounded Perkins, Jensen and Evans are still alive and lying near the back of the plane. Fran hears the wounded moaning and the intense hail of bullets ripping through the ship.

Fran wonders if he will hear the shot that gets him.

Arvid Ambur administers morphine and Fran's head is in a cloud right now. Maybe that is the best way to navigate through battle. Arvid stops the bleeding and wraps Fran's head and eyes in bandages. Shrapnel is sticking out of his face, so Arvid is careful. As he is no stranger to nursing wounds, Arvid's experience as a farm boy is paying off.

Patterson and Wyckoff rapidly go back to firing positions on the planes as the U-turn is complete and the enemy is spitting deadly fire into the **Daisy Mae**.

Fran reaches out next to him and feels Lt. Jensen's upper arm. "I cannot see you, Sir, but when we ditch in the water; I'll get you up to the top and keep your head out of the ocean. I'm a strong swimmer and I can help you. I'll use our buoyancy to keep us afloat."

There is no sound coming from Lt. Jensen.

The Battle to Return Home

The Big Girl struggles to keep up with the remaining three bombers heading back to Midway Island. The Zeros are attacking relentlessly as **Doity Goity**, **Sky Demon** and **Wicked Witch** run for their lives. Attackers on their heels, the bombers are pulling away, leaking fuel but can still maintain enough speed to put distance between them and Wake Island. The Zeros find **Daisy Mae** an isolated target. **Daisy Mae** is trailing the bomber formation by a huge margin now and the enemy is coming in for the final kill. **Daisy Mae** needs more speed to get distance from Wake Island and the attacking Zeros. Gall clearly sees that the inboard number two engine right out his side window is about to catch fire. Both Gall and Van Horn know the fighter planes have to eventually break off the attack or ditch into the sea. "I hope that it will be soon," Gall thinks to himself.

Van Horn reports, "Joe, according to my calculations the Zeros have to break off soon. We can feather the number two engine in about thirty seconds."

"How do you know it is thirty seconds?"

Van Horn laughs, "I have a talent for numbers, Sir."

Joe Gall smiles, "Hah, whatever you say, John. You understand I have complete confidence in you. We've been through a great ordeal, but we need more help to get us safely back to Midway."

"Hey thanks Joe. We'll make it through somehow. There's always hope."

If only the **Daisy Mae** can withstand the punishment, a few more long seconds. Just like Joe Louis, the heavyweight boxer going against a superior opponent, **Daisy Mae** is waiting for the bell to end the round. The **Daisy Mae** has taken the best punches Japan can throw at her and is giving back all she's got. The gunners on the ship cannot communicate with each other because their intercom is destroyed. They now rely on instinct, training and hope to keep on firing their guns at these deadly targets. They are throwing punches and jabs at high speeds.

With hunks of metal sticking out of his legs, Robert Patterson from the left waist gun battle station passionately shouts, "It's either them or us, damn it. Someone's going down for the count and we're not throwing in the towel!" It has been over a hundred years since the Battle of the Alamo in Texas. It was a battle to hold off Santa Anna's Mexican forces to give time for Sam Houston to train a new Army. Right after the Pearl Harbor attack in December of 1941, fifty-seven men fought and died on the Wake Island invasion by the Japanese. The Alamo of the Pacific gave the American forces in the Pacific a chance to train, defend and protect the Hawaiian Islands and the United States from Japan's conquering empire.

Now 17,000 feet above the Alamo of the Pacific, there is a tiny band of eleven air warriors fighting at their Alamo in the Sky. As they slow down, they are presenting an easy target and allowing time for the other three bombers to put distance between them and their attackers.

Suddenly the enemy backs off. The gunfire stops. Maybe the enemy fighters leave because they lost nine aircraft and pilots to the battling bombers or perhaps the last bomber in formation, the **Daisy Mae**, limped out of their range. The fighters are low on fuel and need to land quickly on their island fortress or they will perish at sea along with the **Daisy Mae**.

In this ten-round slugfest, prizefighter Japan is first to throw in the towel.

Just before turning around, a lone Japanese fighter pilot, "Shōsa" or Major Osumi glances at his fuel gauge and then ahead at **Daisy Mae**'s tail gunner, Earl Conley, as he is loading another ammo belt. Conley's head is emerging out the destroyed rear-turret that is shot up so badly that there are bullet holes coming out of every conceivable spot above, below and all sides of the tail gunner. Osumi sees more man than metal as he gazes at the rear-turret of the B-24D Liberator Bomber. Conley does not see the lone Japanese fighter pilot salute him and the brave crew of the **Daisy Mae** in admiration of how they overcame the adversity of a superior foe.

At one time, they were outmanned fifteen to one by some of the best Zero pilots Japan had to offer. The pilots were from the famous Black Dragon Squadron. Osumi feels these Americans are an honorable foe and he privately wishes these brave warriors be spared from death. He prays they will make it back safely on a long journey that will take another miracle to succeed. He then turns his damaged Zero and bloodied body around and lands safely on Wake Island. He and his fighter plane are wounded. They will never fly again. Major Osumi will remember the experience through the rest of the war and the rest of his life.

In the cabin of the **Daisy Mae**, Lt. Gall feathers the number two engine. Now only three engines can carry the broken ship four to six hours back to Midway. The destroyed engine is leaking fuel badly. At this rate of loss, the brave Brown Bomber will surely be lost at sea hours before it reaches their destination island at Midway. All hope is lost.

Or is it?

Daisy Mae Crawls Across the Sky

Daisy Mae is all alone. The remaining three bombers and the enemy fighter planes are out of sight. The three bombers are doing their best to get safely back to Midway. Suffering structural damage themselves, it is going to take a miracle for them to make it. Back on the **Daisy Mae**, guns stop firing.

"She is Not Dead Yet"

Gall and Van Horn try to get information from their shot-up gauges. Gall orders Arvid Ambur to examine the entire aircraft and assess the structural damage. Navigator Weiss goes up to the cabin and reports on the damage and the wounded shipmates. Ambur returns with Weiss to the cabin, taps Gall on the shoulder and proclaims loudly, "Sir, she is not dead yet! If we can transfer enough fuel from the dead and leaky number two engine to the other engines, then we may have enough fuel to fly very close to Midway Island. We may even make it all the way back. We'll have to lighten the load as much as we can because we're still leaking fuel from the other engines. We'll also have to descend to a lower elevation so that we can pitch our oxygen canisters and reduce the chances of more fires breaking out. After all, we have damage everywhere on board the **Daisy Mae**."

Gall tells his Flight Engineer, "You know the ship better than anyone, Sergeant. Go ahead and get us started. Do what you have to do to get us back alive."

Arvid finds that the hydraulic system is destroyed, making the brakes inoperable. That means that if they are lucky enough to make it back and land on the Eastern Island at Midway, they will be racing down the runway at over 200 miles per hour, 60 miles per hour too fast. They should be traveling at speeds of only ninety to 140 miles per hour. The monster bomber will drive right through the island and crash into the shark infested waters after reaching the small band of sand piles lined on the outer edges of the runway. First things first, however, as Gall and Van Horn, assisted by Weiss, do everything they can to get back as close to Midway as possible. Ditching the **Daisy Mae** at sea within a short range of Midway Island may be the best plan, although they need to consider that the entire crew could die in a landing at sea.

On long missions like these, even minor wounds can prove fatal as rapid blood loss in combat can induce shock and shock can be a major killer. Many of the missions for the 42nd Squadron of the 11th Bomb Group were eight and nine hours long, with nowhere to land except the originating bomber base. All of the men on board know the danger they are facing. They buy into helping their shipmates and their country every time they climb aboard.

Daisy Mae Limps Across the Sky

"Sergeant Ambur, I order you to go back and talk to each of the crew. Tell them to pray for a safe return to Midway," Gall says.

Ambur salutes Gall, "Yes Sir, you can count on me for that."

As the Flight Engineer approaches each man, Ambur finds him in compliance. They are willing to listen to their older brother. One by one, each shipmate nods, understanding Gall's order. Each young man silently turns away and closes his eyes. There are no political or religious differences today. Some men make the sign of the cross in the Catholic tradition. Whether they are religious or not is not the point. Gall's order is part of their duty to their country and, by God; they are going to carry it out for themselves and the other brave brothers, some living and some dying on board the **Daisy Mae**. They all respect Gall and each other. They are All American Boys on an All American Mission. No one complains. Complaints are just something you see in the movies to make the movie more interesting. These heroes have flown every mission together, even ones on other bombers, the same exact way. They work together and they die together. No questions asked. No explanations are needed.

The heroes of the **Daisy Mae** are determined to complete their mission, today.

With the hopeful news about the fuel, there is no time to celebrate aboard as Ambur, Gall, Patterson and the others keep improvising on the way back to Midway. The pilot created a plan. All of the remaining crew have jobs to do in order to survive.

Gall orders Nose-Gunner Storts and Top-Turret Gunner Wyckoff to stay in what is left of the shot-up greenhouse in the nose of the plane, using their body weight to balance the bomber when it goes down into the ocean. They stay there the whole time without any intercom contact with the pilot or the rest of the plane. Their jobs as gunners change into jobs that are necessary to save lives upon landing. Doing their jobs in this way will prove just as important as battling enemy aircraft a few terrifying hours before.

Navigator Weiss pours over his maps, looking for any alternative places to land the severely wounded **Daisy Mae**.

Picture yourself looking over Ben's shoulder as he looks at his maps. Today if you could study a world globe or a world map, you will see exactly what Navigator Weiss is looking at on July 24, 1943. You and Ben are looking at the clear blue Pacific Ocean with no landmasses between Wake Island and Midway Island. There are four hours of sea below if the **Daisy Mae** had four healthy engines. Now Gall and Van Horn are forced to limp back with only three. It may take five or six hours at their reduced speed and there may not be enough fuel to make it. It is possible to locate a US submarine somewhere between them and Midway Island. It is also possible to be tracked by one of two Japanese submarines who are the early warning system between Midway and Wake Islands. The Japanese submarines will take no prisoners. Navigator Weiss goes over his findings with Gall and Van Horn.

What the crew does not realize right now, and we had better not tell them, is all four engines are leaking fuel.

The Deadly Storm

The storm is right where they left it, waiting for them. Thunder, lightning, rain and black skies attack the ship and due to the lack of windshield wipers, Gall and Van Horn have their heads out their side windows. The shipmates toss about the wounded bomber. High winds, not Zeros, are now attacking the ship. At least no one has to look out the windows at the storm, as they all know there are no other aircraft in the sky. All aircraft are grounded under these conditions and the other three bombers are hours ahead of the **Daisy Mae** if they are airborne at all.

Minutes seem like hours and hours seem like days as the wounded **Daisy Mae** limps across the sky. Someone on board is singing the official song of the 11th Bomb Group. You can hear these words right now:

> "Remember Pearl Harbor as we go to meet our foe."
> "Remember Pearl Harbor as we did the Alamo."

Joe Gall and Arvid Ambur successfully work out a system to transfer fuel from the dead engine to the working ones. Arvid returns to the cabin, "Sir, all of the fuel is transferred from the number two to the other engines. We should be okay, now."

Gall responds, "Thank you Sergeant. You give us hope again."

With the transfer complete, the crippled **Daisy Mae** has a slim chance to make the long journey back to Midway, if the damaged aircraft has enough working parts to survive that long. Instead of the planned four-hour trip back to Midway, they will have to allow for five or six hours, providing the fuel will suffice and the ship remains airborne. With all of the damage onboard, the odds are not in favor of the crew ever reaching Midway safely, but at least, the crew has a glimmer of hope. Sometimes hope is all you need.

Lt. Gall orders the men to lighten the load on the **Daisy Mae**. Cheerfully, they throw all of their machine guns, ammo, provisions, bombsights, cameras, helmets, gas masks and spare parts into the Pacific Ocean. They walk around ankle deep in spent machine gun shell casings, which they pitch as well. Flight Engineer Ambur carries the heavy Norden Bombsight toward the rear of the bomber where one of the gunners throws it out the left waist window to the sea below. Everything they have on board drops into the sea, except handguns and

Tommy Guns stay with the men in case a shootout is eminent, but everything else is expendable.

Some of the men are actually smiling and laughing for the first time all day. The fun they have pitching things, after staring death in the face repeatedly, actually uplifts their spirits. It gives them hope. They are ready to crash land at sea, face off with enemy submarine crews, or survive fighting off hungry sharks. These airmen feel like the Supermen they really are.

Finding no other place to land except Midway Island, Navigator Ben Weiss walks back to the rear of the plane and helps the badly wounded. Fran Perkins is weak from his tremendous loss of blood. Lt. Jensen and Pop Evans are in the worse shape and unconscious.

"Sergeant, do you have a girl back home?"

Nineteen-year-old Perkins nods. "Yes, Sir. Her name is Elaine." He hesitates and adds downcast, "I'm blind now though. She won't want me anymore."

Ben Weiss thinks for a moment and then speaks as a much older and wiser combat veteran would speak yet he was just slightly older than Perkins was. Smiling yet assuming the persona of a superior officer, Weiss orders, "Sergeant Perkins, ten years from now after this war is over, I want to visit you on Thanksgiving Day. As your superior officer, I order you to invite me over to your Thanksgiving dinner and I want Elaine to cook for us."

Fran responds loudly. "Yes Sir!" as he is trained to do when given a command by a superior officer.

Then Weiss kneels down and his voice softens as he says, "Remember this too, Fran. Joe Gall is the best pilot in the Army Air Corps and the **Daisy Mae** is the best bomber in the Grey Geese Squadron. You remember the crash landing at Barking Sands a month ago with the other

197

bomber, **Tail Wind**? We lost our number three engine and should have never walked away from that landing. Gall set us down so softly Lt. Jensen was sound asleep in the greenhouse. I could hear your buddy, Conley, snoring all the way from the tail gunner position to the cabin. Fran, we will get back safely. I promise you we will."

After a long pause, "Sir, can you navigate by the stars?" Fran says in a whisper.

"Sergeant Perkins, on all of our night missions I navigated by the stars. Today, we will be back in the late afternoon so it won't be dark enough for that. I need to go back to the cabin now, but we'll talk more at a better time, I promise."

Ben Weiss stares at Perkins, lying on the floor for a moment and then says loudly, "Never underestimate the power of hope."

Lt. Benjamin Weiss turns and walks quickly back to the cabin to work his navigational magic. The Navigator's words give Perkins encouragement coming from a respected officer. Fran instantly feels hope. Hope is a driving force and alive on the mission.

Officers and men did not fraternize, so the conversation makes Perkins smile a bit through his painful and weak condition. Fran is thinking that along with this lovable hunk of metal, **Daisy Mae** herself, they are united in getting back safely whether the bomber makes it all the way back to Midway or if they ditch the plane at sea short of their goal. If it is time for Fran to die, it is an honor to die with this amazing ship and extraordinary crew. He feels a sense of pride and a sense of peace comes over him. It feels like the warm Pacific waters washing over his body when swimming on the tropical beaches of Funafuti.

Fran thinks about the mysterious voice in his shot-up ball-turret. The voice assured him that this was not his time to die and he truly believes that voice now.

The Battle to Return Home

Daisy Mae Walks Across the Sky

Gall instructs Ambur to order Conley to ready the inflatable boats. If the **Daisy Mae** lands in the sea Conley's job is to dive out of the waist gunner window with the rafts and gather the wounded, get them into the rafts and help any other survivors as well. Just before diving out the window, both waist gunners will attach parachutes to both waist window gun mounts to help slow the plane. Everyone knows what to do. The odds are that the plane will ditch at sea after it runs out of fuel. Maybe they will land close enough to Midway that a submarine or patrol boat will see them. The airmen know the odds are slim the further out to sea they find themselves so they need to ditch close to the island.

Gall thanks Ambur for his service and orders him to stand on the catwalk over the bomb bay doors. Ambur's job is to dive out of the aircraft through the biggest hole he can find and then swim to the rear of the wreckage in the ocean to help Conley get the wounded into the rubber rafts. Gall viewed enough Pacific wrecks including the **Green Hornet** and **Superman** that he knows the light aluminum bomb bay doors will tear off in a water landing. Ambur will have a huge hole to swim out of the bomber, providing he can keep his balance and position during the crash landing. There will be a myriad of wires and cables in the wreckage, in which Ambur could get snarled. He must keep his eyes open underwater to make sure he doesn't get stuck or dragged down with a sinking ship.

Minutes seem like hours and the hours seem like days, as the severely wounded **Daisy Mae** slowly walks across the sky. Patterson is busy at the radio trying to get a signal from the tiny island of Midway across the many miles of open sea. The rest of the crew near the tail section of the **Daisy Mae** take care of the wounded. They say very little to each other as they sit on the plane, recovering from the shock of an unbelievable air battle held a short time earlier. Their thoughts are more personal now. When the able-bodied are not busy, they go back one by one to give the wounded men words of hope. Storts and Wyckoff are unable to go back

199

because they are using their bodies in the greenhouse to balance the ship and Ambur is balancing on the catwalk.

Wyckoff asks, "Why can't we go back there and help out with the wounded?"

Snuffy replies, "We are dead weight up here in the nose. I wish we could go back there and help the guys. But you know how easy it is to lose control of a Liberator. Gall and Van Horn have their hands full just keeping us in the air. These high winds and rain can be our undoing, long before we land at Midway."

The standard procedure in a normal landing situation is to raise the nose up and drop the tail. If Storts and Wyckoff are viewing the sky, they will be landing on a runway and the only runway they can be landing on would be at Midway Island.

The two men smile at each other and get as comfortable as one can when staring into the face of death.

Midway Air Control Tower

The storm has passed the island but the heavy dark clouds nearby and the reflection of lightning linger. The soft rumble of thunder is a frequent and a familiar sound.

In the Midway Air Control Tower, a young Army Air Corps private is operating the radio that sends out the audio beacon signal that bombers use to focus on to bring them back to the airfield safely. The young private is sending out the beacon and radio signal to find the missing plane.

No signal is coming back from the **Daisy Mae**.

It is very difficult for the Big Brown Bombers to find these remote coral atolls because they are just small rings of land surrounded by water and a lagoon in the center. They look like small Cheerios from the sky. If just less than one degree off in a compass reading, the **Daisy Mae** will never find the island. Honing in on the radio signal is the best bet for the crew of the **Daisy Mae** to find her way home.

After talking to Fran, Navigator Ben Weiss moves from the rear section of the **Daisy Mae** to the pilot's cabin to go over some last minute map readings. From Ben's calculations, they should be in range of the radio beacon, however **Daisy Mae**'s damaged radio is unable to receive transmissions.

It is close to 1700 hours and that is the end of the shift for the tower crew back on Midway when the signal is retired. Without the signal, the chances of the bomber finding Midway Island are remote and it might have to ditch at sea.

With repeated attempts from the Control Tower, still no signal is returned. A Captain comes up the ladder to check with the private. "Have you heard anything from the last B-24 Liberator, the **Daisy Mae?**"

"No, Sir. It's almost 1700 hours when I'm supposed to turn off the radio. They'll bust me if I leave it on, especially if any Japanese Betty Bombers are in the area, but I don't want to leave the **Daisy Mae** without a signal. Captain, what should I do?"

"Sign out at 1700 hours. I'll keep the beacon on. I will stay here all night if I have to. Those boys on the **Daisy Mae** deserve it." The Captain sits down in the chair facing the private and begins to tell a story.

The Pearl Harbor Connection

"I was on shore leave at the Army Air Corps barracks at Hickam Field in Hawaii when it was bombed on December 7, 1941," says the Captain. "The barracks was called the Hale Makai which means 'Inn by the Sea' and was three stories tall. It housed over 3200 men. It was the largest barracks in the world at the time. Airmen felt like they lived in a resort hotel. The sailors and marines stationed on Oahu hated us because they felt slighted by their living conditions as compared to ours.

"Many of my friends died in that barracks' attack. Over two hundred airmen out of three hundred in my group died during the Pearl Harbor and Hickam Airfield attacks. I still can see a B-18 bomber on fire on the runway and a maintenance man in one of the hangars running out toward the flight line. He jumped into the nose of the B-18 bomber while strafing machine gun bullets were raining down around him. The lone airman fired his machine gun at the Japanese fighter planes. The airman was a maintenance man, not a combat trained airman and on this day of infamy, he was a hero. He had to do something to get rid of those damned Zeros. The B-18 was on fire and exploding and the nose gun was still firing. I could hear the screams of the airman but the machine gun did not stop firing until the plane blew up. As sad as I felt for the maintenance man, I felt a sense of pride and hope at the same time. I found myself punching my fists at the menacing images in the sky. That nightmare meant that no matter how much we are outgunned and losing the battle, we can still win the War. We'll never give up. The men of the 11th Bomb Group are the bravest people alive. Private, did you know there are images of three Grey Geese on their patch insignia and their bomber rudders? Their unit motto stands for 'Progress Without Fear or Prejudice'.

"After the first wave of Japanese attackers moved off the island somebody handed me a shotgun and told me Japanese marines are landing on the beaches. That wasn't true, we found out later; however, we were ordered to find cover and stay and defend our foxhole until relieved.

"My shotgun didn't have any shells, but I figured the ammo would come later. I found a bomb depression that I used as a foxhole and another officer with his .45 caliber 1911 Colt pistol stayed with me all night. We were situated on the parade ground facing the flagpole.

"All night long shots were being fired in the air by all of us guys as planes were flying around everywhere. These were American planes we were shooting at, going up on patrols all night expecting to see Japanese ships and men invading our island."

"You were shooting at our own planes?" asked the private.

"We were flat out scared. We were shooting at anything that moved in the sky. No one was in charge. We felt all alone. Other airmen, civilian workers and sailors, stayed awake all night manning our makeshift battle stations.

"I don't think I slept at all, Private. Neither did the officer sharing my foxhole. At first light, there was a calm in the air. I guess many of the soldiers finally fell asleep as they ran out of ammo firing at the phantoms in the air or, perhaps like me, they were just overwhelmed by what they just witnessed. We were all in a state of shellshock. I looked at the flagpole about fifty yards away in the middle of the parade ground and I saw a tattered and torn Old Glory, still waving in the soft Pacific breeze.

"Just then, my new found friend and I witnessed something that stays with me right now. We both heard the voice of an Angel. It was a young teenage Hawaiian girl singing our National Anthem. She was escorted by two MPs armed with Thompson submachine guns. A ten-year-old Hawaiian boy was playing the ukulele to the Anthem. There were no buglers or military bands around, just a young girl singing and the little boy playing the ukulele. The girl sounded like an Angel. Immediately, I thought about my history lesson in elementary school where the teacher taught us about the flag at Fort McHenry where Francis Scott Key penned the words," And the rocket's red glare, the bombs bursting in air, gave proof through the night that our flag was still there."

"After the song, cheers exploded like rockets from all of the GIs hiding in bushes, under burning wreckage and in their foxholes all around Hickam. I saw men shaking their fists, yelling and punching the air.

They were resolved to come back and win the war. We lost the first round of the prizefight, but it's going to be a ten-round fight. We're not beaten. Not by a long shot.

"I owe it to those men to wait all night if I have to, signaling for the **Daisy Mae**. I don't care if they bust me down to private. Three beat up bombers landed today. I have no idea how. All of them except the first one, **Doity Goity**, were damaged beyond repair. They carried a dead crewmember out of **Wicked Witch**. They flew through hell. I overheard the briefing from the pilots. They talked about all of the remaining Zeros attacking **Daisy Mae**, as their bombers were putting distance between the **Daisy Mae** and the Zeros. There had to be 15 or 20 Zeros swarming all over the bomber. The pilots wished they could have bucked orders and helped the sitting duck, rather than flying straight home. All of the bombers had spent their ammunition and if they went back, they would only have been sitting ducks themselves. They would have not been able to save the **Daisy Mae**."

The private thought for a second and then asked permission to stay with the Captain.

"You know the risks, son. We could both be thrown out of this man's Army. I appreciate the company."

Taking a drag from his cigarette, the Captain adds as he nods towards a huge black cloud with flickering lightning far out at sea, "Private, the **Daisy Mae** is NOT dead yet. I can feel her in my bones. In fact, this sounds silly, but I can hear her singing to me right now."

The control tower picks up a weak signal in Morse code. Was this the missing ship? The three remaining bombers in the raid landed on Midway hours before. Only one, **Doity Goity** will fly again. The **Wicked Witch** and the **Sky Demon** made it home but were damaged in the raid and may never fly again. Marines push the planes off the runway.

The Battle to Return Home

Both Private and Captain listen intently as the weak signal gains strength.

They copy down the Morse code and it says, "Big Girl Coming Home… Big Girl Coming Home…" The Captain and Private jump for joy almost knocking over the table between them. The Big Girl can only be one ship still in the air.

The signal is coming from Staff Sergeant Robert Patterson, the wounded radio operator with hunks of metal still sticking out of his legs, aboard the wounded **Daisy Mae**! Patterson's shot-up radio is sending a stronger signal now. Patterson receives no signal back due to the damaged condition of the radio, but the air control tower on Midway will alarm the marines and sailors to get their medical people ready in the airfield hospital.

A Lanky Marine

A young lanky marine sits on the beach staring at the vast Pacific Ocean, pensively watching the waves go in and out. He is lonely for his girlfriend back home and misses his Mom and Dad and the rest of his family. He hasn't seen them in over a year. He thinks about his friends fighting and dying as the Americans begin their advance toward Japan. He examined the three bombers that returned today and studied the damage. One Liberator was sitting near the end of the runway too tired to move a few feet further. The marine knew they went through hell in that clear Pacific sky. He envisions the **Daisy Mae**, alone in the sky fighting off a swarm of Japanese Zeros, going down in the Pacific. He only wishes that the men had quick deaths and felt no pain. He is alone and depressed. Like flames, fear engulfs his body and hopelessness floods his very soul. He can't remember a time in his life when he felt this depressed. He has just reached the lowest point possible.

The Battle to Return Home

As he scans the skies for the **Daisy Mae**, all the lanky marine can see is an enormous dark cloud with occasional flashes of lightning and the rumbling of thunder off in the distance. The rumbling makes him think the air battle is continuing. The wind is blowing from behind his back; therefore, if the ship is nearby, he will not hear the three struggling engines working as hard as they can to get back to the safety of Midway.

Aboard the **Daisy Mae**, the crew in the cabin is getting ready to crash land. Through a small crack in the clouds, Van Horn, spots Midway's Eastern Island, the same airfield from which they began their long journey many hours before. Navigator Ben Weiss confirms the location on his map. There are no brakes to slow down the **Daisy Mae** once it reaches the air base. Van Horn looks out his window at engines three and four. They seem tired but they have only a few more miles to go and a few more rotations of the blades to end their deadly ordeal.

Young men in those days worked with metal a great deal because even all of the childhood toys were made of metal. As the young men fixed their baby brothers' or sisters' toys, they learned that metal has memory.

Daisy Mae is a big hunk of shot-up metal, but she has a memory. She remembers back on May 27, when carrying another crew piloted by Lt. Joe Deasy, she overshot three men in a lifeboat from another B-24, the **Green Hornet**. The **Green Hornet**'s crew was the same crew that crashed landed Superman just days before. **Daisy Mae** did not have a way to signal Deasy's crew, searching for the stranded men in the life raft directly below. **Daisy Mae** also fondly remembers when Gall landed her friend, Tail Wind gently on Barking Sands on Kauai after her landing gear would not come down affecting minimal damage.

Gall has a loving touch at the controls. Today the **Daisy Mae** has a chance to help her favorite crew. Along with Van Horn sitting just above her image, she can see Midway's Eastern Island as she is peeking through the clouds just below his viewing position. **Daisy Mae** wonders how she can help this brave crew. So far, she has done everything possible and she only has a few miles left. She gives it all she's got.

In the cabin, all you hear are huge engines and the air whistling through more than 800 bullet and cannon holes in the aircraft. It is an eerie sound, almost as if **Daisy Mae** is trying to calm the crew by singing a song.

Daisy Mae Marches Across the Sky

Now there are three pilots in the cockpit, Lt. Gall, Co-pilot Van Horn and Navigator Ben Weiss.

Weiss sports a huge grin as his confidence in Joe Gall's flying and landing skills is evident. Weiss thinks, "Now we have a chance. Now we have hope."

With damage to the altimeter and other instruments, Gall does not want to leave anything to pilot error. He orders Weiss to call out the altitude as they are descending in one-thousand foot increments and then one-hundred foot increments and finally, call out in 10-foot increments until the bomber touches the runway.

After over nine straight hours in the air, all the men are worn out. Gall desires a perfect landing for the valiant crew, some of them wounded and possibly dying. The rest are at their positions and fighting to do their jobs in spite of the fear and shock they had experienced a few hours before.

Evergreen Park, Illinois

At this very moment, 10:55 PM Chicago time, young Elaine Birmingham is at home at 9336 Clifton Park Avenue Evergreen Park, Illinois. It is nearing 11:00 PM and Clarence and Mae Birmingham want young Elaine to get her sleep, even on a weekend. Elaine enjoyed the movie, *Cabin in the Sky*, with her friends Marge and Sophie a few hours earlier. What she never found out was that a B-24 Bomber with the same name, **Cabin in the Sky**, battled for its life over the Pacific Ocean around the same time Elaine and her friends were watching the movie. Elaine is very restless so she decides to pray the Rosary for her true love, Fran, and the rest of the crew of his favorite ship, the **Daisy Mae**. Elaine is a good Catholic girl. Tonight she feels a sense of urgency in her prayers and prays as hard as she can.

Let's pretend we can travel back through time and watch young Elaine praying. She is kneeling beside her bed with the rosary beads interlaced among her fingers. If you listen closely, you can hear her soft voice saying the words in Latin. Elaine feels that speaking in a language that sounds holy may get God's attention quicker. Maybe God will really hear her prayers. Maybe God will answer her prayers.

As Elaine presses one of the rosary beads, listen to her say, "saecula saeculorum." In English, these words translate to" world without end." If any of Fran's shipmates make it to Midway alive, life for future generations of their descendants will be possible. The crew labors to pay life forward. Whoever returns alive may truly begin a world without end. This is the goal now for the airborne band of brothers. "If I don't make it, please help my shipmate get back alive so he can live his life for me." This is the prevailing silent thought of each **Daisy Mae** crewmember.

About halfway through her beads, Elaine climbs into bed and she falls into a deep, sound sleep, exhausted from her big day.

At this very moment over the blue Pacific Ocean, the **Daisy Mae** is preparing for her final descent on the Eastern Island of Midway. Gall orders Navigator Benjamin Weiss to call out the altitude one last time, **loud and clear**.

The Final Descent

In the greenhouse, Nose Gunner Storts and Top-Turret Gunner Wyckoff are using their bodies as ordered by Gall to balance the ship. If they land on the runway, they will be the last to touch ground. If they land at sea, the pilot's job is to go in nose first. Storts and Wyckoff will get the first look at the Pacific Ocean and perhaps a pelting of broken Plexiglas from the turret making contact with the sea. Both heroes consider themselves lucky, however, to see the familiar Eastern Midway Island coming up quickly ahead. Most crash victims are never that lucky.

In the cabin, Gall and Van Horn are at the pilot and co-pilot controls. Navigator Ben Weiss is standing centered and just behind them. Weiss is getting ready to call out the altitude as Gall and Van Horn prepare to land this twenty-ton comet. Just outside Van Horn's window is the cartoon image of **Daisy Mae** from the Li'l Abner cartoon painted on the co-pilot's side of the B-24D Liberator. She is standing with her left hand outstretched as if to say "Howdy." There is a smile on **Daisy Mae**'s face.

In the bomb bay area, Flight Engineer Arvid Ambur is trying to balance himself on the catwalk. It is too narrow to put his feet side by side so the flight engineer has to balance himself with one foot in front of the other and shift his body weight back and forth or side to side to keep from falling on or through the bomb bay doors. Ambur concentrates on getting through a landing at sea and swimming to help the wounded in the rear of the plane. His thoughts are on his men and the saving of lives.

In the rear of **Daisy Mae** Tail-Gunner Earl Conley and Radioman Robert Patterson are helping the wounded. Conley is still able-bodied and is securing the parachutes to the machine gun mounts in an effort to slow down **Daisy Mae**, once she touches down. She will be barreling down the runway at over 200 miles per hour with nothing to slow the momentum except for the friction of her wheels touching the pavement. Now Conley is getting the two inflatable rafts ready to throw out the window as close to the projected crash site as possible.

209

The Battle to Return Home

Conley turns to Perkins as he is readying the clumsy parachutes and says, "Fran, we will hit land or water in just a few minutes. With all of the holes in the ship right beneath you, do you think you will be able to tell whether we land at sea or on land?"

Fran becomes wide-awake now and responds, "Yes, Earl, I'll yell out if we touch down in water. Right now I can feel warm outside air shooting up my back from the bullet and cannon holes."

"We're still a good team, Fran. I promise to get you out of here alive."

Bombardier Lt. Jensen and Photographer Joseph "Pop" Evans lie next to the wounded Belly Gunner Fran Perkins. Evans and Jensen are unconscious and Perkins is blind and weak from loss of blood, but he fights to stay awake, as he knows he is on the best ship flown by the best pilots in the US Army Air Corps. He is confident Gall will save the day with another perfect crash landing. If not, he feels lucky he was able to crawl back into the **Daisy Mae** and die with his shipmates. A spirit of peace fills his mind, body and soul.

With the Eastern Island of Midway in view, the **Daisy Mae** begins her final descent. Fran feels it as his ears begin to ring with the steep decline of every few hundred feet of elevation. He swallows to relieve the pressure. Fran feels safe, as he knows the long, bloody fight will soon be over. Whether he lives or dies, the personal drama will vanish.

Then Fran begins to hear a beautiful male voice. He recognizes it is a tenor, as he remembers Elaine teaching him various vocal types at a concert they attended in Chicago a summer before. The voice is singing *Nearer, My God to Thee* made famous by sinking of the Titanic back in 1912. Fran knows that this is it.

In the cabin, Navigator Ben Weiss is counting off the altitude in hundreds of feet as Gall and Van Horn begin a gradual descent. Weiss shouts so the pilot and co-pilot are sure to hear and react accordingly, "1000! ... 900! ... 800!"

As the Navigator counts aloud, Van Horn turns to Gall and gives him a salute. Flight Officer John Van Horn says, "Sir, it has been an honor and a privilege to serve you and the entire crew of the **Daisy Mae**." With a lump in his throat, Gall returns the salute and then refocuses on the landing. Both Gall and Van Horn are determined to get **Daisy Mae** back to earth safely. Everyone aboard braces for the crash.

Near the airfield, the lanky marine on Midway looks in the direction of the long dark cloud. He sees an image in the heavens above. He blinks and shakes his head a couple of times; maybe it is just a mirage. Is he daydreaming? He keeps watching and he makes out the unmistakable profile of a large four-engine bomber with twin rudders. This has to be the **Daisy Mae!** It is coming out of the cloud at the very location the lanky marine was hoping and praying it would. The marine's body snaps to full alert! The awareness of a soldier responding to an emergency overcomes all other emotions right now. A United States Marine always knows what to do in an emergency.

Ben Weiss continues with his count. "600! ...500! ...400!"

In the rear of the bomber, Perkins hears the end of *Nearer, My God to Thee* and then the beautiful tenor voice switches to something more alive and upbeat. The new song is the ever-popular *Boogie Woogie Bugle Boy of Company B*, a hit song by the Andrew Sisters that became an anthem for every fighting man in World War II.

Lying on his back weak from wounds, blind, and expecting his death, Fran Perkins smiles.

Chapter 13

The Last Landing of the **Daisy Mae**

The mission began on Oahu, Hawaii yesterday. Today **Daisy Mae** took off from Midway just before 0800 hours and then engaged the Japanese Zeros near Wake Island in the early afternoon. Driving through a killing storm on the way to Wake and most of the way back, these men are exhausted, but all of the men execute their jobs to save each other. They sacrifice and are willing to sacrifice even more if it is needed.

"I must survive," each man thinks privately. "If I don't make it, I will make damn sure my brother makes it." That brother includes all of the faithful crew that fought so long together and it also includes Sgt. Joseph P. Evans, the Aerial Photographer who is not a member of the crew but is now a brother just the same.

The men work together to make sure one or all will make it back to Midway safely.

Everything happens quickly. In the air, the **Daisy Mae** marches across the sky. As the Big Girl is reaching the ground, without any brakes, she will accelerate like a high-speed racecar that is out of control.

Storts and Wyckoff in the greenhouse see the marines with stretchers racing toward the opposite end of the runway. Even the marines and sailors stationed at the anti-aircraft positions are abandoning their guns and racing flat out toward the end of the runway where the sand on the beach meets the shark-infested waters. Everyone on the base is in motion. Men in their hospital gowns are walking or limping toward the aircraft. The walking wounded are going to do anything they can to help.

The lanky marine is also in motion. The Big Girl filled him with hope just a few minutes before and, by God, he is going to run through fire, if

212

he must, to save the crew. "This is what marines do," he remembers. "I'm going to be the first responder to the ship! I'm going to save lives!"

Weiss is still calling out the altitude numbers, by tens of feet now, "100! ...90! ...80!"

Encouraged and more exhilarated than ever, Gall, Weiss and Van Horn feel the landing gear engage the pavement on Midway's short runway. Gall has the Brown Bomber's nose facing slightly upward and **Daisy Mae** waving "Howdy," to all the young marines, sailors, and airmen racing to help her and the precious cargo she protects.

No one remembers how fast **Daisy Mae** was racing across the runway that day. It was a streaking comet. Perkins, lying on his back pressed against the hull, could not feel the touchdown. Gall is making one of his patented soft landings. This is Gall's way of showing a deep appreciation for the wounded and dying inside. Even though **Daisy Mae** is shot full of holes and all engines are sustaining total damage, he lands the **Daisy Mae** exactly where you would expect the "best damn pilot in the whole damned Army Air Corps," to land a plane.

Gall softly touches down dead center on the runway!

Dead ahead at the end of the runway, stands one of the three destroyed bombers from the mission. The marines did not push this one off into the sand. Gall makes quick movements with the stick and gives gas to the number one engine, and **Daisy Mae** performs a do-si-do around the twenty-ton giant, as if she is at a square dance in Al Capp's mythical cartoon town of Dogpatch.

Parachutes deploy from the waist gunner machine gun mounts perfectly but **Daisy Mae** is not slowing down as quickly as needed. Instinctively, Gall and Van Horn keep trying the brakes, even though they remember what Flight Engineer Ambur said hours before, "There will be no brakes upon landing."

Perkins, lying on his back feels the plane go off the runway, possibly into the ocean. As the **Daisy Mae** strikes sand in the minefield guarding the air base, he feels the force of the sand and water exploding against his back. Water and sand come flying through the windows and the bullet holes at a rapid pace.

Perkins shouts, "Water, Conley, Water!"

Conley dives head first out the window to ready the rafts in the sea. Explosions are caused by the **Daisy Mae** touching off mines located in the minefield along the runway where Lt. Gall wills the veering steel bomber. Conley is going to make sure he is ready to help any crewmembers should anyone survive at the end of this wild ride. Instead of landing in the shark-infested Pacific Ocean, Conley lands head first in the exploding mine field.

Simultaneously, **Daisy Mae** completes her last duty. She stops before breaking up at sea. The nose wheel on the mighty B-24D Liberator collapses in the deep sand and the **Daisy Mae**'s mission is over. The Big Girl stops dead and rocks back and forth in the sand gently, as if she is rocking her crew to sleep, cradling them in her loving arms.

Twice in his military career, Staff Sergeant Earl W. Conley flies out of a speeding airplane without wearing a parachute. This time it is his own choice. Landing in a minefield, he bounces and rolls in the sand. He rumbles, bumbles, stumbles catching his balance, and finds himself on a small hill in the middle of the sandy and scratchy coral beach. He is covered from head to toe with beach sand and debris from the numerous explosions around him. He looks at his feet and sees a rope tied from his foot to one of the life rafts about fifty feet away. He remembers tying a parachute to his foot while in Aerial Gunnery School months before, which saved his life. Earl W. Conley is good at tying knots.

Sitting on his sandy hill, Conley watches a surrealistic scene of marines and corpsmen frantically risking their lives by running through the exploding minefield in **Daisy Mae**'s wake. They will reach the injured men or die trying. **Daisy Mae** used her body to set off explosions, giving the trailing marines safe passage to her endangered crew. Skidding along the runway and through the sandy beach, her aluminum bomb bay doors, considered the weak link of the ship, proved her strength in keeping Arvid Ambur safe.

Conley laughs aloud as he thinks about the last thing his friend, Fran, said to him, "Water Conley, Water." Laughing, Earl leaps to his feet, extends both arms straight up in the air just like Joe Lewis the Brown Bomber. Jubilantly he shouts at the top of his lungs, "CALHOUN'S THE NAME!" Running flat out at top speed now to complete his vow to help Fran Perkins and his other brothers aboard the **Daisy Mae** arms still raised in victory, he joyfully shouts, "Calhoun's the name!"

Daisy Mae Waves Her Last Goodbye

As **Daisy Mae** stops in the deep sand, resting on the beach just a few feet from the ocean, Conley and pursuing United States Marines hear a long, loud hissing sound coming from the Big Girl. It sounds like a defiant statement to her attackers back on Wake.

"You can't stop me, Japan! I am a champion. Hear me roar!"

The Brown Bomber wins the ten-round fight and completes her mission. Now pursuing marines hear a loud groan from the beached bomber as it stops dead in the sand. The **Daisy Mae** is finished. She will never fly again, nor some of her loyal crew.

Marines, risking their lives by running through the exploding mine field to help the struggling crew on board, gently carry the wounded from the **Daisy Mae**. They give reassurances to the wounded. Help is on the way.

Navigator Ben Weiss, points out the men at most risk being the first carried through the minefield back to the emergency field hospital. As Evans and Jensen are carried to the field hospital, Weiss gently whispers

215

in each of their ears. The Navigator wants to make sure they understand they both were heroes and saved the lives of the rest of the crew.

Perkins wants to stay until Evans and Jensen, the most critically wounded, are carried off. He reaches out one of his hands to touch the metal doorframe. He cares about the ship and the men bringing him back to the living. He pets the frame with his fingers as if he is petting a dog or a horse. He wishes he could stay with **Daisy Mae** forever.

Fran is trying to peek through the mountain of bandages on his face, but it is of no use. Perkins is blind. Two marines place Fran on the stretcher. When a person is stricken blind, other senses begin to take over immediately. Fran develops his sense of sonar to figure out size and shape by sound. One sound comes from a long, lanky marine supporting his upper body at the head of the stretcher. The other is a shorter but more muscular frame at the foot of the stretcher.

He thanks the marine supporting his head and privately names him Lanky.

13-1 Port side of Daisy Mae

*13-2 Starboard side of **Daisy Mae***

"You Are Guarded by United States Marines"

As the two young marines pick up the stretcher with young Fran onboard, they wait near the door for the rest of the crew to leave the wreckage. The marine at the foot of the stretcher, speaks in a loud and clear voice with determination and authority.

"Determined", as Fran will refer to him later says loudly, "Sir, you are safe...you are guarded by United States Marines." Lanky reached the **Daisy Mae** first with Determined a scant second behind him. Both marines are ready to die if needed be to protect their wounded man. That is what marines do.

Conley catches up with Perkins languishing on the stretcher, "We're all safe now, Partner. You get yourself fixed up and I'll see you sooner rather than later!"

For the first time in the nine-hour mission nineteen-year-old Sergeant Francis J. Perkins Jr. falls asleep. A lanky young marine carries Fran out gently. This marine was hopeless while sitting on the beach just a few minutes before. Now, he radiates hope. Lanky passes near the door of the **Daisy Mae** and sees a small piece of shot up metal hanging from a thin strip of steel from the ceiling. He takes a pocketknife, cuts down the piece and puts it in his pocket. Lanky thinks, "This is going to be my good luck charm."

Lt. Myron W. Jensen, Staff Sergeant Francis J. Perkins Jr., Staff Sergeant Robert Patterson, and Staff Sergeant Joseph "Pop" Evans are carried to the field hospital. Evans dies in transit and Jensen dies at the hospital, both understanding their sacrifice and bravery helped save the lives of **Daisy Mae**'s crew, as well as the other crews in the bombing formation.

Bombardier Lt. Jensen volunteered to shoot from a waist gunner position. He saved the ship by firing a gun. Pop Evans saved the crew by waving a dismissing arm, letting Sergeant Arvid Ambur do his job and get Jensen's waist gun back in service. Both men died heroes on the beach of the small Pacific island known as Midway.

Chapter 14

Hospitals and Hope

Fran is still groggy from the trip on a medical evacuation airplane from Midway to the hospital in Hawaii. He doesn't remember what happened to the rest of his crew. He remembers he heard marines carrying Lt. Jensen and Staff Sergeant Evans out of the plane. "What happened to my buddy, Earl Conley?" Fran anxiously thinks to himself. "He's my brother. I hope he is okay."

An emergency team of doctors scrubs up and unwraps the emergency bandages very carefully. They ask Fran what he recalls of the battle. Disoriented Fran hesitantly speaks; he wants to know who these people are. Since Fran has no sight, could these people be Japanese? Is he in Hawaii or on Wake Island?

Out of his blind darkness, Fran hears a young woman's voice. "I see from your dog tags you're from Chicago. I lived in Chicago while studying at John Hopkins for many years before becoming a nurse here in Hawaii. Tell me, are you a Cubs fan or a White Sox fan. You can't be both."

The female voice passes the first test. The Japanese would never know the simple facts each Chicago Cub and each Chicago White Sox fan shares.

"I'm a White Sox fan," Fran says through the bandages. "I live on the South Side of Chicago.

The young woman gives him a sip of water. "Good answer, Sergeant," the young nurse says in a soft but firm voice. "Last summer, I took my family to a game and watched Shortstop Luke Appling foul off ten pitches before he hit a line drive double down into the left field corner. I

219

was hoping the ball would bounce in our direction so I could give it to my little son, David. My oldest, Mary Jane also loves the Sox. I had to leave my youngest, Robin, at home with my sisters Hilda and Marge.

"Luke Appling is the best player on the White Sox. I hope I get to see him play again," Perkins says glumly.

"I will be straight with you, Sergeant. Because of the gun sight embedded in your skull and all of the shrapnel, you may never gain any vision at all. There is just too much damage. However, if you give me your complete attention at all times and listen to your surgeon, we will give you a fighting chance. Your surgeon is from Australia and he is the best in the world at repairing massive eye damage."

"I will take a fighting chance every day of the week. That is what Lt. Gall gave us on every mission. He gave us a fighting chance."

"Well, think of me as Lt. Gall or as your drill instructor. You must do everything I tell you and not question why. That begins with staying inside your head brace at all times. The doctors did not remove all of the shrapnel nor the front gun sight yet. It is going to take time and it is going to take obeying orders from the doctors and myself. Do you understand?"

"Yes, Sir," Perkins replies with hope coming from his heart and soul.

"You are not to address me by name at any time. Call me Nurse and I will call you Sergeant. Do you understand?"

"Yes, Nurse!"

Nurse, the consummate Chicago White Sox fan, tightens the brace around Fran's head. He is looking straight ahead with considerable pain.

"You are not allowed to have visitors, Sergeant. This is to keep your head still and to help you heal quicker so you can go home. Think of this

220

as a Top Secret mission. Can you carry out a mission without divulging Top Secret information?"

"Yes, Nurse! I know it is a long shot to get my vision back, but I always bet on the long shot." At the same time, he remembers the Top Secret information presented by Major Perry 'Tosh' McIntosh about the capabilities and manufacturing behind the B-24 Liberator. "Yes, Nurse, I always bet on the long shot."

The Nurse replies, "You have your orders. I will have marine guards posted outside twenty-four hours a day until we have the all clear. The all clear comes when we have all of the shrapnel out and you are ready to move on. These are your orders, Sergeant, and that is all."

Instinctively, Perkins salutes Nurse as she gives commands the same way his Air Corps officers present theirs. The medical team leaves and they come back several times in the next week to dig around in Fran's head. He complains loudly until his favorite nurse reminds him who is boss on this floor.

"You are the Nurse and you are the boss of me," Perkins submits.

Daily, after the nurse and doctors leave, Perkins tries to sleep. His logical brain knows it is the best way to heal, but the rest of his body wants to join his crew in another Liberator. His head is constantly hurting because of the doctors digging around in his eyes and the steel head brace pushing in hard on his head.

The Sound of Whispers

One night Fran hears the *Sound of Retreat* on Armed Forces Radio. He enjoys listening to entertainers like Bob Hope, Bing Crosby and the Andrew Sisters. He remembers how Clarence Birmingham, Elaine's dad, loves to hear Jack Benny. While listening to the bugle play *Sound of Retreat*, he remembers a long time ago when he stopped to salute at a flagpole in Texas. Fran remembers very vividly his meeting with Major

McIntosh. He remembers McIntosh told him he wishes Fran should see the clear water while taking off from Midway. Fran remembers leaving Major McIntosh and hearing the *Sound of Retreat*. He remembers reading McIntosh's kind note when Perkins sat down on his bunk.

"I never returned the Major's salute while taking off at Midway. Now I never will. I wish I had. I wish I could have done more during the battle. I wish hadn't got hit and blinded. I should have done more for my brothers."

The only way Fran can tell whether it is night or day is the amount of noise, he hears coming from the hallways and other rooms. Fran cannot turn his head. He remembers Nurse's order, not to even try turning it.

The radio seems to lose volume late at night and now Fran can barely hear a sound. No more Jack Benny or Bob Hope. No more Bing Crosby or any of the wonderful entertainers who volunteer to be in the line of fire, trading their talent for a front row seat on America's front lines. Fran thinks about the best-traveled front line USO entertainer. He is a man whose last name epitomizes the gift he gave to the men and women who served their country. His name is Hope... Bob Hope.

Radio volume is lost now and Fran scoots up in his bed. He hears the sound of his door opening. "Who is there?" Fran blurts out. Fran hears tiptoe footsteps coming close to his bed. He hears a whisper in his right ear.

"Fran, listen to me. Do not turn your head. Keep your eyes and head forward. I have information you need to hear right now. First, in a few days, they will take your bandages off. You will be able to see again but only in one eye. The other one will move with your good eye, but you will never see out of it again. Having just one eye will not burden you much after you get used to it. You will be able to go back to Elaine and have a long and wonderful life together. You will be able to hold a job, have kids and maybe you will even build your own house from scratch.

222

It will be hard work but you are up to the task. You have the fighting spirit of a ball-turret gunner! Am I right, Fran?"

"Yes, Sir. I will do whatever it takes to get back to normal."

The voice continues. "I have to leave now, but you must promise me you will never tell a soul about my coming here. Do you understand me?"

"Yes Sir," he says skeptically.

The whispered voice continues, "Put your right hand out."

Fran opens his hand and feels a small object placed in the center of his hand. It feels like a coin of some type.

The voices whispers, "Don't take any wooden nickels."

"Sir, can you tell me your name?" Perkins asks.

There are sounds that evoke emotions. There is the sound of a newborn baby crying. There are sounds of coins pouring through a slot machine when you hit the jackpot. Then, there is the unmistakable sound of a three-letter word when that sound spelled F-U-N.

Fran hears the visitor walk to the door, turn and face him lying helplessly in the bed and then hears the most beautiful unmistakable sound he will ever hear again in his life. What must be coming from some hidden loudspeakers, Fran hears in the loudest and clearest tones imaginable.

"CALHOUN'S THE NAME!'

The door closes and then opens quickly as the marine guard and the nurse burst into Fran's hospital room. "Who was here?" Nurse angrily asks the marine guarding the door.

"No one, Nurse," the guard replies. "I have been here all by myself. There was nobody here except the patient. He was sleeping in bed all night."

"I don't believe you," Nurse says sternly. She turns to Fran and says, "Sergeant, are you awake?"

Yes, Nurse. I just woke up. You two made a lot of noise." Fran says while not trying to laugh.

The nurse demands, "Was anyone here?"

"No, Nurse, that big lug of a marine guard read me a bedtime story and then he left," Fran, responds.

"Nurse, what is this?" Fran opens his right hand and presents the Nurse the round object left in his hand by his secret night visitor.

Nurse turns on a bright light over Fran's bed and reads the coin to herself. After a moment, she says. "It is a coin from Buffalo Bill's Wild West Show.

"Now everyone, who is not supposed to be here, get out! Sergeant, please go back to sleep immediately. Do you understand me?" Nurse sounds enraged. Then she says something that takes Fran off guard although she says these words in the same lecturing tone. "Don't take any wooden nickels."

"Yes, Nurse, I won't," says Perkins while restraining a well needed laugh.

The door in Fran's room closes and he can hear Nurse and Big Lug Marine Guard arguing in the hallway. Fran is trying to hold back laughter the same way he and Conley tried to restrain their laughs back on the **Daisy Mae** during their pajama party one scary night on Guadalcanal.

224

Fran holds both hands over his mouth, as he does not want Nurse to come back in while in the chewing-out mode. Fran's body shakes. The heavy steel framed hospital bed sits on wheels. The wheels have a lever that locks them in place in order to keep the bed from moving by itself all over the room. Night visitor Larry Calhoun quietly took the brakes off while whispering to Fran. Fran's vibrating action from laughing is causing the bed to move across the room like a broken field runner in football. Fran feels the true power of laughter as his suppressed laughing is moving the bed all over the room, bumping into things before it instantly changes direction.

He knows that Calhoun's words are true. He will get better. Life is too much fun to have it any other way. "At least Calhoun didn't set off firecrackers," Fran laughs even harder at the thought.

Finally, after the hilarity dies down and he becomes exhausted, Fran whispers to himself, "Thank you, Larry, for saving my life."

Sergeant, What Is My Name?

The next day is hectic. The Doctor was supposed to be in at 9AM but he had another emergency eye surgery case to work on. It is now past 11AM. Fran becomes agitated. One way or another, he wants those bandages removed today. If he is going to be permanently blind, so be it. Although he does like the option, he thinks he heard from his friend, Larry Aloysius Calhoun III. If my Flight mate has inside information, I am betting on that information.

Finally, Nurse and Doctor come in Fran's room a little after noon. Without any fanfare, Nurse unwraps the bandages and says, "Sergeant, keep your eyes closed until Doctor tells you to open them."

"Yes, Nurse," Perkins replies.

She takes off the bandages and then retreats by the door. Doctor is sitting right next to Fran on the bed waiting for Fran to open his eyes.

225

"Sergeant, climb out of bed and then I will count to three. At the count of three, open your eyes.

"Yes, Doctor," Fran replies.

Fran is standing now and facing the door.

The Doctor counts, "One, two get ready now, and three. Open your eyes." Fran opens his eyes. He now has one black eye and one blue eye staring out in space.

Nurse takes over now as Doctor is just a few feet away watching Fran's eye movements very closely. "Sergeant, look across the room at me and do your best to read my name tag. Tell me my name." Nurse points at her own nametag with her right forefinger. "Tell me my name."

Fran tries to focus his one good eye on her nametag. He turns his head to the left slightly as if ignoring his left eye, now black in color, and focuses on the nametag with his right eye. "Nurse, your name is O'Connor. Nurse O'Connor," Fran whispers weakly as if he thinks this is just wishful thinking.

"Sergeant, I need you to speak louder so I can hear you," Nurse O'Connor commands as if she is a drill instructor.

Perkins says forcefully, "Nurse O'Connor!"

"You are correct, Sergeant."

The last thing he saw was a second Japanese Zero, exploding from his deadly aim. Now he is safe from harm, watching caring doctors and nurses. Fran's mind, body and soul are overwhelmed with joy to the point of tears! He has his life and his dreams back. A life in which he can see. Just before tears of joy explode, Nurse O'Connor's facial expression changes from compassion and gratitude to a stern game face and gives Fran direct orders.

"Sergeant, I need you to lubricate both of your eyes. I can go ahead and shove some eye drops in your eyes but I have a better plan. Your own natural fluids are better than eye drops. Here is a towel. Doctor and I have to make the rounds and we will be back in an hour. I expect you to lubricate your eyes with your natural tears. They work better than water because they contain your own antibodies. Do you understand me, Sergeant?"

Emotion overcomes Fran. He is too emotional to speak, so he nods and buries his head in an enormous towel. Doctor and Nurse leave the room. Fran plans to carry out the orders given to him by Nurse Virginia O'Connor, a fellow Chicago White Sox fan. He plans to do a good job at filling his eyes with his own personal lubricant.

Chapter 15

The Second Bombing of Wake Island

After Fran was loaded onto the medical evacuation plane on the night of July 24, the surviving **Daisy Mae** crew met with Gall. All of the men were in a state of shock. They just needed to be together and to grieve silently. Few words were spoken. They were just glad to see the remaining shipmates and remember those who will never join them again.

Sunday July 25, 1943, on the Eastern Island of Midway, the Chaplain assembles the crew in formation for a burial ceremony. The chaplain begins with, "On behalf of the President of the United States and the People of a grateful nation..." These were some of the words heard by the remaining crewmembers of the **Daisy Mae**. The surviving crew accompanies their dead brothers out to sea, where in accordance to Naval Regulations at Midway at the time, the flag-draped fallen heroes are quietly slipped into the peaceful Pacific Ocean.

*15-1 The last crew of the **Daisy Mae***

Lt. Gall and Flight Officer Van Horn silently stand next to each other during the military ceremony as they accompany their shipmates out to sea. Lt. Gall wears dark aviator glasses. He wants to appear strong for his remaining crewmembers and dares not to reveal his eyes.

Van Horn remembers Perkins and Conley plugging his co-pilot chair with .45 caliber bullets back on Guadalcanal after a scary night on guard duty. Van Horn smiles to himself. He is too choked up to talk. "The gunners saved my life. Working together, we saved as many lives as we could. I hope we will meet again when it is our time to go."

After the short service and burial at sea for Bombardier Lt. Myron Jensen and Aerial Photographer Staff Sergeant Joseph "Pop" Evans, the crew walks around the Eastern Island of Midway in a daze. At 1800 hours, they meet for a briefing with the rest of the squadron to discuss Day 2 of the remaining mission tomorrow. This is the second bombing of Wake Island. Only four of the ten assigned bombers made it to the target on Day 1 leaving much of the work that was planned for this operation unfinished. The unexpected dogfights that were encountered on Day 1 negatively affected the results of the operation. New defensive strategies need to be formalized for this bombing. The Grey Geese need to finish the job they began on Saturday.

On the beach where the **Daisy Mae** finished her mission, a mechanic drains the engines and the fuel tanks. The engines that served the **Daisy Mae** so well were totally fried. None of the engines can be salvaged. The mechanic walks over to his supervisor and shows him there are only thirteen gallons of gasoline left on the ship.

The supervisor, Steve, chews on a sloppy, wet cigar and scratches his head as he looks at the gas can and then back at the **Daisy Mae**. "I can't believe it!" said Steve, scratching and shaking his head. "How was that ship able to fly?"

The **Daisy Mae** had barely enough fuel for five more minutes of flight. In the air, Gall and Van Horn squeezed out every bit of life out of this

229

amazing ship with Navigator Ben Weiss calculating and recalculating his bearings while making stuff up along the way to perfection. If he calculated only a fraction of a degree off, Gall and Van Horn would have ditched at sea. All would have been lost, as they would have landed in shark-infested waters.

What a glorious ride, indeed! Eleven men and a heroic ship made it home together.

The following day, Monday July 26 1943, the remaining crew without any rest or recovery saddle up a new bomber to finish what they started on Wake Island just two days earlier. Since they needed three new gunners, three young marines volunteer to shoot down some Zeros. Standing outside his quarters are three young marines.

"What do they want?" Joe Gall asks his trusty Co-pilot Flight Officer John Van Horn.

"I think they want to man the ball-turret and waist guns for Perkins and Patterson. Let's see what they have to say."

The tallest marine brings the other two marines to attention and they give their finest military salutes to Lt. Gall and Flight Officer Van Horn. "Sir, we are the best marksmen in the Marines and want to join you on your Wake Island mission. We know we cannot replace your wounded men. We just ask for a chance to get even with Japan. They took our friends during the battle of Midway and the Alamo of the Pacific, Wake Island. Can you help us?"

Gall orders, "Report to the third bomber in line. We will be happy to have you men join us. We have two gunner spots open, but all three of you can come. We never want to be short handed in battle as we were on Saturday. You will report to Technical Sergeant Arvid Ambur. He will show you what to do."

The Second Bombing of Wake Island

Sergeant Arvid Ambur stands outside a new ship with his fire extinguisher resting on a dolly. Van Horn climbs in his Co-pilot seat and looks down at him from the open window, as Arvid gets ready to turn the propeller on engine number three. Van Horn smiles and yells out his window overlooking the cute bunny cartoon image painted below the passenger side window.

The new B-24's co-pilot yells, "6 good turns, Ambur, 6 good turns!"

The new crew, a new Bombardier and three marines along with the remaining crew including Ambur, Conley, Storts, Wyckoff, Weiss, Van Horn and Gall, are ready for another adventure.

Their mission is to fly to Wake Island and finish the job.

The Last Mission to Wake Island

"Down we dive spouting our flame from under, off with one helluva roar"

– From the United States Air Force Hymn

On Monday, July 26 1943 at 0800 hours, the second bombing mission prepares for take-off on Midway's Eastern Island. Again, the target is the Alamo of the Pacific, Wake Island.

This time ten B-24 Grey Geese are revving their engines to 2700 RPM.

The remaining crew from the **Daisy Mae** is on board a new ship. Ironically, the new ship is **Thumper**, named after the cute bunny from the classic movie titled Bambi. There were several **Thumpers** in the Grey Geese so we will call this one, **Thumper II**. The ship was built in the Consolidated Factory in San Diego, California. The ship's ball-turret gun mounts sport a note from Molly Alphabet.

On Monday morning as the bombers take off from the Midway runway, they begin to gain altitude. When they reach the proper altitude, they

231

lower their left wings dropping engine number one and engine number two to allow the ship to bank and head southwest toward their targets on Wake Island.

The airmen are quiet during takeoff. They get their game faces on for battle. The only man speaking is Arvid Ambur as he instructs each marine on his duties aboard the ship. The marines give Arvid Ambur their complete attention. They are highly motivated to show their skills and help **Thumper** complete her mission.

Quietly, each man on the Brown Bomber understands he has a score to settle.

Thumper does too…

Each of the ten metal giants looks down during their turn and stares at the **Daisy Mae**, lying on the beach just two feet short of the calm Pacific Ocean. The wings dropping down from the level position looks like a salute to the Big Girl, lying below. As each wing levels out again it looks like a soldier returning his salute to the original position, hand and arm to his side.

Marines below on Midway see the spectacle in the air and react emotionally. From the ground on Midway, the marines return their best salutes to the circling Grey Geese Squadron. The marines shout and wave at the crews on their flying carpets made of steel. Some men are punching their fists in the air and as though they are cheering at a sporting event. After all, three marines are taking up gunnery positions on this bomber and more marines on other bombers. It is a united effort to defeat the enemy. It is a proud and an historic moment for the US Marine Corps, the U.S. Navy, and the US Army Air Corps.

The second mission over Wake Island is to be another milk run. What happens on long missions over vast stretches of water? Many aircraft usually turn back or ditch into the sea because of mechanical failure or pilot error.

That scenario will not be the case today.

Unlike the mission two days earlier, the sky is clear blue all the way to the target. Conley in his tail gunner position sees most of the 42nd Squadron flying in perfect formation. There will be no mid-air collisions today for lack of visibility. The plane ride is so smooth and comfortable in contrast to the wild storm they experienced just two days earlier that the crews laugh and talk all of the way to the rallying point, Peacock Point about eighty miles from Wake Island.

As the bombers approach the sprung paper clip in the middle of the big blue ocean, Wake Island, or as the Japanese call it Bird Island, they are intercepted by all of the remaining fighter planes from the attack two days earlier.

Beginning at high noon, the attack is like an old Western shootout. For a South Dakota cowboy/rancher like Arvid Ambur this is right in his wheelhouse, playing to his strength.

Conley spots them first. "Twenty Japanese Zeros at ten o'clock!" as he pulls the bolt back and readies his twin fifty-caliber machine guns. He lets fly with a long burst of machine gun fire and he shouts loudly over the intercom, "This is for you, Fran, and for the crew of the **Daisy Mae!**"

Once again, the enemy flies out of the sun at the ten o'clock and two o'clock positions, after being warned by patrolling submarines of the approach of the air armada. They use the same tactics of the figure eight skating through the formation. Today, however, would not be a Central Park pleasure skate. All the gunners including Conley, Storts, Ambur, Wyckoff and three United States Marines open fire.

Twenty Zeros skate through the fighting 42nd and twenty Zeros splash into the sea!

The bombardiers from all ten Liberators take over the controls with their Norden Bombsights. The pilots and co-pilots of the bombers rest easy and become passengers on the ride. The bombs drop and the ships speed back to Midway in a tight military formation. As the Grey Geese Squadron nears Midway, waiting marines and sailors marvel at the sound of ten heavy bombers with their forty engines purring like large kittens as they begin their descent. Pilots check their engines and all are functioning at 2700 RPMs. Oil pressure is perfect.

Navigator Ben Weiss comes down to the engineering station and shakes Sergeant Arvid Ambur's hand and slaps his back. They both smile at each other. This is one for the books. If any mission is supposed to be perfect, this is it.

Out of the mid-afternoon sun, Gall and Van Horn land softly and dead center on the runway. Lanky is on the beach, smiling as each airship lands. He counts all ten aloud and recognizes the cartoon character *Thumper* on the left side of the plane just below Van Horn's smiling face. This is a personal victory for Lanky. His heart and soul are filled with hope that America is winning the War and he will be with his family soon. He feels close to the crew because he helped carry out wounded Fran Perkins and kept a souvenir from the **Daisy Mae**, a small piece of metal from the mighty metal hero. He will keep this symbol of hope and remember his experiences for the rest of his life.

Van Horn points past the far edge of the runway where the **Daisy Mae** rested just nine hours before. She is not there! During the day, the **Daisy Mae** had been disassembled, placed on a barge and dumped out to sea. **Thumper**'s crew wants to see the Big Girl again, but they know that just like Pop Evans and Myron Jensen, she is considered just another casualty of war.

The Second Bombing of Wake Island

Summary of the Wake Island Raids

July 24, 1943 on the raid against the 28-30 enemy fighter aircraft, the **Daisy Mae** and four other bombers accounted for nine kills. The ball-turret gunner, Perkins, had two confirmed and two probable kills.

July 26, 1943 with the help of the marines riding along on the next attack, 20 Zeros find a new home at the bottom of the sea. This time all ten of the Grey Geese Squadron make it to Wake Island and safely back to Midway and none would have to fly a mission to Wake Island ever again.

Everyone on the mission is thankful and filled with hope.

The Return of a Friend

Early Saturday morning, a week after the last mission over Wake Island, Lanky is asleep in his bunk when his platoon leader shakes him from a deep, peaceful slumber. "On your feet! There's an enemy submarine detected by radar coming in slowly from the northwest side of the airfield. Grab another marine and one of those rubber rafts. I will direct you by radio from the radar battery."

The submarine is moving very slowly in order to remain undetected. All of the marines knew how Japanese soldiers move just a few inches in an hour if they are stalking their prey at night. They are very patient. During the battles on Guadalcanal Island, a few months earlier, the marines and these same B-24 Liberator Bombers were parked along the airstrip. Often they experienced this type of sneak attack in the middle of the night.

Lanky wakes up Determined and together they load their M1 Carbines and head for the beach. Before shoving a round in the chamber, Lanky grabs the small rectangular shot-up lucky charm that he had carefully removed from the **Daisy Mae** only a few days before. He kisses his lucky charm and puts it in his pocket as they pass under the archway on Midway that reads, "Hold Midway until hell freezes over." These marines are ready for battle.

Both men race flat out with the small rubber boat to the shore. Lanky does not feel his feet touch the sand. He cannot believe the speed he has developed since arriving on Midway. His heart is pounding so hard he wonders if the silent enemy will hear him coming.

The two marines paddle their small raft in the dark while their platoon leader is directing the men by radio toward the enemy submarine that is hiding in the shallow water offshore. At the same time, the marines focus on being the first responders to the attack. They are glad about being chosen to defend Midway until hell freezes over. Lanky now feels the same way he did a week ago when **Daisy Mae** completed her mission. He feels honored to be able to serve in such an important role.

Other men are scurrying about the airfield and are loading three bombers with depth charges.

An aircraft carrier Commander far out at sea, orders his ship to turn into the wind and get ready to launch. Six fighter planes lift off the aircraft carrier about 100 miles out to sea while the remaining planes are preparing to launch. A destroyer is steaming full speed ahead toward the island from about ten miles out and two PT Boats are heading to the Eastern Island from Sand Island at Midway a short distance away.

Midway is Ready for Action

Every soldier, sailor, airman and marine is on alert and every anti-aircraft gun battery readies with guns swinging around toward the Northeast. There will be no surprise attack today either by sea or by air. There will be no successful invasion of Midway by the Japanese.

Lying prone on the beach with rifles trained toward an anticipated invasion, one marine rifleman turns to his buddy and whispers, "Hold

236

Midway until hell freezes over. Pass it on!" Marines whisper the phrase to each other as they set up a ring of protection in foxholes and bunkers around the island. There is a certain look in the eyes of a marine as he goes into battle. This look is on the face of every defender on the island.

Lanky and Determined paddle their boat right over the top of the enemy submarine lurking under water. The water is so shallow here that it must be a very small submarine beneath their tiny rubber boat. Lanky bends down to stick his head underwater to get a better look. Determined covers him with his M1 Carbine. He also has two hand grenades at the ready attached to his pistol belt.

The early morning sun is rising and illuminates the water up to about six feet under. The marines see just about everything under the still early morning waters off the Eastern Island. Lanky sees small fish, a sea turtle, a small squid and some ripples bubbling up from below. Pulling back with shock, he sees a human hand reaching toward the surface! The human hand is almost glowing as the illumination from the sunrise is causing it to sparkle. At the same time, he is hypnotized and paralyzed by the clear view of the mysterious hand.

Slowly the realization hits him that this is not a human hand! This is much better. It is the hand attached to the waving arm of **Daisy Mae**, smiling and waving at the two marines just a few inches over her head.

Lanky quickly backs his rear end into the boat, and because of the sudden movement, it sends Determined heels over head, backward into the sea while the raft somersaults Lanky forward right beside the playful **Daisy Mae**. The continued rocking sent both men, with their M1 Carbines and two grenades each, rumbling, stumbling and tumbling overboard in a hysterical reunion for the US Marines and US Army Air Corps.

You can almost hear **Daisy Mae** coyly ask the waterlogged marines, "Why, boys, did you come for a swim with me? You are such big, strong, handsome marines!"

237

The complete cabin side panel of the **Daisy Mae**, the one that looked out over the number three engine, the one that rested just below Co-pilot Van Horn's waving arm and included all of **Daisy Mae**'s artwork, had slowly floated back toward Midway's Eastern Island almost at the very point the Big Girl entered the water a few days earlier.

"What is going on?" Determined shouts to Lanky as both are splashing around.

"The **Daisy Mae**," Lanky replies as he spits out a mouthful of seawater. "The **Daisy Mae** came back!"

Now one of the PT boats arrives alongside the small boat and finds both marines laughing, splashing, and frolicking during this heightened state of military alarm. Confused at the chaos, the PT Boat Commander suspects the Japanese set off a chemical weapon to disorient the marines, but then throws caution to the wind as he personally looks down at the playful image of the Big Girl.

Lanky pulls his metal relic out of his pocket and waves it back and forth in front of the baby blue eyes of **Daisy Mae** yelling "**Daisy Mae**, thank you for coming back! Thank you, Big Girl. Thank you for giving us courage and hope."

He continues swimming, laughing and just having fun while the rest of the Navy pulls alongside the bouncing rubber raft. They watch as Lanky and Determined are laughing hysterically and taking turns waving the piece of metal that once was part of the 1,250,000 parts assembled in Molly Alphabet's factory in San Diego, California a year earlier.

The PT Boat Commander and several of his sailors study the scene. How? Why did this piece of the wreckage end up here? The Commander will have to tow **Daisy Mae** back out to sea but not before he ferries several other servicemen out to this point as he personally declares World War II over at least for this Saturday morning on this beautiful

238

Pacific island paradise. He makes a special trip to take the wounded out to see their new special friend. It brightens their day.

Even though Lanky did not use proper wartime procedure over the radio to explain to his platoon leader what he discovered, there would be no punishment today. The Commander of the racing destroyer and the Commanders of the area PT Boats find a reason to celebrate that early Saturday morning on Midway.

Trying not to laugh over their radios from the control tower on Midway, the captain and the private, with tears rolling down their faces, call off the six fighter planes racing to quell this dangerous invasion. Each fighter pilot takes a sigh of relief as he banks his speeding aircraft and heads back to the carrier.

One mischievous fighter pilot continues on to Midway and after seeing the playful display below, he buzzes the PT Boats and barrel rolls over the island. Sailors and marines shout and cheer at the impromptu air show.

All of the tension and stress of World War II takes a break on that hysterical Saturday morning. Everyone on the base are laughing and talking about their early morning visitor. The men tell funny stories of their own to add to this wonderful day. They all wonder if she wanted to get back into the war, or was **Daisy Mae** looking for her favorite crew? In any event, **Daisy Mae** is a welcome friend for the Joint United States Military Forces stationed at Midway Island on a warm, tropical Saturday morning in the summer of 1943.

Today is a unique day. It is the only day in history on Midway when hell froze over.

What they did not know then, but you know now, is that this was the last scare they would ever have of an impending invasion during World War II. The Japanese forces were far away. By this time in the War, the 11th Bomb Group 42nd Squadron and the United States Marines have the

239

enemy on the run as they approach to dismantle the Japanese Empire many thousands of miles to the North and many miles to the Southwest in the Solomon Islands.

Lanky and Determined will remember their intimate moments with **Daisy Mae**, their new best friend, for the rest of their lives.

In the meantime, Gall, Van Horn, Weiss, Ambur, Storts, Conley, and Wyckoff, along with a new Liberator built in the San Diego factory, **Thumper**, are ready to fight once again focusing on other targets.

On December 7, 1941 while Pearl Harbor was in flames, the 42nd Squadron and the 11th Bomb Group were wiped out. Now it is time for payback.

The Grey Geese and many other new flocks of larger birds called B-29s began the long, difficult migration north to end World War II.

Chapter 16

Joe the Mailman

Once Fran Perkins leaves the hospital with a clean bill of health, he is anxious to rejoin his crew. Before leaving the hospital, he writes letters home to Dad, Elaine's Mother or "Mom" and Lady Elaine. Fran does not go into detail about the battle, in fact, he never wants to talk about it again.

He told Elaine he injured his eyes so he could not write much but now things are okay. He is excited at seeing his crew again even if he cannot be a gunner anymore.

Fran hitches a ride on an Air Corps transport plane and reaches Funafuti around noon on a Monday. He goes back to the familiar group of tents reserved for the 42nd Squadron. All of his crew are out on assignments and the only shipmate he runs into is Sergeant Thomas Wyckoff who has Fran's new assignment and mail safely tucked away in his footlocker.

"Fran, it is good to see you! Can you see okay?"

"There are things I have to get used to. They will not put me in a bomber again. The doctor told me that with only one eye, I don't have my depth perception anymore. Sometimes I feel sorry for myself because I want to be up there with you and my other shipmates. There is nothing in life I want to do more."

Thomas says, "Yeah, I understand. In fact, we understand. We were decorated back on August 6 at Hickam while you were in the hospital. Gall, Van Horn, Weiss, and all of us gunners went to visit you but some battle axe of a nurse told us she would bust us out of the service if we went up to your room."

"Did that battle axe have a nametag that said O'Connor?"

"Yeah, that was her. I was kidding. She was nice to all of us. Virginia O'Connor explained how you were in a metal harness and the doctors were still trying to get shrapnel and the gun sight out of your head. She told us to be patient and they have a good shot at restoring your right eye. She gave Conley a big towel because he was sporting some huge crocodile tears. Remember the big crocs back on Guadalcanal?"

"Yes, I do! Conley and I had a crazy night guarding **Daisy Mae**. Conley is a real card. I am so glad I served with him and you, Brother Thomas. The crew will always be my brothers no matter what happens to me in life."

"I feel exactly that way, too," returns Wyckoff.

"I don't think you know this yet, but Flight Officer Van Horn is dead. He was flying a twin-engine bomber from Kualoa Airfield and had some kind of mechanical problem. He ditched at sea, but only after he maneuvered to get his shipmates near enough to swim safely ashore."

"Oh, no! That's horrible," Fran replies. "Van Horn was a good man and always kind to us. I loved the way he teased Arvid whenever we were starting up the engines."

"Six good turns, Ambur…Six good turns," both Fran and Thomas chime in together.

"He was a good man," Thomas reflects. "I'll never forget him. Lt. Gall is taking it very hard. He was scheduled to ride as a co-pilot as John Van Horn needed more piloting hours to keep his certifications current. But, for some reason Gall was scratched at the last minute. Lt Gall thought if he rode with Van Horn, they would have made it out alive."

"I know how Lt. Gall feels. You and I have seen many good pilots go down in training or just taking off on missions. In fact, I will bet more men in the 42nd died without any enemy gunfire at all. My brother Bob in the Eighth Army Air Corps is finding the same thing happening with B-24s and B-17s flying on missions in Germany. Maybe it was just that time for Flight Officer John Van Horn. I think if Gall rode on that training exercise, we would have lost two of the best pilots the Air Corps has ever had instead of just one. I feel sorry for Lt. Gall. He may feel guilty about that the rest of his life. It isn't fair but life isn't always fair."

"I understand." Brother Thomas tries to change the subject from this dismal memory about a lost warrior and friend. "I think you are ready for this, Fran."

Thomas hands Fran an envelope. "Just call me the mailman, Fran. Lt. Gall wanted to sit down and talk to you personally about it but they just called him away on another mission. Sometimes the rest of us fly together but they split us up quite a bit. I think they're afraid some of us will freeze up after the last mission on the **Daisy Mae**. They understand none of us should have made it back. It took a miracle. They think we may reach a breaking point where we all crack. I don't blame them one bit. Every night I have nightmares about all of the Zeros attacking us and having nowhere to hide. I hope I don't crack."

"Yeah, I have the same nightmares. I still see the face of the pilot firing his machine guns at me. When I think about it, I know it was not a personal thing. He was doing his job and I was doing mine. In battle when you do your job someone dies. That's the reality of war."

Perkins changes the subject. "Sit down Brother Thomas and let's see where I'm going next. Maybe they'll drum me out of the Air Corps with my bad eye." Fran holds his written orders out about a foot from his face as he works at using one eye to read. "They're sending me to Jackson Mississippi, Brother Thomas. They're going to make me a trainer."

"That's good news, Fran! You will be a great one."

243

Fran thinks about Major McIntosh returning stateside to train young men after becoming a hero at Midway. Fran sees this assignment as an honor and a privilege. They could have discharged him with a medical discharge. At least Fran is still valuable to the Army Air Corps.

"I'm going to do the best job I can, Brother Thomas. Training is important as we have both found out in battle."

"Do you know what classes you will be teaching?"

"Not yet. I don't really care, but I promise I will be the best trainer in the Air Corps. After all, I may be training one of your new shipmates and I have a responsibility to keep **Daisy Mae**'s old crew alive. The Big Girl would have wanted it that way. I'd better get over to the flight line. I'm leaving in about an hour. Make sure you tell Conley I was the guy who nailed that Japanese soldier on Guadalcanal."

"What Japanese soldier?" Wyckoff asks.

"Exactly," Fran replies with a smile.

On the way back to the Hawaiian Islands, Perkins had to spend the night on the big pork chop called Canton Island. He was hungry for chops when he landed but all they serve today is chicken. It takes four full days to make it from Funafuti to Jackson Airfield. Four days and no pork chops for Fran. On his final leg of the trip, Fran hitches a ride on a mule-drawn wagon from a sharecropper and his wife. It is an adventure just getting to the base.

Fran reports to the company clerk who immediately calls for Joe the Mailman to meet with Sergeant Perkins. "Come with me," Joe says after shaking Fran's hand. "I'll take you to the barracks right after I show you the training assignment. Joe is older than Fran by several years but has a great smile poking through his whiskbroom mustache. Fran spots an Italian last name on his nametag but he is unable to make it out at the angle he faces Joe. Joe tells Fran his life story during the ten-minute walk it takes to reach the classrooms.

Joe wanted to fight for his country after Pearl Harbor, but he was already forty years old at the time. An officer took a liking to Joe and found an excellent way he could serve his country by helping the returning Veterans acclimate to training assignments stateside. At the same time, Joe is receiving credit for time served at the post office department in Jackson where Joe was Head Post Master prior to enlisting. Joe will receive a healthy retirement once the war is over and he rejoins the United States Postal Department.

Joe helps support his younger sisters and his mother who live in a small home in Jackson. His Mom, Della, enjoys cooking homemade Italian food and asks Joe to invite the airmen stationed there to join them for Thanksgiving dinner. She cooks traditional turkey and ham as well as stuffed manicottis, homemade raviolis and other great Italian food.

Although Joe and Fran know each other for only ten minutes, Joe invites Fran to his Thanksgiving dinner that is only a few weeks away. Fran likes Joe right away and does not hesitate when he accepts Joe's invitation. Fran thinks, "I bet I'm going to love Jackson, Mississippi."

"We will be glad to have a War Hero at Thanksgiving dinner," Joe says enthusiastically.

"Oh, I'm not a War Hero, but I flew with ten heroes on a bomber called the **Daisy Mae**, who IS a hero in my book. Our pilot Lt. Joe Gall is the best pilot in the whole damned Air Corps."

"The hell you ain't a War Hero!" Joe pauses realizing he came on a bit strong to a sensitive veteran and concedes, "Ok, Fran. You'll be our designated non-war hero at our Thanksgiving table."

"Sounds good, Joe, I'll put the ol' feedbag on," laughs Fran.

245

Joe the Mailman

Joe and Fran turn the corner to stand directly in front of a large wood building housing the classrooms. It looks like a converted two-story barracks. Joe nods toward the building, "We're painting a new sign for you so young airmen can find your classroom. I'll show you inside so you can see your training assignment first hand."

"What classes will I teach?

"You'll see…"

"What's all the secrecy about?" young Fran inquires. "I'm just a ball-turret gunner. I don't think I feel qualified to teach anything."

"You ain't just…"

Joe pulls a brown envelope out of the blue mail satchel he carries everywhere with him. "I have a letter here written by your pilot, Joe Gall, and signed by your shipmates from the **Daisy Mae**. It's a strong letter of recommendation. It's the best I have ever read. Do you want to read it for yourself?"

"Thanks. No, I still struggle with reading because of my one eye. I'll read it later," Fran says to cover for the real reason he doesn't want to read it right now – because he knows it will touch his heart and he wants to keep a strong front.

"I think you will appreciate it, Fran," Joe smiles.

As Joe the Mailman opens the door to the classroom, Fran sees fifty-caliber machine guns on portable gun mounts and a sign over the repair counter that reads, "You are a gunner in the United States Army Air Corps. You must WANT to be a gunner!"

Fran slowly shakes his head from side to side in disbelief and takes an oath to himself right now. That oath promises his shipmates, he will do his best to teach young gunners to assemble and disassemble these fifty-caliber machine guns, just as Sergeant Masters taught him over a year earlier. Fran is smiling from his face all the way down to the very depths of his soul.

Just as Larry Calhoun found the best way to serve his country in the entertainment field, Fran Perkins finds his best way to serve. He will motivate and train these men in Armorer School. Fran will turn these men into the best gunners in the Army Air Corps. He understands from personal combat experience why it is so important to assemble and repair guns while blindfolded.

"Joe, can you do me a favor?" Fran asks.

"Anything," Joe smiles. "Anything."

"I need you to spend five minutes with me right now, Joe."

"Take as long as you need. This is my job. My job is to help war heroes, and you, the non-war hero, achieve their dreams. Men just like you, Fran, training from real combat experience is the reason we are winning the war over Japan and Germany. I love this job."

Fran opens a large drawer marked spare parts and dumps the contents on the floor. He finds a black hood to put over his head and a stripped down fifty-caliber machine gun. He puts the hood over his head. So that he cannot peek at the gun, he tightens the hood around his neck until he attains the gag reflex. Sitting cross-legged on the floor, spare machine gun parts are strewn everywhere. Fran quickly and quietly assembles and disassembles his fifty-caliber friend. Joe smiles to himself and thinks, "Bless you Fran, you are going to make it just fine."

"Fran, you will be initially training gunners from the Netherlands with the Royal Dutch Air Force. Do you remember the Battle of Java Sea?"

"No, I don't." Fran replies while completing the machine gun assembly with the black hood still tied securely over his head.

"At the end of February of 1942, just two months after Pearl Harbor, the Japanese attacked the Dutch Fleet sailing near Borneo. Dutch, Australian, British and American ships were destroyed by the Japanese Fleet. Most of the ships were World War I vintage ships and were severely beaten by the modern Japanese technology. The worst part about it was the Allies felt the Japanese were so powerful they just gave up all hope of winning the War. Ten allied ships were sunk from guns, torpedoes and air strikes. There weren't many survivors. It was officially the Dutch version of Pearl Harbor.

"Also, as you know, the Germans invaded the Netherlands in 1940 and have controlled it ever since. The gunners you will be training escaped from the Nazi invasion. They are here to learn from you. They want to be a major part in liberating their own country from their German invaders.

"Fran, the Dutch Airmen have a motto. In Latin, it is 'Parvus numero, magnus merito,' which means 'small in numbers, great in deeds.'

"It is your job as the official non-war hero from the **Daisy Mae** to give these small numbers of gunners the chance to take revenge for the Battle of Java Sea and return to Europe to liberate the people of the Netherlands, also known as the Dutch.

Fran takes off his hood and focuses his good eye on Joe.

"I sure know what it's like to lose, like when I got hit in my ball-turret on the **Daisy Mae**. I also know what it feels like to win as most of us got to Midway alive and when the doctors in Hawaii got one of my eyes to work again. Maybe that's why I have one eye. The one good eye represents all of the good that can happen when you have hope. The bad one reminds me that sometimes you have to lose before you can win. Joe, I'm going to help these Dutch gunners get their country back. It'll also help my brother Bob who is bombing Germany with the Eighth Air Force. I guess we're all working together.

248

Joe the Mailman

"I feel good about this job, Joe. I can't wait to get started."

"Fran, why don't you go to your barracks now and get unpacked. Or if you want, you can stay awhile and work in the classroom."

"I want to stay here in my new home awhile longer and get ready for class."

Joe tosses him the keys and says, "Should I tell Della to count you in for Thanksgiving dinner in a few weeks?"

Fran replies, "You bet. Tell her I will be there with bells on!

Chapter 17

Top Secret Revealed

England April of 1945

Several British, Polish, American and Canadian bombers take off from bases in England on a special mission. Leveling off at 17,000 feet, they fly across the English Channel to Western Europe. Normally, they would not be flying that high, except today there is an incredible air stream allowing the bombers to glide to their targets.

One B-24D bomber marked with the word "Manna" painted on the nose is flying in a squadron of mixed bombers. Some are B-24Ds but most are B-17 Flying Fortresses with Lancaster Bombers flown under the British, Polish and Canadian flags.

Ferdi, the ball-turret gunner whose name means brave and peaceful in Dutch, hears a voice over his headset, "Belly gunner, test fire your guns." Ferdi does not know that these will be the last bullets he will ever fire again. He aims his twin fifty-caliber machine guns straight down toward the sea below. Ferdi, who is known to obliterate German Messerschmitt fighter planes with long concentrated bursts, only uses two ten round pops to test his guns.

Ferdi's best buddy, Van Geehm, who is the tail gunner, hears in his headset, "Tail Gunner, test fire your guns." He, like the belly gunner, reacts with two ten round pops. Van Geehm and Ferdi have teamed up many times flying on missions on a variety of B-24s and B-17s under many Allied Flags. They know each other's strengths, weaknesses and fields of fire.

Descending to a lower altitude as they reach the coast of the Netherlands, they skim over the treetops toward their targets. Van

Geehm calls to Ferdi in English, "Belly Gunner! Vindmills, Ferdi, vindmills! Vindmills, Ferdi, vindmills!"

Ferdi pulls his circular lucky charm out of his pocket and shouts loudly, "Don't take any vooden nickels!" He remembers his Gunnery School instructor in America telling him, "Ferdi, you were born to be a ball-turret gunner. Take this token and it will keep you safe. It kept my father-in-law safe during World War I and it kept me safe over Wake Island"

Down below Ferdi and Van Geehm view large windmills, the distinctive Dutch countryside and the retreating German Army many miles ahead of the armada in the sky. Ferdi and Van Geehm's mission is different today. This is the last flight for **Manna** in "Operation Chowhound." There will be no bombs dropped today.

Together they see their Dutch homeland with barren farm fields decorated with large formations of colorful flowers. These were flowers secretly grown inside private homes, as the Dutch citizens were not allowed to grow anything. The German Army was starving them to death. Today in April of 1945 with World War II coming close to an end, the Dutch citizens, along with Jews, who were hidden by their Dutch neighbors for the last five years, took every flower they could find to spell out their appreciation.

Each colorful floral arrangement Ferdi and Van Geehm see spells one word.
LIBERATORS

For miles and miles in every direction, the word from the People of a Grateful Nation can be seen over the barren fields. Every Liberator Bomber is carrying thousands of pounds of food. Loaves of fresh baked bread, blankets and other food drops by parachute from B-17s at higher elevations while the B-24's are pouring out food at a more direct route flying less than fifty feet off the ground.

251

"Beans Away"

Both Ferdi and Van Geehm are ecstatic as they spot their friends and families below for the first time since the Germans invaded Holland over five years earlier. Although the Netherlands was neutral, the Germans wanted Dutch airfields to attack England. They also wanted to eliminate over 700,000 Jews, including Anne Frank who lived in this neutral country.

Church bells ring in Amsterdam, Rotterdam, and the small villages, around the countryside. **Manna**'s bombardier flies over a barren field, ringed by irrigation ditches flooded with water. Taking over from his pilot and co-pilot who now become spectators for the bombing mission, he looks through his Norden Bombsight. The Bombardier waits until he is flying over a decorative flower arrangement spelling out the words "Many Thanks." As he lines up the words "Many Thanks" in his crosshairs, he yells loudly over the ship intercom, "Beans Away!"

17-1 Many Thanks spelled in flowers

The farmers below watch at a safe distance, as the finest soybeans, coming from a large farm in DeKalb, Illinois gently, fall onto the silent Dutch fields to germinate for a new spring planting. Other bombers are dropping food from parachutes bursting from their bomb bay doors.

Some B-17s break from their formation to fly dangerously as low as the B-24s, with skillful pilots stalling their engines and risking death, to make sure the food gets to the people safely and does not land into the hands of retreating Germans or fall onto the flooded fields and water canals that ring each dry growing parcel.

Later in the week when Molly Alphabet in San Diego, California, reads the newspaper stories of Operation Chowhound and Operation Manna, she sees the word "Liberators" spelled in flowers in one of the pictures and tears of joy shower her face. The love of her life, the "Liberator," is doing a job she hoped for and the job Major Perry McIntosh revealed as Top Secret information for a young Fran Perkins.

This is exactly what the aircraft was engineered to do, as it became the most manufactured bomber in the history of the United States of America. The B-24 had a job to bomb enemy targets, and she is designed to restore life in the war-torn countries. Now Molly and her co-workers understand why it was so important to build the B-24. She carries the bombs for war and the food for peace. For Molly it was not for the LB-30 or Land Based Bomber Project that she gave her heart and soul to Consolidated, nor was it for the Lib. It was for the "Liberator" that she toiled for those long years. When asked by people, "Why work at Consolidated? Molly always responded the same way. "There is nothing in life I want to do more."

The sacrifices of the ten-man crews of the battling bombers and the thousands of workers building them during World War II were not in vain.

Ferdi's bomber is dropping soybeans for the next planting. The Dutch fields have been barren since the German occupation of the Netherlands in 1940. It is now April of 1945. In less than a month from Operation Chowhound and Operation Manna, the War in Europe will end on May 8, 1945.

The Netherlands and other war-torn countries will rebuild and flourish.

Chapter 18

Many Years Later

Joe Gall

Lt. Joe Gall fought in many battles after the last flight of the **Daisy Mae**. Many of the missions included his Navigator Benjamin I. Weiss and Flight Engineer Arvid B. Ambur.

Like most of the remaining crew, Gall left the Army Air Corps at the end of World War II, married and started a family. However, the world was still a dangerous place. The Iron Curtain fell in Europe and the Communist Chinese and North Koreans were rattling swords in Asia. With the drums of War beating again, where do you expect the best-damned pilot in the Army Air Corps to find his place in history serving his country?

Lt. Gall joined the fledgling United States Air Force, previously the Army Air Corps. It was the beginning of 1947. Joseph Gall served through the Korean War and the Vietnam War. Not many young men served their country in three major wars in a single century but Gall was up for the task. He had a score to settle. Two of his assigned crew in the beginning, Myron Jensen and John Van Horn died in World War II, and Ben Weiss sustained serious injuries from enemy flak exploding on his Navigator's desk. This was on a bombing run piloted by Gall over Betio Island in the Tarawa chain to kick off the bloody invasion the next day. The marines below were fighting and winning one of the bloodiest battles of World War II. Weiss lost the use of a hand and received a medical discharge. Gall was the only active survivor of the four original officers assigned to the **Daisy Mae**. What better way to honor his shipmates then to continue and finish the job of fighting for liberty. He always remembered the lessons he learned while serving with all of his crews and especially the fine crew of the **Daisy Mae**.

Many Years Later

Joseph Gall retired at a rank of Lt. Colonel and trained countless airmen who took their lessons into a new Air Force and a new century. The lessons taught by Gall span generations of the fine men and women of the United States Air Force.

The Lanky Marine

One day, almost a half-century after the last flight of the **Daisy Mae**, a lanky (former) marine is looking through an old photo album with his wife of many years. They are out with friends just down the block from their home. The friends ask Lanky about a small piece of metal he had fastened to the album. "What is the piece of metal from?" they inquire.

Lanky begins to tell his friends and his wife the story you just read. His wife is hearing the story for the very first time. Lanky tells the story of The Last Flight of the **Daisy Mae**. He fights to choke back tears as he remembers sitting on the beach, all hope lost in despair on July 24, 1943. He remembers it all too well. It is a story that stays with him along with other battles he still faces every night when his house is quiet.

Now Lanky composes himself and brags about how the men made it back, flying through hell. He continues about how the sight of seeing **Daisy Mae** descend through the dark clouds of war gave him a sense of hope. Everyone listens intently as Lanky tells his wife and friends the story about **Daisy Mae**'s miraculous return to Midway Island that affected the entire base. He laughs as he recalls how he and Determined fell out of the rocky boat and playfully splashed in the warm Pacific waters on a suspenseful yet satisfying Saturday morning. He said it was a joyous bomber baptism for both men.

All the friends laugh together one half century after the event. They all cheerfully toast the marines and the gallant crew of the **Daisy Mae**.
Lanky smiles as he says, "**Daisy Mae** gave every airman, sailor and marine the same wonderful gift of hope." Then he adds, "Hope is a good thing…in fact, hope is a great thing!"

255

His wife turns to Lanky and whispers in a soft voice, "Do you know what you need to do?" Lanky knows what to do. Marines are always Marines; they never really retire. A marine instinctively knows his duty no matter how many years separate active service. He puts down the photo album and runs flat out to his house, feet barely touching the pavement, to look through his files and make some telephone calls. He instantly remembers running the same way toward the **Daisy Mae** to carry nineteen-year-old Fran Perkins to safety many years earlier.

To complete a mission, Lanky remembers he will run through fire if necessary. This feels just like when he and Determined ran through a minefield risking their lives for just the opportunity to save lives aboard the **Daisy Mae**. Lanky prepares to run through danger again. "After all," he thinks to himself, "This is what marines do."

He remembers his life long wartime friend and best man at his wedding, Determined. As he is running with reckless abandon on winged feet, Lanky remembers what Determined shouted to Perkins as he was facing the blind and wounded warrior. "You are safe. You are guarded by United States Marines."

Lanky remembers his favorite verse from the United States Marine Hymn as his feet fly down the street:

"If the Army and the Navy, ever look on Heaven's scenes,
They will find the streets are guarded by United States Marines"
– From the United States Marine Hymn

As soon as Lanky runs through the doorway, he riffles through his files, grabs his telephone and begins making calls to track down names, addresses and phone numbers of the surviving crew of the **Daisy Mae**.

Many Years Later

Sacramento, California

At Retired Lt. Colonel Joseph Gall's birthday party, a package arrives. There is a message that this package is to be opened on Joe Gall's' birthday and not before.

Inside the package is the piece of metal, the last surviving hard evidence of the existence of the beloved B-24D Liberator Bomber...the **Daisy Mae**. Along with the relic is a letter from Lanky thanking Joe Gall for bringing his ship in safely and sending hope to all of the men stationed on Midway.

Daisy Mae finds another way to reach the servicemen she so fondly tried to find again after she was towed out to sea.

The reunion is perfect...

Joe Gall loves the gift and promptly sends it off to Arvid Ambur with orders to forward the gift to all of the surviving shipmates. After being out of the service since 1945, Arvid Ambur still remembers how to obey orders from a superior officer.

As this amazing package bounces from home to home, each shipmate has a story to tell his family. A copy of Lanky's letter arrives with the relic. Each personal story includes a little sadness. Each story contains a great deal of humor and hope at the same time. The men are uniquely aware how hope can save lives and create new lives in the process.

The small piece of metal has been lost over time and maybe that is a good thing. This mysterious piece of metal will be a constant reminder of hope for generations to come. All of these brave men are gone now. A stranger in a new generation may find the gift and keep it. Who knows what new story and what new wonders may emerge from that old piece of metal? The piece of metal is part of a magnificent machine, manufactured by loving spirits and blessed by the ages. Maybe the spirit of the crew, or **Daisy Mae** herself, will find a new friend to inspire.

257

Fran's Thanksgiving

It is Thanksgiving Day, November 26, 1953. This is ten years after the Fran's last mission aboard the **Daisy Mae**.

Fran's wife is preparing Thanksgiving dinner and there is the sound of a loud knock on the door. Fran is sitting opposite the door, propped on a chair against the dining room wall and deeply consumed in thought. Fran's good blue eye and bad black eye are staring off together into space. This look will follow him through the years. Fran is sitting in an odd position on a kitchen chair leaning on one leg, three legs in the air with his body balancing on one leg of the chair. His body is curled as if in a confined position and pinched against the wall. He picks at a small scar over his bad eye. Every once in a while through the rest of his life small pieces of shrapnel from the **Daisy Mae** will emerge and work their way to the surface of the skin. Fran always keeps the small bits of metal in a coffee cup in the bedroom. It is a reminder of what he will always refer to as his personal Day of Infamy. It also reminds him of the greatest mission of his life, defending the soft underbelly of the B-24 Liberator... **Daisy Mae**.

While I was researching this book, it finally occurred to me what that unusual sitting position meant for former Staff Sergeant Fran Perkins. In a cutaway diagram located in an Air Corps training manual for the B-24 Liberator, there is a picture of a gunner sitting in the ball-turret. You can see the gunner pressed up against the glass in much the same position Fran is sitting right now in our living room. He is sitting between two imaginary fifty-caliber machine guns spinning in an imaginary turret.

Fran is deep in thought as he finally hears the second door knock. He springs out of his chair like a Jack-In-the-Box and opens the door. Standing outside, is a handsome man a few years older than Fran, smiling the biggest smile I have ever seen. Fran shows the man in and first introduces him to his wife. "Elaine, this is Ben Weiss, the Navigator of the **Daisy Mae**.

"Ben, this is my wife, Elaine. She is my Lady Elaine. This is my daughter, Linda, and my son Wayne. Linda and Wayne, this is your Uncle Ben."

Navigator Weiss smiles as he replies, "I have waited ten years to see you again Fran and I'm especially happy to meet you, Elaine. I had a strong feeling we would all meet someday."

Ben opens a bottle of Mogen David wine and begins a Thanksgiving tradition in the Perkins family lasting long after our new visitor was gone and even after Fran and Elaine have three more baby girls, years later.

The conversation is lively, but conspicuously does not include talk of the War. Fran talks of a new promotion. He is now a Plant Manager at an aluminum factory in Chicago. He brings out blueprints of a new home he is planning to build all by himself at the corner of Maple and Cedar streets in rural Lake in the Hills, Illinois, just as our old friend Larry Calhoun predicted on a quiet and hopeful night in Fran's hospital room ten years earlier.

After dinner, Ben has a surprise for the family. Weiss commands, "Saddle up everyone, we have a mission to complete. We must complete our mission."

Uncle Ben opens his car door and loads us into his rental car. He takes the Perkins family to an airport in Chicago as he has a surprise for all. During World War II, the airport was called CIT, or Chicago International Airport. Today Chicago International Airport has had a recent name change. It is now named after the most significant battle of the Pacific Front during World War II. It was the defining battle in putting the Japanese on the run for the rest of the war. It was a battle fought from the sea and the air by many heroes, including Major Perry 'Tosh' McIntosh. The airport was named after the same place from which **Daisy Mae** took off and landed after fighting her "Alamo in the Sky."

Many Years Later

Midway!

At Midway Airport, Uncle Ben loads the family onto a Piper Cub airplane with two seats in the front and a long bench seat in the rear, where Wayne and Linda can barely contain themselves as six and eight-year-old children during their first ride on an airplane.

As Uncle Ben picks up little Wayne to put him in the back seat, Wayne asks, "Uncle Ben do you have a name for your airplane?"

"Yes, I do," as he winks at my Dad. "I call her the **Daisy Mae**."

The Last Flight of the **Daisy Mae**

The late afternoon sun is at an angle as Uncle Ben's airplane is racing down the runway. Fran Perkins looks outside and salutes an imaginary officer along the airstrip. Fran's dream comes true at Midway fulfilling a prophecy from years earlier. The apparition he is saluting is Major Perry 'Tosh' McIntosh.

Now we have two former crewmembers of the **Daisy Mae**, once again taking off from a place called Midway. This time they will be flying in peacetime for pleasure not for combat. Now there is no rank or decorum separating officer and enlisted man. They fly as two brothers, talking, laughing and having fun while enjoying precious moments that only they can fully comprehend. Flying in place of bullets and blood, there are heroes and hope.

Ben takes us low over the tugboats churning up the Chicago River just as Fran and his brothers Jim and Bob did the summer before they enlisted to serve their country. Wave upon wave of wonderful memories flood Fran's brain. Since Uncle Ben's smile has never let up even for a second, he is enjoying these moments as well.

As the sun sets, Ben's **Daisy Mae** flies over the City of Chicago. After circling the bright lights of Chicago at night several times, she flies over Comiskey Park, Fran and Nurse Virginia O'Connor's favorite ballpark, and home to the Chicago White Sox. Fran says, "Joe the Mailman is a Cubs fan," so Ben heads for the North Side of Chicago over Wrigley Field. He flies over Soldier Field in Chicago, the place where Mae Birmingham's father received a Blue Ribbon at the World's Fair many years earlier for World Class Butter.

During the Battle of the Beans held in the summer of 1942, Fran's friend Private John Paul Olsen told Fran that he would get his chance at piloting a small plane over Lake Michigan. Private Olsen's promise rings true on this Thanksgiving Day. After leveling off at the required altitude, Navigator and fellow wounded War Hero, Benjamin Weiss says something over the radio headset and then switches places with Fran.

Ben Weiss is teaching Fran to how to fly. Fran is at the stick.

Can you imagine learning how to fly from a man who flew large B-24 bombers many times relieving Gall and Van Horn? Can you imagine Ben Weiss teaching you how to navigate your plane after navigating over hundreds of thousands of miles over featureless ocean, both night and day while never losing his way?

Ben orders Fran to fly over a dark Lake Michigan. Fran Perkins cannot comprehend it all. He feels he is in heaven. Fran remembers on the beach on Midway when he never wanted to leave the **Daisy Mae**. Now he is piloting his war brother's own version of his beloved ship called the **Daisy Mae**. He feels the spirit of the **Daisy Mae**, is flying with him, right now.

Upside Down

Uncle Ben gives Fran some instructions and soon the plane rolls over and Fran is flying a much smaller namesake of the **Daisy Mae** upside

261

down! It was only for a minute or two but created a memory for a lifetime for young Wayne and Linda giggling from the rear seat.

After righting the plane and helping Fran level off to the prescribed altitude, Navigator Ben Weiss says, "Fran, I remember the last time we were on the bomber together. You asked me if I ever navigated by the stars? Do you want me to show you how?"

Fran Perkins can barely speak. An emotional lump fills his throat. Fran nods "yes," and Ben points to the star filled November skies. Fran Perkins learns how to navigate the stars by the best Navigator in the whole damned Army Air Corps. Ben Weiss delivers on a dream and a promise he made ten years earlier in a desperate battle when the odds were neither Fran nor Ben would survive.

Ben begins his instruction. "Fran, the secret to navigating at night involves mastering two tools.

"What are the tools I need to learn? I'm ready," Fran replies determined. Fran feels the same excitement he experienced when his best buddy Conley and goof-off Calhoun first climbed inside a B-24 Bomber many years ago.

Ben points toward his windshield and to his right "First, you need to find the North Star, which is located close to that frying pan formation over there, and then you need the most important tool of all."

"OK, what tool is that, Ben?"

Ben smiles, "You need hope. Never underestimate the power of hope."

18-1 Fran and Elaine together for life

Epilogue

The Sound of Taps

The B-24D Liberator Bomber lives on in the hearts and souls of the surviving families of the brave men who flew and fought on the last flight of the **Daisy Mae**. Four generations of names like Gall, Ambur, Perkins, Storts, Conley, Wyckoff, Patterson, Jensen, Van Horn, Evans and Weiss are the living legacies of true and lasting heroes. The sacrifices of Jensen and Evans on board that day assures these new generations of Americans would spring forth. The power of hope and the power of prayer by these winged warriors on that fateful day also assured life for these future generations.

Sixteen-year-old Elaine Birmingham prayed the Latin words *saecula saeculorum*, meaning world without end. Her prayers were heard and answered at that very moment while Lt. Gall was landing a bloodied, yet unbeaten **Daisy Mae** on the Eastern Island of Midway. Clarence and Mae Birmingham, Elaine's parents, and all of the millions of workers on the home front are the unsung heroes. It was their contribution of injuries, extra hours, dedication, attention to detail and their hard labor that helped these bombers take tremendous punishment and bring their crews safely home.

Also, among the unsung heroes are the maintenance men, and the men and women in all areas of industry who worked together to win the war. They worked, prayed, hoped and died for the airmen and for successful missions to end World War II.

I can visualize thousands of arms extending upward with hands lifting toward the blue Pacific sky, passing the **Daisy Mae** from worker to worker, as she crawled, limped, walked and finally marched across the Pacific skies on July 24, 1943.

264

Epilogue

The 42nd Squadron of the 11th Bomb Group of the Seventh Army Air Corps protected the Hawaiian Islands from invasion, found stranded soldiers and sailors, and moved the Bomber Line across the Pacific all the way to victory over Japan in World War II.

The Grey Geese were wiped out during the Pearl Harbor attack to start World War II for America on December 7, 1941. The Grey Geese regrouped and rebuilt to finish the war and were flying proudly in formation over the signing of the Peace Treaty on the Battleship Missouri to end World War II in 1945.

You may watch movies or read comics about Superman, The Green Hornet, Thumper, Dog Patch, or Daisy Mae. You might smile when you remember images or memories attached to these names. I have different memories when I see those names.

Now you do, too…

The story ends far away from the battle site.

On a warm, dark July day, not far from a quiet ocean, the marines are escorting an airman to his final resting place. At the *Sound of Taps*, four marines in uniform fire their M1 Carbines into the sky, during a twenty-one-gun salute at the National Cemetery in Bushnell, Florida.

Francis Joseph Perkins Jr. lays in an open casket ready to be laid to rest with a plastic model replica of a B-24D Liberator Bomber with the nose art image of the **Daisy Mae** created by his youngest daughter, Wanda. The replica lays against Fran's heart to accompany him on his next mission.

Along with the *Sound of Taps*, the Chaplain recites the familiar speech that begins with, "On behalf of the President of the United States and the People of a grateful nation…"

Epilogue

The diminutive guardian of **Daisy Mae**'s soft belly is in uniform and ready to climb into her body and reply to Joe Gall's order over the intercom by saying "Belly Gunner, checking in." Nothing would have made my dad happier, except for one more mission with the brave ship and crew. The **Daisy Mae** was Fran's *Field of Dreams*. Just before Fran died, he told his family, "There is nothing in life I'd rather do more."

There is a familiar rumbling in the dark clouds in the distance. The weather conditions are appropriate at this time marking the exact same conditions of the bomber raid on Wake Island, the "Alamo in the Sky", and the heroic landing on Midway Island sixty-nine years earlier, almost to the day. The burial detail personnel at the National Cemetery in Bushnell, Florida are decorated and uniformed United States Marine Veterans of World War II, Korea and Viet Nam.

A lanky marine in uniform is handing me the folded US flag. He appears to be in his late eighties. He is old enough to have been one of the marines serving in the Pacific during World War II. He could have been at Guadalcanal, the Solomon Islands, Midway, Wake, Funafuti, the Gilbert Islands, or any of the other campaigns listed on the back of the photographs lovely Lady Elaine kept for the rest of her long, happy life with her sweetheart from Calumet High School, Fran Perkins.

Now, I receive the folded flag with spent M1 Carbine shells neatly and efficiently tucked inside the flag while a lanky marine stares directly into my eyes. I instinctively salute him.

I mirror his long, sweeping ceremonial salute in a fashion that would make Larry Aloysius Calhoun III proud. The salute takes the entire bugle *Sound of Taps* to complete from the time I raise my hand to the time I finish with "fingers extended and joined, thumbs curled at the fore-finger," just as I learned serving as an infantryman in the United States Army back in 1966.

I am saluting all of the men in combat during World War II and especially all of the United States Army Air Corps, Navy, Army,

266

Epilogue

Marines, Coast Guard, and the crew of the **Daisy Mae**. Without their brave deeds, my family and other loving families of those men would simply not exist.

From just one day in history, life and hope springs eternal.

I wonder if this lanky marine saluting me is the same young lanky marine who helped a younger Fran Perkins off the wreckage of the **Daisy Mae**. Is he the same marine who cut a piece of metal from the **Daisy Mae** and carried it as a good luck charm through the rest of World War II only to restore it to its original crew many years later? Is the brave marine the same one who **Daisy Mae** visited after she was towed out to sea? Did he experience a hysterical reunion with the Liberator in the warm, shallow waters on Midway Island a long, long time ago? Was this lanky marine there on the official day when hell froze over on Midway and turned that hell into a joyous memory for thousands?

I wonder and I hope…

"Never underestimate the power of hope."
　　　—Lt Benjamin I. Weiss, Navigator, The **Daisy Mae** July 24, 1943

Special Features

You will find Special Features for *The Last Flight of the **Daisy Mae*** by clicking on this link while connected to the Internet or by going to the following link:

http://thelastflightofthedaisymae.com

These features include history and stories about the 42nd Squadron 11th Bomb Group 7th Army Air Corps. Special Features also includes a blog and welcomes questions and remarks from the readers. You will find more information about the Big Brown Bomber and stories about other missions of the B-24 Liberators during World War II.

New variations of the book as well as formats such as trade paperback, hardback and audio books are listed there as well.

Highlights and special features are found online at *The Last Flight of the Daisy Mae* website. Type in the URL below when connected to the Internet.

http://thelastflightofthedaisymae.com

Group Book Sales: Save on custom orders for 100 books or more!

Get special pricing for your group; when you offer your organization the true story of *The Last Flight of the **Daisy Mae***.

Benefits

1. Give a lasting gift to each member of your organization. Add your logo or mission statement to your customized copy of the book and make it yours.

Special Features

2. Share the story of hope, dedication, and sacrifice. This story helps inspire your special organization.

3. Use the book to raise money for your non-profit organization., giving a story that will resonate with your members.

Call Today!

Wayne Perkins
Cell: 602-647-4280
Email your request to: wayne@wayneperkins.net

http://thelastflightofthedaisymae.com
https://www.facebook.com/wayne.perkins.9235/

Please give complete contact information including telephone contact numbers and email address.

"Never underestimate the power of hope."
    --Navigator Lt. Benjamin I Weiss, the **Daisy Mae**, on July 24, 1943"

About the Author

Wayne F. Perkins is the son of Francis J. Perkins Jr., or Fran, the main character in his books. Wayne grew up in rural Lake in the Hills, Illinois in a house at 1019 Maple Street, that his Dad, Fran Perkins built by himself. He has authored several Hypnosis Training Programs over the years. His passion is writing books in a new series titled "Whispers of Heroes."

After graduating from Dundee High School in 1965, Wayne was drafted into the Army. He spent two years' active duty military in the United States Army. In 1967, Wayne served as an "Imjin Scout," patrolling the Demilitarized Zone between North and South Korea. He was in the 32nd Infantry Brigade, 7th Division. He is a graduate of Northern Illinois University in DeKalb, Illinois. Wayne taught Business Education courses at Elgin High School in Elgin Illinois and taught Self-hypnosis at Triton College in River Grove, Illinois

Endnotes

Endnotes

"Heroism and Hope" notes
1. Wayne Perkins interview with Francis J. Perkins Sr. in Chicago, IL.
2. Ibid.
3. Interview with Clarence and Mae Birmingham in Evergreen Park, IL.
4. Donald L. Miller, "The Story of World War II," (New York, Simon and Schuster, 2006) p.99

"Molly and Her Lib" notes
5. Boone, Andrew R, "The Liberator," Popular Science May 1943 p.90
6. Linder, Bruce (2001), San Diego's Navy, Naval Institute Press, Annapolis, Maryland, p.122
7. Herman, Arthur, "Freedom's Forge: How American Business Produced Victory in World War II," pp. 219-34, 242-3 (Random House, New York NY 2012
8. Donald L. Miller, "The Story of World War II," (New York, Simon and Schuster, 2006) pp.60, 70-76, 430, 488-486.

"The Farm Boy" notes
9. Camp Grant (Rockford, Il.), Soldiers' Shirt Pocket Handbook of Camp Grand and Rockford, Ill," Rockford Ill (The Camp), 1918 OCLC 13042782
10. Louis, Joe; Edna Rust and Art Rust, Jr. (1978). My Life. Brighton: Angus & Robertson

"Advanced Airman Training," notes
11. "Davy Crockett, His Own Story," Applewood Books, 1993
12. Miller, Donald L., "The Story of World War II," (New York, Simon and Schuster, 2006) pp.120-126
13. Alef, Daniel, "Henry J. Kaiser First in War First in Peace," Enhanced Digital Edition (Titans of Fortune Publishing, 2010) Santa Barbara, California
14. Interview with Elaine Esther Perkins, Lake in the Hills, IL.
"Armorer School Training" notes

15. AAF 1943 Training Film "Flexible Aerial Gunnery: Making a Gunner" (full) Retrieved on July 30, 2013 YouTube.
16. Toland, John, "The Decline and Fall of the Japanese Empire 1936-1945 (Modern Library War). May 27, 2003 p. 61-63

"Water Conley Water" notes
17. Hutchinson, James Lee, "Through These Eyes: A World War II Eight Air Force Combat Diary," Authorhouse, 2006
18. Donald, David, "The Complete Encyclopedia of World Aircraft," New York: Barnes & Noble, 1997.
19. Newman, Alexander (November 28, 2003) "Metal Building Systems: Design and Specifications." McGraw-Hill Professional, p. 2

"Thumper" notes
20. Lundstrom, John, B. "The First Team: Naval Air Combat from Pearl Harbor to Midway," Naval Institute Press, 2013.
21. Maurer, Maurer, "Air Force Combat Units of World War II." Washington, DC: U.S. Government Printing Office 1961, Republished 1983, Office of Air Force History
22. Eckersley, R. J. "Amateur Radio Operating Manual," Radio Society of Great Britain, 1985
23. Holiday, James, "PT Boats at War," Carleton Press, 1995

"Meet Daisy Mae" notes
24. Daws, Gavin, "Prisoners of the Japanese: POWs of World War II in the Pacific," Quill Press, New York, NY 1996 p.135
25. Tregaskis, Richard, Guadalcanal Diary, Random House, New York, NY 1955
26. Dorr, Robert and Rolfe, Mark, "B-24 Units of the Pacific War," (Combat Aircraft) 2012, p.29

"Missions of the Daisy Mae" notes
27. Air Force Historical Association, "Reports for the 42nd Squadron (H) Missions: 20 May 1943 to 5 March 1944." 42nd Bombardment Squadron (H) 11th Bombardment Group. Seventh Air Force. IRIS No.44028

28. Ibid., 27-31.
29. Ibid., 32-33.
30. Jersey, Stanley C., "The Battle for Betio Island, Tarawa Atoll," (2004-02-29)

"Mischief and Duty" notes
31. Air Force Historical Association, Reports for the 42nd Squadron (H) Missions: 20 May 1943 to 5 March 1944." 42nd Bombardment Squadron (H) 11th Bombardment Group, Seventh Air Force. IRIS No. 44028
32. Ibid., p.32-33.

"The Alamo in the Sky" notes
33. Ambur, Arvid, "The Last Flight of the **Daisy Mae**," The Midway Mirror, February 1993.
34. Perkins, Francis J. Phone Interview February 28, 2004.
35. Ibid.
36. Ibid.
37. Ibid.

"The Battle to Return Home" notes
38. Ambur, Arvid, "Hell in the Sky Part II. Capital News, South Dakota, July 19, 2012
39. Ibid.
40. Ibid.
41. Henderson, Dale A., "The Gray Grey Geese Remember," 11th Bombardment Group (H) Association, Pronto Print, Inc. Portland, Oregon, pp6-12.
42. Ibid.

"The Last Landing of the **Daisy Mae**" notes
43. Ambur, Arvid, "Hell in the Sky Part II." Capital News, South Dakota, July 19, 2012
"Hospitals and Hope" notes
44. "Chicago Team History & Encyclopedia," Baseball-Reference.com, Retrieved April 7, 2014.

Endnotes

45. Hope, Bob, "Don't Shoot Its Only Me," Putnam Adult; First Edition, 1990.

"The Second Bombing of Wake Island" notes
46. Air Force Historical Association, Reports for the 42nd Squadron (H) Missions: 20 May 1943 to 5 March 1944." 42nd Bombardment Squadron (H) 11th Bombardment Group, Seventh Air Force. IRIS No. 44028 pp. 32-40

"Joe the Mailman" notes
47. Cox, Jeffrey R. Rising Sun Falling Skies: The Disastrous Java Sea Campaign of World War II. Osprey Publishing, 2014
48. Bowman, Martin W. US Eighth Air Force in Europe: Eager Eagles 1941 to Summer 1943 Going Over, Gaining Strength- Volume 1, Pen and Sword Aviation, 2012

"Top Secret Revealed" notes
49. Dando-Collins, Stephen "Operation Chowhound: The Most Risky Most Glorious US Bomber Mission of World War II" Palgrave McMillan Trade, 2015

"Many Years Later" notes
50. Phone Interview with Arvid B. Ambur on July 19, 2012 from Tampa, Florida to Presho, South Dakota
51. Interview with Benjamin I. Weiss on Thanksgiving Day, November 26, 1953

Photo Credits

1-1 and 1-2: Courtesy of the Clarence and Mae Birmingham Collection
2-1: Courtesy Library of Congress
2-2: Courtesy United States Air Forces
3-1: Courtesy Library of Congress
3-2: Courtesy Library of Congress
4-1: Courtesy United States Army Air Forces
4-2: Courtesy Library of Congress
6-1: Courtesy of the Francis J. Perkins Family Collection
6-2: Courtesy Library of Congress
8-1: Courtesy Wikipedia.com
8-2: Courtesy World War II Memorial
9-1: Courtesy United States Air Force
10-1: Courtesy Library of Congress
13-1: Courtesy Stan, Dona and Michael Thompson and Family Collection
13-2: Courtesy Stan, Dona and Michael Thompson and Family Collection
15-1: Courtesy Stan, Dona and Michael Thompson and Family Collection
17-1: Courtesy also noted for Library of Congress
18-1: Courtesy Francis J. Perkins Jr. Family Collection

Bibliography

Air Force Historical Association. Mission Reports IRIS 44028, Maxwell AFB: Air Force Historical Association, 1943. Microfilm Copy.
Alef, Daniel. Henry J. Kaiser First in War First in Peace. Santa Barbara: Titans of War Publishing, 2010.
Ambrose, Stephen E. The Wild Blue. New York: Simon and Schuster, 2001. Book.
Ambur, Arivd. "Hell in the Pacific." Capital Journal 22 July 2012: 3. Newspaper.
Ambur, Arvid B. Betio Bombing Mission Wayne F. Perkins. 19 July 2012. Phone.
Ambur, Arvid. The Last Flight of the **Daisy Mae**. The Midway Mirror, 1995. Article.
Birdsall, Steve. Log of the Liberators. New York: Double & Company, 1974. Book.
—. The B-24 Liberator. New York: Arco, 1968. Book.
Birmingham, Clarence. Evergreen Park Wayne Perkins. 25 December 1956.
Birmingham, Mae. Talk about the War Wayne Perkins. 25 December 1956.
Boone, Andrew R. "The Liberator." Popular Science May 1943: 90.
Bowman, Martin W. Eighth Air Force in Europe: Eager Eagles 1941 to Summer 1943 Going Over Gaining Strength. Pen and Sword Aviation, 2012.
"Chicago Team History." 2014. Baseball Reference.com. 7 April 2014.
Cox, Jeffrey R. Rising Sun Falling Skies: The Disastrous Java Sea Campaign of World War II. Osprey Publishing, 2014.
Crockett, Davy. His Own Story. Applewood Books, 1993.
Dando-Collins, Stephen. Operation Chowhound: The Most Risky Most Glorious US Bomber Mission of World War II. Mac Millan Publishing Mac Millan Trade, 2015.
Davis, Larry. B-24 Liberator in Action. Carrollton: Signal Publication, 1987. Book.
Daws, Gavin. Prisoners of the Japanese: POWs of World War II in the Pacific. New York: Quill Press, 1996.

Bibliography

Donald, David. The Complete Encyclopedia of World Aircraft. New York: Barnes & Noble, 1997.

Dorr, Robert and Rolfe, Mark. B-24 Units of the Pacific War. Combat Aircraft, 2012.

Eckersley, R.J. Amateur Radio Operating Manual. Radio Society of Great Britain, 1985.

Fain, James E. The Flying Circus. New York: Commanday-Roth, 1946. Book.

Flexible Aerial Gunnery: Making a Gunner. Dir. Army Air Force Films. Perf. AAF. 1942. Video.

Getz, C.W. The Wild Blue Yonder: Songs of the Air Force. San Mateo: The Redwood Press, 1981. Book.

Greene, Jack. The Midway Campaign. Conshohocken: Combined Books, 1995. Book.

Henderson, Dale A. The Gray Grey Geese Remember. Portland: Pronto Print, 1991. Book.

—. The Gray Grey Geese Remember. Portland: 11th Bombardment Group (H) Association Pronto Press, 1983.

Herman, Arthur. Freedom's Forge: How American Business Produced Victory in World War II. New York: Random House, 2012.

Hillenbrand, Laura. Unbroken. New York: Random House, 2010. Book.

Holiday, James. PT Boats at War. Carleton Press, 1995.

Hope, Bob. Don't Shoot It's Only Me. First Edition. New York: Putnam Adult, 1990.

Hutchinson, James Lee. Through These Eyes: A World War II Eighth Air Force Combat Diary. Authorhouse, 2006.

Lewis, Joe and Edna and Rust, Art Jr. Rust. My Life. Brighton: Angus & Robertson, 1978.

Linder, Bruce. San Diego's Navy. Annapolis: Naval Institute Press, 2001.

Lundstrom, John B. The First Team: Naval Air Combat from Pearl Harbor to Midway. Naval Institute Press, 2013.

Maurer, Maurer. Air Force Combat Unites of World War II. Office of Air Force History. Washington : U.S. Government Printing Office, 1983.

Bibliography

Miller, Donald L. The Story of World War II. New York: Simon and Schuster, 2001. Book.

Newman, Alexander. Metal Building Systems: Design and Specifications. New York: McGraw Hill Professional, November 28,2003.

Perkins, Elaine Ester Birmingham. Mom and Dad Wayne Perkins. June 1956.

Perkins, Francis J. At Home Wayne Perkins. November 1953.

Perkins, Francis J. Battles in World War II Wayne Perkins. February 2004.

Scearce, Phil. Finish Forty and Home. Denton: University of North Texas Press, 2011. Book.

The Camp. Soldiers Series Shirt Pocket Handbook of Camp Grant and Rockford Illinois. Rockford: The Camp, 1918.

Toland, John. The Decline and Fall of the Japanese Empire 1936-1945. Modern Library War, 2003.

Tregaskis, Richard. Guadalcanal Diary. New York: Random House, 1955.

US Army Air Corps. Flight Manual for the B-24 Liberator. Appleton: Aviation Publications, 1977. Book.

Weiss, Benjamin I. Flight in the Piper Cub Little **Daisy Mae** Wayne Perkins. 25 November 1953.